CARTOOS SAAB

Ian Cardozo was born in Mumbai on 7 August 1937 and studied at St. Xavier's School and College. After a year at college, he joined the National Defence Academy in July 1954 where he was awarded the gold medal for being the best all-round cadet, and the silver medal for being first in order of merit. On being commissioned from the Indian Military Academy he joined the 1st Battalion the 5th Gorkha Rifles (Frontier Force) and moved to the North East Frontier Agency (NEFA) with his battalion where he was the first officer of the Indian Army to be awarded the Sena Medal for gallantry on a patrol on the Sino-Indian border in 1959.

He took part in the Sino-Indian war of 1962 and was part of the team that re-raised the Fourth Battalion of his regiment in the aftermath of that war. As part of 'Four Five' he fought the Indo-Pak wars of 1965 and 1971. Disabled during the 1971 war at Sylhet, in Bangladesh, he overcame the disability of losing a leg and changed the mindset at Army Headquarters by proving that losing a leg did not take away his ability to command troops in the army.

Gen. Cardozo was the first war-disabled officer to be approved for command of a battalion and a brigade. He thereafter commanded an Infantry Division on the Line of Control and retired as Chief of Staff of a corps in the Northeast. After retirement, he worked with an NGO taking care of persons with disability and was chosen by the Government of India to head the Rehabilitation Council of India.

'General Ian Cardozo is from that rare breed of men, who marched out of the Academy with a gold medal pinned on his chest only to excel not just as a scholar in uniform but to exhibit courage that defies definition. This account of his life and times tells us why this book must be read by all, especially those who wish to understand what makes soldiers go beyond their call of duty.'

MAROOF RAZA, FORMER ARMY OFFICER,
TV COMMENTATOR AND MILITARY HISTORIAN

'General Cardozo's memoirs are as extraordinary as he is. This book chronicles the remarkable journey of a remarkable man. His courage and compassion are the stuff of legend. Except it all happened for real. *Cartoos Saab* is inspirational reading for every Indian.'

BARKHA DUTT, SENIOR JOURNALIST

'This is an amazingly inspirational life story of the evolution of a soldier, leader and a crusader over a lifespan. The story is about valour, grit, emotions and overcoming odds and seemingly insurmountable hurdles. This will surely motivate and inspire a range of readers.'

SOM MITTAL, CHAIRMAN, NATIONAL COUNCIL FOR PROMOTING EMPLOYMENT OF
DISABLED PERSONS; FORMER CHAIRMAN, NASSCOM

CARTOOS SAAB

A SOLDIER'S STORY OF RESILIENCE IN ADVERSITY

MAJ. GEN. IAN CARDOZO

ROLI

Sketches: Ian Cardozo (except on pages 331–32)

First published in 2022
This paperback edition published in 2025

ISBN: 9789349474062

Roli Books Pvt. Ltd
M-75, Greater Kailash II Market, New Delhi 110 048
Phone: +91 (011) 40682000
E-mail: info@rolibooks.com
Website: www.rolibooks.com
Also at Chennai & Mumbai

Typeset in Minion Pro by Roli Books Pvt. Ltd

Dedicated to the Indian Army
whose officers lead from the front
and whose soldiers are the best in the world

Contents

Preface

*Fill your life with adventures not things. Have stories
to tell not stuff to show.*
UNKNOWN

Through this book I have tried to tell the story of a young school boy who grows to be an army officer, takes his place in the Indian Army, and how he puts his life together again after getting disabled in war.

Although this is the story of my life, it is also a reflection of the lives of most army officers of that period who walked along similar paths of time and space.

My journey starts at a time when India had yet to attain freedom from British rule and touches upon issues we faced as young children against racial prejudice. The story continues through the exhilaration of Independence, the disaster of Partition, the wars with China and Pakistan, the liberation of East Pakistan, the birth of Bangladesh and the inimical situations in the Northeast and in Jammu and Kashmir that continue to the present day.

On 15 August 1947, India had become independent, but the transition to be a free country has been a turbulent one. Partition soured the joy of freedom, and the wars with Pakistan and China that followed fragmented the vision of harmony and the dream of building a peaceful future based on the culture and vision of India's ancient past.

Each of these wars had its own effects on the development and economy of the country. Being in the ringside seat of some of these events, one was able to see the effects of how these wars impacted the national scene and the impression they made on the minds of young officers of the Indian Army of that time.

Looking back, it seems a long while ago that I joined the army and yet it also seems that it was only yesterday. Most of us who joined the army were looking for adventure. Little did we realize that instead, adventure would come looking for us!

It all started at the National Defence Academy (NDA), 'The Cradle of Leadership'. It was here that we learnt that adventure was there for the asking, that the shortcut to good leadership was 'Service before Self', and that not only was co-operation a principle of war but also that it was the essence of our lives in uniform. The Academy also taught us the principle of 'unity in diversity' for which our country is justly famous. It brings people of different castes, creeds and communities to the level of brotherhood that engenders togetherness and camaraderie, contributing to the strength of the armed forces and ultimately of the nation.

My early years in the army were spent on the borders of Tibet and Pakistan. On our way to our posts on returning from a course or from leave, we broke journey at 'Transit Camps' which were akin to the sarais on the old Mughal roads. After a bath we would walk across to the Transit Camp Officers' Mess where on a winter evening, in front of a warm fire and over a drink, we would listen to the stories of old timers about life on the North West Frontier; about exciting events during the Second World War on the battlefields of

Africa, Europe and Asia and the Indo–Pak war of 1947–48. As young officers, we wondered whether we would ever have our own stories to tell. Little did we know, that we would have more than our fill of dramatic adventures in the years that lay ahead.

After a journey of thirty-nine years in uniform starting from the day I joined the Joint Services Wing of the Armed Forces Academy, to the night I said goodbye to my battalion and the Indian Army at a lonely railway station in Assam, I have my own stories to tell.

This is a true story, however, it has not been possible to mention the names of all the wonderful people I have worked with, but let it not go unsaid that my respect and friendship for them remains without bounds, for without them there would be no story to tell. I have combined historical facts with anecdotal narratives while telling this story. I have changed the names of some of the characters where I felt such change was necessary to protect their privacy and because the aim is not to belittle anyone.

I hope this story will be useful to the young officers who have recently stepped across the threshold of Chetwode Hall into the great adventure that the Indian Army is all about. I hope they realize that in time to come, they too will have their own stories to tell.

The average Indian citizen holds the armed forces in high regard but knows very little about the lives we truly live. This story hopefully would enlighten them and bring them closer to life in the armed forces – a way of life that has no equal!

Ian Cardozo, New Delhi, May 2022

Prologue

We live by chance, we love by choice,
and we kill by profession.
OFFICERS TRAINING ACADEMY, CHENNAI

The men were holding on resolutely to the perimeter of the ground that had been captured by us at Sylhet. We were at war with Pakistan and our battalion, the 4th Battalion the 5th Gorkha Rifles (Frontier Force) had landed deep behind enemy defences in East Pakistan on the afternoon of 7 December 1971, in the Indian Army's first heliborne operation.

Pakistani forces were doing their best to evict us from the ground that we had captured but their counter-attacks had been effectively repulsed. War cries of *'Allah o Akbar'* mingled with energetic responses of *'Ayo Gorkhali'* from our men. Our men were being restrained from launching counter-attacks with their khukris.[1] They had used this weapon very effectively in earlier battles of the previous weeks but this was not the time and place. The strength of the Pakistani forces seemed to be more than what was told to us; in fact, their numbers seemed to be overwhelmingly large.

Our task was to capture Sylhet in East Pakistan. We were informed that Pakistan's 202 Infantry Brigade that had been defending Sylhet had moved for the defence of Dhaka, the capital of East Pakistan, and that there were just a few *razakars*[2] defending Sylhet. But there seemed to be something radically wrong with that intelligence report. The ground which we were holding on to so desperately was being plastered with enemy artillery, mortar, machine guns and small arms fire. Surely, this could not be the response of a small body of irregular troops? It appeared that Pakistan's 202 Infantry Brigade had not moved to Dhaka after all! But at that moment we did not know.

The Mi-4 Indian Air Force helicopters that had landed us had managed to get away safely despite the best efforts of the Pakistanis to destroy them on the ground and in the air; but now that we were on our own, we increasingly became the target of enemy fire.

Our strength was just 384 all told, and if Pakistan's 202 Infantry Brigade had not moved out, then we were in the inadequate ratio of 1:6 and they could overwhelm us with sheer numbers. In addition to the seemingly incorrect intelligence on the basis of which our battalion had been launched, we had also been assured that we would be linked up by friendly forces within 48 hours. However, after 36 hours of being under fire, there was no indication whatsoever that help was at hand.

I looked at the sequence of events that had led to the present impasse. Our battalion had launched two successful attacks at Atgram and Gazipur where khukris were used with abandon. We began to realize however, that success sometimes has its own convoluted outcomes. Because we did a great job in the first attack at Atgram, we were tasked to capture Gazipur and because we succeeded in capturing Gazipur, where an attack by another unit had failed, we were now ordered to capture Sylhet!

Success, however, had not come easy! The price we paid was heavy. Two young officers, a Junior Commissioned Officer (JCO) and three men had been killed in the first attack at Atgram; and our second-in-command (2ic) and ten men killed and four officers and fifty-seven wounded at Gazipur. Out of eighteen officers when the war began, only eleven were left and things had only just begun! Our Commanding Officer (CO), Lieutenant Colonel Arun Bhimrao Harolikar, a very brave and competent officer, was barely coming to terms with his losses and trying to reorganize the command and control of the companies when he received orders for the battalion to capture Sylhet. The CO felt that this was an unfair order. To do well in the next battle, he needed time to reorganize the rifle companies because of the large number of casualties. The officers and men had been without rest ever since the war had started. He said as much but his objections were overruled. The Corps Commander, Lieutenant General Sagat Singh, was a man in a hurry! He felt that Sylhet was thinly held and that this was an opportunity that was too good to pass up. His orders were: 'Send in the Gorkhas. I know them well. They are best suited to this task. I want Sylhet to be occupied before it is reinforced.'

In the Indian Army you can protest up to a point. After that, orders are orders!

Meanwhile, we who were holding on to the ground at Sylhet, had no time to think of what was happening. We were doing our best to hang on to what we had captured and to extend the perimeter of our defences.

Based on the assurance that we would be linked up within 48 hours, the CO had decided, after consultation with our officers and JCOs, that instead of food, water and clothing, we would take more ammunition and hand grenades. In those cold nights all that we had were our own water bottles and a handful of *shakarpara*[3] as food and no protection against the weather except our *barsatis*.[4]

We were taught at our schools of instruction that troops which are para-dropped or heli-landed behind enemy lines have necessarily to be linked up within 48 hours, otherwise the force would gradually degrade and disintegrate due to casualties and lack of reinforcements, ammunition, food, water and medical facilities. It looked as if our present situation was exactly this.

Our platoon commander at the Indian Military Academy (IMA), Captain Desmond Hayde had dinned into our heads that '*Battles are won or lost in the minds of men before they are won or lost on the ground*'. He had proved this as a CO at the Battle of Dograi in the 1965 War under impossible conditions and it appeared that our battalion would have to prove this once again at the Battle of Sylhet in 1971.

Notes

1. A sharp knife which Gorkhas use very effectively in battle. It has a sharp slightly curved blade with the cutting edge on the inside and heavier on the outer edge. The blade has a notch near the handle that prevents blood from flowing on to the handle that could make it slippery. The handle could be of bone, wood or metal. The blade of a battle khukri is approximately 14 inches long.
2. An irregular Pakistani soldier.
3. Small sweetmeats made of wheat, milk and sugar.
4. Rain cape.

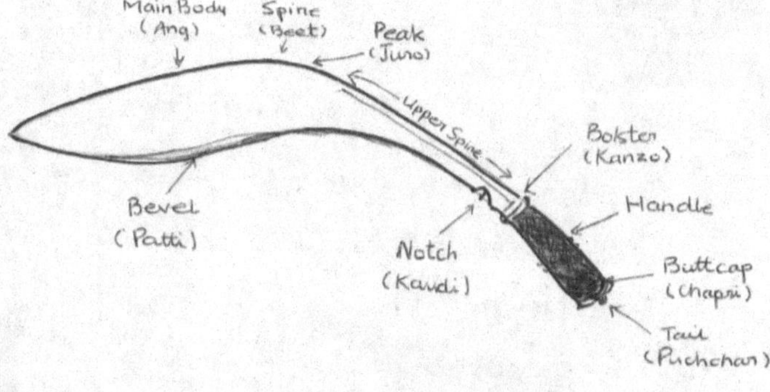

GORKHA KHUKRI

CHAPTER ONE

The Beginning – Cradles of Leadership 1954–1958

The evening of life is determined by the morning of it
The end is determined by the beginning
The decisions you make today, will play
out tomorrow.
Anonymous

Bombay Central Railway Station – July 1954

The rain had eased up a bit, as travellers scurried towards their respective platforms at Bombay Central Railway Station. It was 3 July 1954, and the hands of the enormous clock that hung from the rafters of the roof of the platform indicated that it was a few minutes to 4 p.m.

The Frontier Mail had just backed alongside Platform No. 1 in preparation for its long journey and it shone in

Bombay Central Railway station, Platform No. 1, 3rd July 1954

the rays of the evening sun. The engine driver had not yet finished polishing the brass work of his machine that looked resplendent in black and gold. The wheels of the engine were huge, each standing higher than an average man. There were four of them on each side linked to each other by rods that moved the wheels in unison to give the engine the great muscle power that made it the fastest train on the Bombay Baroda & Central India Railway Line. Wisps of steam hissing from the valves and pipes emphasized the tremendous power of the locomotive. Two firemen with black bandanas around their heads were sweating from their exertions of shovelling coal into the maw of the roaring furnace, their rippling muscles shining in its red reflected glow.

Standing alongside an inter-class[1] compartment were

groups of men and women speaking in low undertones. In the centre of each group was a teenager who was, in fact, a prospective cadet for the Joint Services Wing (JSW), the precursor of what was to become the National Defence Academy (NDA).

Six weeks earlier, a buff, coloured envelope from the Government of India, had arrived at the doorsteps of these young men, bringing news of them being selected to be trained as officers of the Indian Armed Forces at the Joint Services Wing at Clement Town, Dehradun. A railway warrant was attached to the letter that provided for inter-class travel to Dehradun. The letter also had details of the basic clothing that would be needed prior to being outfitted with various uniforms and other matters associated with what was expected of cadets.

These small groups at the railway station comprised of families from different communities that underscored the secular nature of India in general and the armed forces in particular. I, too, was there with my parents who had come to see me off. My father had taken leave from his office. After a while, the fathers and mothers and the younger lot got together in their respective age groups – the elders to exchange their views on what the future held for their sons – and the teenagers to get to know each other.

The minute hand of the big clock moved in relentless jerks towards departure time and at 4.25 p.m., a blast from the engine signalled that the train was ready to leave. The groups broke up once again with families giving last-minute instructions to their sons who felt embarrassed at the display of such parental concern. The guard blew his whistle and waved his green flag and we scrambled aboard and waved our goodbyes, as our train left bang on time for its long journey to the Frontier. We continued to wave to our parents till they disappeared from view. We had embarked on a railway journey, but also on the journey of our lives, full of hope and oblivious to what destiny held in store for us.

The parents said their goodbyes with a silent prayer. Similar farewells were taking place at different railway stations all over India as 150 young men gravitated towards a common destiny. Farewells were at the railway stations. No parent ever came to the Academy. At that time, it was 'just not done'!

The Frontier Mail took off at the speed it was famous for. Launched in 1928, at Bombay, it was meant to carry British troops that had disembarked at Ballard Pier from ships to the garrisons on the North West Frontier – hence its name. The ultimate destination was Peshawar, now in Pakistan. After Partition, its destination was changed to Amritsar, an Indian frontier town on the Pakistan border. The only train that rivalled the Frontier Mail in speed and distance was the Punjab Mail, which worked its way up the subcontinent from Bombay to Punjab on the other railway line – the Great Indian Peninsula line.

The boys who had embarked along with me were from Bombay State,[2] but from different communities. Two were bound for the Indian Air Force, one for the Indian Navy and two for the Indian Army.

All of us were between the ages of sixteen and seventeen headed for the only institution in the world that carried out joint training of cadets of the army, navy and the air force. The bonds between this group of teenagers assembled at Bombay Central that evening have lasted to the present day.

The landscape through which we travelled is a blur but I do remember that we passed through green fields, brown sandy plains, villages with bullock carts and dung fires, deserts with long lines of camels and forts perched on hilltops. We thundered across iron bridges and whooshed past towns and cities and through dark tunnels. As the train rumbled across state boundaries, the scenario kept changing like the patterns in a kaleidoscope and we gazed with wonder at an India we never knew existed.

The windows had three different frames, one behind the other – one of glass to keep out the coal dust from the engine, the second of wire gauze to keep out the insects and the third of latticed wood to keep out the sun. Most mail and express trains those days had dining car coaches. These were empanelled in wood and had a 'touch of class', with tables for four on each side of the aisle. Each table was decked with crockery, cutlery and napery. The waiters were very generous to us hungry young teenagers, and even served us multiple helpings, all for the munificent sum of Rs. 2.50 per meal!

We landed at Old Delhi Railway Station the next evening at 8.30 p.m. and had to wait for the Dehradun Express which was scheduled to leave in two hours. More prospective cadets from northern India trooped into the railway station accompanied by their families. One of them was decked with garlands of flowers. This boy was apparently as surprised at his selection as his neighbours (hence the garlands of flowers), but he and his parents could not stop telling everyone within hearing, that he happened to be the cream of Indian youth, hence his selection.

We had nothing to do, so some of us walked up and down the railway platform. What was amazing was the large number of people resting on the floor of the platform. Families had staked claim by spreading durries or bed sheets. It was unclear whether these travellers had reached their destination and had nowhere to stay, whether they were waiting for a connecting train or if they had yet to commence their journey. Entire families seemed to be on the move with bag and baggage.

The Dehradun Express left on time and we went off to our designated berths, worn out after an eventful day and full of anticipation of the life that awaited us. We were now on a metre-gauge railway track and the train was slow when compared to the Frontier Mail. Lulled by the *clackety clack* of the wheels, we soon fell asleep dreaming of new adventures. Early next morning, the train slowed down to a snail's pace as we approached the Doon Valley – we were now passing through a forest where elephants frequently crossed the railway tracks. After a while, the forest gave way to tea gardens and valley streams. Farms dotted the landscape and life seemed peaceful and laid-back. I would think of these tranquil homesteads often when we were subjected to the rough, strenuous training routine that was to follow.

We reached Dehradun station to be met by a Havildar[3] holding a list of names which he rapidly read out and ticked off after we confirmed our presence. I was allotted to 'Able' Squadron and told to remember that.

We had to carry our baggage ourselves. Each of us had been asked to bring along a steel trunk with our name painted on it. We also had what was known as a 'hold-all' which contained a light mattress, sheets and a pillow. At each end of this contraption were pockets that could carry shoes, slippers, pillows and night suits. The whole thing could be rolled up and secured with leather straps. In those days the Indian Railways did not provide bedding.

After we had collected outside the porch of the railway station, blinking in the bright sunshine, we were confronted by a giant apparition in a glittering olive-green uniform, a highly polished Sam Browne belt and a smart dark navy-blue peak cap. He literally towered over us, fair with a ruddy complexion. He looked at us with blue narrowed eyes which we could barely get a glimpse of from below the visor of his cap. The apparition waited till we all had gathered in front of him. Then he said, 'I am Regimental Sergeant Major George Ayling. I belong to the Grenadier Guards of the British Army. I am 6ft 4in tall and I happen to be the shortest man in my regiment. Now that you are here, you better get used to the fact that you are no longer tied to the apron strings of your mother. From now onwards, I am your father and your mother. I am not "Sir" to you, I am "Staff", and when I say something, I expect an immediate answer. Is that clear?' Nothing could be clearer! So, we all kept quiet. But the apparition apparently was not happy with our awed silence. He bellowed, 'When I ask a question, I expect you to shout an immediate answer. Is that clear?' and we quickly shouted in unison, 'YES SIR!!' We were being initiated – thereafter for the next six months it was nothing but shouting 'Yes Sir', 'No Sir' and to salute anything that moved!

He continued, 'It does not matter here what level of society you come from and how many servants you had at home. From now on, you will do everything yourselves and the first thing you must learn is the meaning of cooperation. It is a principle of war. You will now help each other and load all bag and baggage into these trucks. When I say "move", you will move in double-quick time.'

'MOVE!' he roared. We started to move. 'HALT!' he shouted again. We now wondered what we had done wrong. 'When I say move, I expect you to move like greased lightning. Is that clear?'

'YES SIR!' we yelled and jumped to it in double-quick time.

The boy who had arrived at the Old Delhi Railway Station generously garlanded found this to be very different from his expectations. He had apparently presumed that he had already become an army officer! He muttered something under his breath which the Regimental Sergeant Major (RSM) clearly heard. 'HALT!' he roared once more.

All of us froze. RSM Ayling marched up to Sandeep Kumar.[4] 'WHAT DID YOU SAY?' he shouted. Sandeep wilted at the onslaught from this mountain of a man. 'Nothing sir,' he squeaked. Addressing one of the drill instructors standing close by, the RSM said, 'Staff, take down his name and have him report to me as soon as we reach.'

'MOVE,' he once again bellowed and we moved doubly fast, and in a jiffy, we were all inside our trucks, bag and baggage loaded.

We felt sorry for Sandeep Kumar, but we had learnt our first military lesson at his expense. You don't question an order in the army or comment on it. You obey first, and then speak if you must; and accept the consequences of what you say.

The trucks moved slowly through the bazaars of Dehradun to Clement Town – a military cantonment on the outskirts of the city. We stood behind the cab of the truck and took in the scenes of this mofussil town with its crowded, smoky streets. Dehradun was said to be the gateway to Mussoorie which was known as 'The Queen of India's hill stations' but from the little that we saw, Dehradun seemed like any other; amongst the hundreds of cities and towns that dotted India.

Clement Town was where the Joint Services Wing (JSW) was located. On arrival, we saw rows and rows of red brick barracks. These, we were told, were the barracks of the erstwhile prisoners of war camp for the thousands of Italian soldiers that had been captured during the Second World War. This was to be our home for the next six months until the NDA, under construction at Khadakvasla near Poona, was ready. The first course had commenced training at the JSW on 17 January 1949. It was now 1954, so that made it five years old. Being a tri-service institution, the terminology for everything was also tri-service. The barracks were grouped into 'squadrons' – Able, Baker, Charlie, Dog, Easy and Fox. The squadrons were grouped into 'battalions' and divided into 'divisions', and the rooms where we stayed were called cabins.

Allotted to 'Able' squadron along with 24 other cadets, we were each given a number. For the next three years, I would be known as No. 1720, Cadet Ian Anthony Joseph Cardozo. This was the number I would have to shout whenever I defaulted on the drill square, PT field, riding school, swimming pool or in the academic classes and whenever an *ustaad*[5] would yell 'Shout Number'!

After we disembarked from the trucks and unloaded our luggage, a mob descended upon us. These were the 'second termers', cadets not much older than us, who started what is euphemistically called 'ragging'. It was in fact a form of torture of the most absurd kind. Within a few minutes we were hanging from fans, perched on top of cupboards, crawling through rainwater drains, doing front rolls, back rolls, singing, dancing – you name it and we did it. Our great fault was that we did not know the names of cadets (who we had never seen before in our lives) and that carried a penalty. This went on for nearly a month. The aim ostensibly was to see how much pressure we could take. However, of the 25 of us allotted to 'Able' squadron, three could not handle it, and decided to leave. Some said that ragging separated the men from the boys i.e., if they could not take the pressure of ragging now, then they would later on not be able to take the pressures of war. I don't know if this is true. I am told that ragging has now become illegal and I think that it is for the better because it brings out the worst in us and proves that power corrupts us in one way or another, even at such a young age. Of the three who left, one became a professor at Oxford, one became a travelling salesman and I don't know what happened to the third.

Brigadier Madhav Prasad[6] of the 1st Course Joint Services Wing has this to say about what happened during his time:

We thought we were quite safe from this ordeal since we had no course senior to us; but one night, some of us indulged in, what was intended and believed to be, a friendly inter-division pillow fight. Some bright spark from amongst us thought of shoving an ammunition boot into his pillow cover – the iron shoe heel of which landed on my forehead with such ferocity that it not only inflicted a deep wound on my forehead needing stitches but also chipped off a bit of my upper incisor…

That evening, the evening of the first day, the Squadron Cadet Captain intervened when the ragging was at its peak. He said, 'That's enough for today. Let them unpack and settle down,' and he ordered the second termers and the rest to lay off for the time being. It was then that I realized the power of cadet appointments and I resolved that I too, would one day use power wisely, if I ever became a cadet appointment.

I was allotted Cabin No. 30. Calling it a cabin was a misnomer – it was a large room that accommodated four cadets. Each of us was given a steel bed with a mattress, pillow, a mosquito net and a cupboard. There was a box-room somewhere, but for the time being, we could keep our box under the bed.

We were allotted civilian bearers. The four of us in Cabin 30 were handed over to a bearer called Ram Swaroop. He took charge of us and said that he was responsible for the *'kaydets'* allotted to this cabin, that he would look after us and try to see that we didn't get into unnecessary trouble. For the moment, he advised us to take a bath and get ready because there would soon be an inspection before dinner.

Good advice, because hardly had he said this when we were told that something called 'ante-room procedure' would take place in an hour and that we would have to bathe and change before that. Announcements like these were made by those of us from the junior-most course, who had to run along each barrack shouting the announcement at the top of our voice.

Between the lines of each squadron were rows of

bathrooms and lavatories. Water was heated on coal fires in huge metal boilers outside the bathrooms and we had to queue up to draw water for ourselves, provided one could find a bucket. The seniors were there ahead of us, with their dressing gowns, towels, buckets, soap and slippers and it seemed that we would never, ever get hot water. The senior-most cadet of the squadron – the Squadron Cadet Captain, intervened once again and had us get into a separate queue at another boiler. Ram Swaroop came to our rescue as he would repeatedly do, and gave me a bucket. The bathroom was devoid of anything except a tap. It was one of a series of cubicles that had a cement floor and a door that originated from two feet above the ground and ended at the top after another two feet. Not too bad, except that you had just five minutes to finish because there were others waiting to take their turn, hollering at us to be quick.

Ram Swaroop proved to be a godsend. He had taken charge of the keys of our boxes, unpacked our clothes and arranged them in our respective cupboards. He had decided what we would wear for dinner that evening and got our trousers, shirts and ties ready. He was quick, and by the time we returned after a bath, our clothes were on our beds, duly ironed, and he was sitting on the floor with our shoes, polishing them and bringing them to some level of respectability.

While we were getting ready, we were told that within a few minutes we would be inspected to ascertain whether we were in a fit state to proceed to the ante-room and then to dinner.

Right enough, within a few minutes, a cadet – a third termer – came around to inspect us. He looked smart in his summer mess kit – a spotless white monkey jacket over a collarless, long-sleeved white shirt. The jacket had a 'bund' collar. On one of his sleeves, he had a single gold stripe of a Flight Cadet. Around the waist of the white trouser he had a red cummerbund and his shoes were brightly polished. Although his was the junior-most rank in the hierarchy of appointments, he carried himself well. We learnt from his attitude and behaviour that in Service you had to act the part of the rank and appointment you were given. I would carry the message that we learnt from the conduct of that flight cadet throughout my service until I finally hung up my boots and retired.

The Flight Cadet inspected each of us minutely. He told us that we needed to shave although one could barely discern the hair on our chins. Our finger nails were inspected – something I resented because no one had ever inspected my finger nails except my mother, but the message from Regimental Sergeant Major George Ayling from the Grenadier Guards was unmistakably clear – no more mother or father – the Academy had taken over their role! He then asked us to lift up our trousers which showed our cotton socks drooping over our ankles. Those days there were no nylon socks with elastic tops to hold them up. Turning to Ram Swaroop who was hovering behind, and speaking in Hindi, he said, 'Buy garters for them. I don't want to see them like this tomorrow.' 'Ji Sahib,' and the very next day we had our garters.

Along with the instructions that came in that buff-coloured envelope to our parents was a note that said that parents had to send a money order to meet the needs of 'pocket money' for their wards. This amounted to Rs. 30/- per month, nothing more, and nothing less. This was to cover the expenses for boot polish, boot brushes, brasso, yellow flannel, toiletry and personal needs. Whatever was left over from this princely sum could be used by their wards at the tuck shop. We were given our 30 rupees every month, out of which each of us had to give the civilian bearer looking after us 15 rupees for polish, brasso etc. Considering that Ram

Swaroop got that amount from all four of us, he must have made a small profit on the side, but that was more than fine considering the amount of extra work that he did.

After the Flight Cadet in charge of us had finished, he marched us to the ante-room. It was empty and we were made to sit on the floor. Not before long, our seniors trooped in, preceded by the Cadet Sergeant Major (CSM), and began filing in and sitting on the chairs that lined both sides of the room. Each time an appointment walked in, we would jump up, until the CSM said, 'Keep sitting down, you jokers, until I tell you when to stand up.' We felt relieved.

The CSM read out the orders for the day of the JSW including the names and numbers of those who had defaulted in the course of the last week of the previous term. He then proceeded to tell us what he expected of all those assembled with regard to attitude, behaviour and discipline. It was the first day in his appointment of CSM, the first day of the new term, and I marvelled at the seamless way in which the appointments assumed their role and duties. Suddenly, he said, 'All stand.'

The Squadron Cadet Captain (SCC) walked in followed by the three Divisional Cadet Captains (DCCs). They looked like young demigods! Dressed in their smart, white, immaculate summer mess kit, the SCC had three gold stars on the top left part of his jacket. The gold stars had a red backing. The DCCs had two stars on their jackets but their backing was blue. They carried themselves well – like Roman centurions! I was very impressed.

The SCC, who was a naval cadet, told us to sit down and spoke to us about what he expected from us and that we should do our best, regardless of what we did, not only as cadets of the Joint Services Wing but also as members of Able Squadron. He hoped that we would do our best for the squadron in the inter-squadron competitions, and said that he expected us to win the championship. He outlined the competitions for the term and allocated responsibilities for each. Then, looking down at us first termers, he said, 'And that goes for you too. According to the schedule, the Novices Boxing Competition is due in September, and I expect you guys to do well.'

He knew what had to be said and he said it well. We didn't see much of him thereafter – he was far away from our level, somewhere 'in the clouds'. However, as I came to know from my later experience, he kept a close tag on all happenings in the squadron.

The next day, we were marched off to the Quartermaster Stores; this time by our drill *ustaad*. Here we were issued our drill boots, web kit, leather belts, PT shoes, riding boots, puttees, socks, shoes for everyday use and optional items like dressing gowns, night suits, bed sheets and towels in the event one had not brought these from home, which we would have to pay for.

Having deposited the kit in our rooms, we were marched to Phelps, the tailor and outfitter of the Joint Services Wing, who measured us for our various uniforms. He also gave us berets and pith hats of the old colonial style for our riding classes. We were quite delighted at this avalanche of new items of clothing. By the time we returned, Ram Swaroop had bought marking ink and pen holders with nibs and advised us to immediately mark our clothes to prevent them from getting lost or mixed-up as there would be no time later on. This was excellent advice because these events unfolded exactly as he had predicted. We were then marched off to the barbers and given our haircuts. By the time the barbers were finished with us, we all looked like shaved crows! We could do nothing about this, except look at each other and laugh.

However, the issue of new clothes and equipment meant endless hours of polishing metal cap badges, shoulder titles and numerals, not to mention polishing of boots and shoes till Ram Swaroop finally took over. In addition to academics, we were also to be initiated into drill, PT, equitation, cross-country running, boxing, obstacle courses, weapon training, map-reading, swimming, workshop training and subjects that we knew little or nothing about. However, some of our coursemates who came from military schools were familiar with all of this and they were 'one up' on the rest of us.

The next day was a Saturday. Classes and all other activities were to start on Monday, so we were taken to the book store and given our text books, exercise books, stationery and khaki cloth satchels. Last of all, we were marched off to the workshop and issued our bicycles. Green cycles with a bell and a lock and chain – the lower part of its back mud-guard was painted white with JSW rendered in red letters, below which came the number of our cycle in black numerals. This was another number that we had to remember. The drill instructor who took us for the issue of our cycles was Naib Subedar Harnam Singh, a Sikh Junior Commissioned Officer (JCO) from the Brigade of the Guards – very fair, very strict and very smart.

Once the cycles were issued, he lined us up in twos and told us that we always had to ride in a squad. Riding alone was not permitted. He then instructed us as to how we would have to mount and dismount. Apparently, this drill conformed to the mounting and dismounting of horses. On the word of command 'Prepare to mount' we had to walk with our cycles in unison, pause, put one foot on the pedal, skip on the other leg and mount on the word of command 'Mount'! After that, we had to ride in dressing, in columns of two and if an officer was passing by, the squad incharge would pay compliments and the rest of the squad had to ride to attention. The dismount drill was on similar words of command but in the reverse order.

This is where disaster struck. I did not know how to mount or dismount from the cycle!

The JCO asked us if there were any questions. No one had any – except me. I told him that I did not know how to mount and was not confident in riding in squad and if I could follow the squad on my own? He seemed surprised and irritated but agreed as there did not seem to be any other option. To overcome the order that no one could ride alone, he ordered the ubiquitous Flight Cadet in charge of our course, who had come along with us, to accompany me. The course left, all mounting and riding together quite well and in proper formation.

I took my cycle to a platform, jumped on it and took off with the Flight Cadet following me. The JCO kept looking back to see if I was keeping up with them. But the exit from the workshop turned right suddenly and angled downwards along a very steep slope. This slope ran perpendicular to the road that ran alongside the quarter deck of the drill square. I went hurtling down the slope and I couldn't turn in time. I sailed across the road and fell down with a crash on to the quarter deck about twelve feet below. Luckily, I was not hurt too badly but the cycle was a mess. The crash must have been noisy because by the time I was able to collect my senses, I saw the heads of the JCO and my coursemates looking down at me from the top of the wall that ran alongside the road. 'What are you doing there?' the JCO asked. It was a silly question and I had no answer, but my coursemates were laughing at my plight. Although the JCO was relieved that I was not hurt, he was very annoyed. Firstly, I was not supposed to be riding alone and secondly, he was responsible for me. 'Get up,' he said. 'Carry the cycle on your back and double up to the Squadron.' Although I was not seriously injured, I was quite sore but, more importantly, my ego was severely bruised – I must have looked very foolish.

Carrying a broken bike on my back, that too for a couple of kilometres, was not easy. By the time I reached the squadron, injured, tired and dishevelled, a report of what had happened had already been made to the Squadron by the JCO. The question was whether a Court of Inquiry (C of I)[7] would be required. The SCC was of the opinion that since I was not injured there was no need for a C of I. However, the workshop made a fuss. They said that the cycle could not be repaired unless it was covered by a C of I.

The next day my agony began. I had to run to the PT Field, Drill Square, Riding School and classrooms with my equipment on my back. I was late every day and everywhere and in consequence, on punishment every night. I skipped breakfast because that would have delayed me further. I could not eat dinner because I would never be able to undergo the punishments on a full stomach. I lost seven kilograms in two months and my cycle had still not been repaired!

It was now early September and by now I was the butt of all jokes of the Wing because I was the only bizarre spectacle seen running from one location to another with my kit on my back, while the rest of the Academy raced away on their cycles.

I was also trailing at the tail-end of my course. I was not doing well at academics because I was too exhausted to pay attention to what was being taught in class. I used to doze off during study period; my notes were incomplete because I was always late, and I had accumulated a huge backlog of punishments.

I wondered as to when this agony would end! I realized that I was not doing well and I was afraid that if I didn't do something remarkable, I would probably be expelled from the Academy. I also recalled my last meeting with the Vice Principal of St. Xavier's College in Bombay, who had told me quite clearly that my leaving the college without completing the course meant that I had denied someone more meritorious from getting admission to this prestigious college and that I should never, ever think of returning. I realized that I had to do something dramatic to survive.

At around this time, the dates for the Novices Boxing Competition were announced. I resolved to turn this challenge into an opportunity and grabbed hold of this opening as a drowning man would clutch at a straw. The SCC had directed a senior cadet to give us the rudiments of boxing so that we did not make fools of ourselves in the boxing ring. I took the training very seriously.

Outside our barrack was a full-sized mirror meant for us to check whether we were appropriately dressed, and in front of it I practiced whatever I was being taught about how to fight in the ring. In my first encounter with another novice, I went for my opponent as soon as the bell sounded. Aggression rather than skill stood me in good stead in all the succeeding bouts which I won one after another until I reached the semi-finals. Here, I came up against a coursemate from a military school – he was more than a match for me. It was a hard-hitting bout and I lost on points but it was announced that it was a good fight and that I was a good loser. My Squadron Commander was there and so were my Squadron Cadet Captain and my coursemates.

My reputation in the eyes of my coursemates and that of my instructors improved slightly. The Squadron Cadet Captain sent for me and said, 'The Squadron Commander, Johnny Shukla, your divisional officer Lieutenant Saxena, and I were aware of your predicament with regard to your cycle, but we let you fend for yourself and to fight your own battle. The officers have asked me to convey to you that they are glad, not only that you survived but also that you managed to redeem yourself in the boxing ring. Now keep it up. We had taken up the matter of your cycle and finally it has been repaired. You will be told when you can collect it.'

It was reassuring to learn that all through those difficult

days I was never alone and that there were people watching out for me and looking to see how much I would endure. This was a test, uncalled for no doubt, but a test all the same. I was glad that I had survived and along the way I had also earned the reputation of being resilient.

On reaching my cabin I was told that the CSM had sent for me. I wondered what I had done wrong but he had only called me to compliment me for my performance in the boxing ring and to tell me that my cycle had come back. He told me that one of the Flight Cadets had been instructed to teach me how to mount and dismount and how to ride in a squad over the weekend and that next week onwards, I could use my cycle for classes and all outdoor activities. He also said, 'It took the SCC a lot of trouble to get it repaired without a court of inquiry, and now you better look after it.'

'Yes sir,' I said happily and went to collect my bike. Within that weekend I learned how to mount and dismount and how to ride in squad and there was no looking back thereafter. I got a lot of ribbing from my coursemates when I joined them with my cycle, but it was all good-natured.

By this time, our uniforms had come back from the tailors, duly fitted and adjusted and we were eager to try them on. In those days, we had cotton uniforms which had to be stiffened with starch by our squadron *dhobis*. The stiffness had to be to a degree that if a properly starched pair of drill shorts were thrown on the floor, it would stand upright when it landed on the ground.

Strangely, during the first NDA Course (1st JSW), cadets were initially issued uniforms in accordance with the choice of their respective Service. Brigadier Madhav Prasad has this to say of what happened at that time:[8]

When we joined the Joint Services Wing in January 1949, far from uniformity of dress, we cadets were fitted out differently; in uniforms of the three Services i.e., cadets who chose to go to the Army, Navy and Air Force were given uniforms of their respective services. Fortunately, better sense prevailed after a while, when it was decided that all cadets should be dressed similarly with the same uniforms. This certainly helped in better camaraderie amongst us which has resulted in abiding friendships that have lasted to the present day.

The SCC had also said that based on my performance in the boxing ring he had given instructions that I should be tried out for squadron boxing, hockey, football, athletics and swimming teams. This taught me that ultimately organizations and institutions, especially in the armed forces, not only recognize talent and skill but also the attitude of persons who are prepared to work hard and not give up easily.

Based on the trials, I was selected to be part of the squadron boxing, football, hockey, swimming, and athletic teams, and also sent for trials for the Academy hockey team, so things started looking up. At St. Xavier's School I had captained the junior hockey team and had won the Dr Viegas Cup. Later I played for the senior school team and also for the St. Xavier's College second string and so I knew that I would do reasonably well at hockey. At boxing I knew that I was still a novice but the boxing captain felt that I was trainable. At athletics I knew I was good at the 400-metre run and I was very good at swimming. In academics, I managed to catch up in all subjects except in math and Hindi.

Before the term break, we were told that we had to report to the NDA at Khadakvasla, on the outskirts of Poona. When we reached there after the term break, we found a brand-new Academy waiting for us. Spread over an expanse of 8,022 acres, donated by the erstwhile Government of Bombay, the Academy was adjacent to the picturesque

Khadakvasla Lake. The other suggested sites considered by a committee headed by General Claude Auchinleck in 1946 were Marve (Bombay), Karachi, Bangalore, Lahore, Dehradun, Belgaum, Bhopal, Deolali, Jabalpur, Nasik, Puri, Secunderabad and Vishakhapatnam. Poona (now Pune) was ultimately chosen because of its climate, terrain, suitability for training, proximity of the lake at Khadakvasla, the sea at Bombay (now Mumbai) and the airfield at Lohegaon.

Earlier in 1941, a generous gift of a hundred thousand pounds was received from the Government of Sudan in recognition of the gallantry and sacrifices made by the Indian forces in the liberation of Sudan in the North African campaign during the Second World War. Initially, the NDA was envisaged as a War Memorial! However, after a period of time, the fact that the NDA was supposed to be a War Memorial and that the Sudan Government had made a substantial donation to this effect seemed to have been forgotten.

When we joined the Academy at Khadakvasla in January 1955, the only buildings that were constructed were the Main Block, the Science Block, the Cadets' Mess and the squadron buildings. Some of the remaining buildings were built while we were there, and others like the auditorium, the museum, the gymnasium and the library came into being only after we had passed out. Sometime in 1957, the Prime Minister of Sudan visited the Academy. I was the Academy Cadet Captain at the time and was required to sit next to the VIP at the top table. During dinner, the Prime Minister, in my presence, expressed his surprise that the name of Sudan did not figure anywhere in the Academy to honour the donation made by them towards making the Academy a War Memorial. To overcome this omission, the Main Block was immediately renamed as the Sudan Block.

Our rooms this time could justifiably be called cabins. Each of us was allotted a separate cabin with brand new, well-designed furniture. The squadron buildings were made of grey stone and had a ground, first and second floor – one floor for each of the three divisions. Four squadron buildings formed a battalion group in the form of a hollow square, the centre of which enclosed four lawns, with cycle racks aligned with the rear of each squadron building. The front of each squadron building overlooked a gravelled parade ground that measured the length of the squadron. At one end of the ground floor of the building was the squadron ante-room and at the other end was the squadron office. We learnt that four more squadrons had been added – George, Hotel, Item and King. Along with some others from 'Able' Squadron, I had been transferred to 'George' Squadron.

The main administrative block was designed on the lines of Lutyens' Delhi in brown and pink sandstone. Suited to a scientific temperament, the science block had a tower that was topped by a stainless-steel observatory type of dome, and the building was built with grey-coloured stone quarried from the Academy estate itself. The drill square was magnificent, measuring 650 x 50 metres – the largest drill square in Asia at the time. At one end of the NDA estate was the glider drome

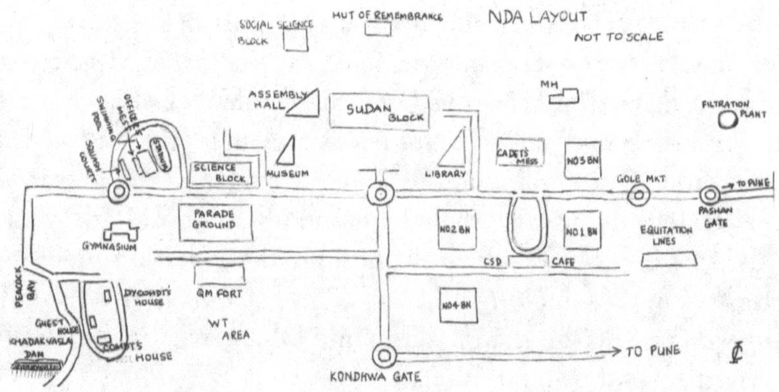

Layout of the National Defence Academy, Khadakvasla

Sketch of Sudan Block – National Defence Academy,
Khadakvasla

under construction and a little closer was the riding school. On the other side of the parade ground were the PT fields. Opposite the PT fields were the stadium and the Officers' Mess, alongside an Olympic-size swimming pool adjacent to the squash and tennis courts. In between the riding school and the parade ground were the squadron buildings, the 'Gol Market' and the cadet's mess. The cadet's mess, which was empanelled in wood and had a wooden parquet floor, could seat the whole Academy at one sitting and had the most modern kitchens in the country.

The officer's family quarters were located on a ridge above the Officers' Mess, which housed the officer's bungalows and beyond this was Peacock Bay and the Khadakvasla dam. But there was no greenery – there was not a single tree, plant or blade of grass to be seen anywhere!

We were told that the second term was the toughest – we had to pass off the drill square, pass our basic PT, riding and swimming tests, all in this term. Army, Naval and Air Force training would also commence and we learnt that we were to have a very tough Training Major.

Now in our second term, we had become senior enough to take note of the organization structure of the Academy and the staffing of its instructors. At the top was the Commandant who at that time was a Major General. The Deputy Commandant was a naval Captain. The officer in charge of administration was an army Brigadier. At the top of the academic infrastructure was a principal, a civilian who headed a sizeable staff of civilian instructors who taught us every subject under the sun – math, physics, chemistry, geography, history, social studies, English grammar and composition, English literature, Hindi, foreign languages, engineering, drawing, carpentry, blacksmithy and foundry work. Military subjects covered military history, map reading, weapon training, field craft, sailing, army, navy and air force organization and administration. Heading the army, navy and air force training was a Colonel. All aspects of military training were headed by service officers and staffed by personnel from the respective services who instructed us in all aspects of army, navy and air warfare, riding, drill, PT and swimming.

Our course had sons of Generals[9] and Junior Commissioned Officers (JCOs), corporate heads and carpenters, professors and teachers, landowners and farmers, businessmen and bank clerks and we all gelled together as one homogenous entity. There was only one cadet who was the son of a bureaucrat or a politician who we knew as 'Tunku' – the son of Tunku Abdul Rehman, the Prime Minister of Malaya! Tunku's father was a wise and revered politician and the first prime minister of Malaya. He sent his son all the way from Malaya to India to the NDA. He felt that some element of military training is essential for any vocation or any walk of life and desired that his son should imbibe values that would prepare him for higher responsibilities in Malaya.

Something new to us in this term was the introduction of nude bathing. The bathrooms were large, modern and efficiently designed, all in white tiles and chromium fittings but had shower stalls without doors or curtains. Nevertheless, we got over our initial shyness and nude bathing quickly became the norm.

Far away on the Khadakvasla skyline was Singhad Fort, one of the forts of the great guerrilla warrior, Shivaji, who troubled the Mughal rulers no end and carved out the Maratha Empire. It overlooked the Academy and loomed on the horizon close to the clouds, a sober reminder of our medieval history.

Drill was something beyond us, hours and hours of it. We were unable to comprehend its great importance. We were told that drill was the key to discipline, and discipline was what helped win wars. While we were tormented on the drill square, we found it difficult to establish that connection. It was only many years later, during the 1965 War, that I understood the importance of the discipline inculcated by our drill routines.

The drill square was presided over by Regimental Sergeant Major George Ayling, MBE, and his posse of proficient drill instructors who were JCOs and Non-Commissioned Officers (NCOs) from different infantry regiments of the Indian Army. Each squadron had a JCO and two NCOs to drill us. That was the time when words of command had switched over from English to Hindi. The Hindi words of command seemed strange – over a period of time we had become used to English. Then again, language seemed irrelevant to us – our instructors screamed at us with words of command that had links with no recognizable language. Although the first few words appeared meaningful, the crescendo was meaningless gibberish! They moved our squad forward, backward, sideward in endless movements that made no sense whatsoever. They marched beside us, screaming at a pace that increased from 120 to 140 to 150 to 160 paces a minute and we tried to comply as fast as our legs could carry us. It was as if they wanted us to fly – faster and faster with words of command, 'dayenbayendayenbayendayenbayendahinemudbayenmud dahinemudpichemudkadamtalpichemudtezchalpichemud bayenmudkadamtal.....' so much so that at times, sections of the squad moved in opposite directions and sometimes marched against each other. But it was no laughing matter. They appeared serious enough to take us to hell and back and they managed to achieve their objective.

Before each drill parade commenced, we had to undergo a dress inspection. For this ritual, we had to stand absolutely still and stiff as statues. Our boots and belts had to shine like mirrors, our brass shoulder titles and numerals had to gleam like burnished gold, our khaki shorts and shirts had to be well starched, stiff and spotlessly clean. Our belts were pulled tight so that the starched shirt remained in place. We were supposed to polish our own boots and belts but truthfully, Ram Swaroop was always at hand to get the necessary shine. Without him life would have been impossible in that second term. We went through great effort to see that our turnout was perfect but no matter what we did, the drill instructors would manage to find fault even when there was none. 'Loose button' they would yell: 'Naked on parade! Shout number!' or the slightest movement of our eyes instead of staring fixedly in front of us would result in a triumphant shout: 'Idle on parade. Shout number!' The words 'idle on parade' covered a whole litany of sins, real or imagined, and there would be some instructor somewhere, who would be noting the cadet's number which meant extra drill on Wednesdays and Saturdays when the rest of our coursemates were off parade. Often, the instructor ordered to note down the number would not have a pencil or a notebook but he would shout 'Yes sir' and go through the pretense of writing it down. Later, he would enquire as to who was the unfortunate cadet whose number he was supposed to note down. Subedar Birlam Gurung was one such instructor who later became the Subedar Major of one of the battalions of the regiment I would one day join. The culmination of all this frenetic pace of drill was called 'passing off the drill square'. If a cadet managed to pass off the drill square it meant that his drill was of an acceptable standard and that he was eligible to proceed on liberty.[10]

The symbol of having passed off the square was the red lanyard worn on the right shoulder, which was given to us only after we passed off the drill square. Once I wore that lanyard, I never took if off until I retired. The same lanyard was used at the Indian Military Academy (IMA) and finally in my regiment. In my regiment, this lanyard was called 'The Royal'. It was bestowed upon us in 1924 when we were declared to be the best battalion in the British Empire – the battalion had won four Victoria Crosses and countless other gallantry awards. The red lanyard for us is a badge of honour, removed from an individual only on punishment due to unbecoming conduct.

Our drill instructors drilled us as though their lives depended on it. In a way they did, because how we fared in the 'passing of the square' would affect their reputation. If we did badly as a squadron on the drill square, their reputation would be tarnished.

Finally, the day of the 'Passing of the Square' arrived. Ram Swaroop laboured on our boots and belts till they shone like mirrors, the length of our hair was down to zero, the stitching on the buttons on our shirts was checked and re-checked, our numerals and shoulder titles were cleaned and re-cleaned till they shone like gold, our black hose tops were folded to measure exactly four inches, with the red and grey garter flashes appropriately placed, the 13 hobnails on the soles of our boots were counted and re-counted and the soles cleaned, we practiced lacing our boots to ensure that our leather boot laces were never twisted, we shaved although there was no necessity but we could not risk it.

On the day of the drill square, we felt that our turnout was perfect and we drilled as though our lives depended on it. The Adjutant was the chief examiner. He belonged to the 5th Gorkha Rifles (FF) – very serious and very strict. Little did I know that one day I would join his regiment and that there he would be a different person altogether. It was only later that I realized that he was playing his part as 'the Adjutant of the National Defence Academy' and that one day it would also fall upon us to play our various parts in the great Indian Army. For today, however, he was dead serious. He had watched our drill movements and made no comments. He then proceeded to inspect us and his keen eyes missed nothing. The RSM followed the Adjutant and tapped the shoulders of those who were passed fit. How we longed for that elusive tap on our shoulder! I did not pass on the first attempt. It took one more parade for me to receive that much awaited tap telling me that I had passed muster. Every cadet ultimately passed off the drill square although some were 'all hands and legs' and very awkward in their movements. Nevertheless, it was an important landmark in our lives and signalled that we had come of age.

At the end of the second term, my Divisional Officer, Flight Lieutenant D.S. Chhabra of the Indian Air Force interviewed those of us from his division. He told me that although he was not there during our first term, he could tell from my reports that I had made some progress. He noted, however, that I had failed in Math and Hindi and that I needed to do better in those subjects, until which time he had no option but to put me up for 'warning for relegation' and he hoped he would not have to do this again next term. I promised that I would do better.

Although I tried very hard, by the end of the third term I

had once again failed in those two subjects. Flight Lieutenant Chhabra was not happy. He said that I was doing very well in games, sports and extracurricular activities and in all other academic and military subjects. If I could only just pass in these two subjects my order of merit in the course would radically improve. I told him that I was too involved in sports and games and that I did not have time to study and that perhaps I needed help to pass these two subjects.

He said, 'Why don't you study at night? The nights are yours.'

I asked him how I could study after 'lights out'.

He looked at me and said, 'Don't ask silly questions; find a way and don't get caught.' He then repeated what RSM Ayling had said to us on our first day when we landed at Dehradun. He had said, 'There is something known as "co-operation". It is a principle of war. You are doing very well in English, History, Geography, Social Studies and some of the military subjects. Why don't you help your coursemates who are weak at these subjects and ask them to help you with Math and Hindi?'

This was a good idea and so, I worked with my coursemates to help each other out during study period and found that it worked very well. I took Hindi and Math seriously and found that they were not so difficult after all. As far as my coursemates were concerned, they found Shakespeare too difficult to appreciate and wanted me to frame questions and write model answers for them. They were delighted with the answers that I wrote for them, which they learnt by rote and managed to do very well in English Literature. Balwant Singh, my coursemate, remembers those answers even today and he recites them verbatim at our course reunions to much back slapping and laughter.

By the time the fourth term was under way, I felt confident that I was doing well academically. Flight Lieutenant Chhabra was following my progress and was also happy. During that term I set up the Academy record for underwater swimming by doing a length and a quarter of the Olympic-size pool. Although it was not a recordable event, I was happy that I could achieve this distance under water. I had also done reasonably well at hockey, football, athletics and boxing.

Now in the fifth term, we were considered to be 'senior cadets', and looked upon as such. I was awarded a 'Blue'[11] for hockey. This was the term when we became eligible to be Squadron Cadet Sergeant Majors and I held this appointment thrice within the term and frankly I enjoyed drilling the squadron, particularly when we had to march to the mess for dinner. When the senior course was away on camp, we fifth termers became the senior-most course and I was appointed as the officiating Academy Cadet Adjutant. I took my job seriously. Too seriously perhaps!

That term, our squadron had done well in competitions and we were close to winning the championship. All that was required was to win the inter-squadron hockey championship to seal being the champion squadron of the Academy. The Squadron Commander, an officer from the navy was very keen that we win the hockey finals – that would certainly clinch our position as the champion squadron. Unfortunately, the boxing championship finals and the hockey finals were on the same day. The events were back-to-back. I was boxing for the squadron and also the captain of the hockey team, the only cadet participating in both events.

I had reached the finals of the boxing championship in the lightweight category and was up against the captain of the Academy boxing team. His name was Lebon Bosco and he was the 'Golden Gloves champion' at Bangalore before he joined the Academy. He was physically tough and had a 'V'-shaped muscular body, with a reputation of winning all his fights by 'knockouts'. Given a choice, I would have not liked to fight him but there was no choice!

During my short tenure as the officiating Academy Cadet Adjutant, I had taken my job too seriously and had given the cadets a tough time. It was now 'payback time' and news travelled fast that the whole Academy would be coming to witness the boxing finals to see me getting thrashed.

We did not have a gym at that time and matches were conducted in a boxing ring on the floor of the Academy workshop.

Talk of this impending bout reached my Squadron Commander and he was most concerned. He wanted me to be fit to lead the squadron in the hockey finals and wanted me to withdraw from this event. I explained to him that I could not walk away from this challenge as it would amount to cowardice. I was able to convince him that I would survive and that we would also win the hockey final. We were told that the Commandant, Major Gen E. Habibullah[12] would be present for both events. Flight Lieutenant Chhabra, my Divisional Officer, ordered me to survive!

The boxing finals were held in the afternoon to be followed by the hockey final soon after. For our fight, Bosco and I had PT *ustaads* to be our 'Seconds'. The rumours were true. The entire Academy had assembled to watch this fight and everyone expected Bosco to make short work of me.

The cadets filed in squadron wise. They were in their PT kit and navy-blue blazers and the workshop was filled to capacity but I could only see a blur of blue and white. To say that I was not afraid would be an outright lie. I was overawed by Bosco's reputation. Our squadron PT *ustaad*, who was my 'second', was a national level boxer and he was giving me tips on how I should fight. I don't know how much of it registered at the time. My mouth was dry and I had butterflies in my stomach. Bosco was sitting in his corner looking very relaxed and confident, his arms extended on both sides on the ropes of the ring, looking at me from the corner of his eye. My Squadron Commander was looking extremely tense.

It is said that when one is in a tight spot one thinks of one's parents. I don't know if that is true, but that day, I did think of what my parents had said to me before I left for the Academy. My mother had said, 'Son, don't do anything for which I would have to hang my head in shame' and my father had said, 'All men have a sense of fear. You are going to be a leader of men and you need to conquer fear.' I resolved to not let my parents down, but I was glad that they were not there to witness my trial.

Most cadets have boxed at some time or the other but I had never asked them about how boxing gloves smell! Somehow, to this day, I hate the smell of boxing gloves. They have an inherent smell of sweat and blood and fear – and that smell churned up the insides of my stomach, particularly when I was up against a boxing champ, far superior to me.

In the Academy, like at Wimbledon, cheering is done only in the breaks. The fight is carried out in total silence.

After what seemed like forever, the referee who was a Major from the Army Physical Training School at Pune and a boxing coach of repute, stepped into the ring and called us both to meet with each other and advised us on how to conduct ourselves in the ring.

The cadets were shouting their heads off. All of them were supporting Bosco. After all, he was seen to be the clear winner and some were even salivating at the prospect of my being knocked out. The only ones supporting me were the cadets from my squadron.

We went to our respective corners and the time keeper said, 'Seconds out of the ring – time' and the gong signalled the start of round one. The noise and cheering stopped, and the silence was palpable!

Bosco and I circled around the ring, sizing each other up. He was taller than me and his 'V'-shaped muscular body was intimidating. He was a southpaw and used his left hand to deliver his typical knockout punch. My second had warned me to watch out for the delivery of that blow.

I had watched Bosco fight before. He normally allowed his opponent to make the first move and then he would wade in, after he discerned a weak spot. I kept my guard up and pushed him to make the first move. Finally, it was I who saw a gap in his defence and went in and delivered a couple of swift blows. This annoyed him and he came for me with a vengeance but I danced out of his way. I was beginning to regain a little confidence now and delivered a few more blows which he parried with his gloves. I went in for the third time and this time he came at me with a succession of three swift blows. I got hit on the nose, my lips and a crashing blow to the head. I was down on the floor and my head was reeling. I got up and felt blood streaming down my nose and mouth. I shook my head and went into him wanting to get it over with, but was saved by the bell.

The whole Academy now broke into a bedlam of noise. All were cheering for Bosco and yelling for the expected knockout punch.

My second, surprisingly, was pleased with my performance and that was reassuring. He warned me once again to be careful of Bosco's left hand. He reminded me that he reserved that for his knockout blow, and said, 'As long as you can avoid that blow you will survive.' I realized now that those who were supporting me only wanted me to survive! That included my Squadron Commander, Flight Lieutenant Chhabra and my squadron mates. I decided that should be my aim – to survive! But I had to survive with honour.

All too soon, the time keeper asked the seconds to get out of the ring and sounded the gong for the second round.

The cheering stopped and once again silence prevailed. Bosco came forward purposefully; head lowered and determined to finish the bout. I was equally determined to frustrate his aim. This time I kept clear of his left hand. Thrice he let fly with that arm of his and each time I managed to avoid those finishing blows. Again, I managed to get in a few good body blows but he landed a couple of punches on my face which got the blood flowing once more and my vest was covered with blood and now, I also had a gash over my right eye. The referee stopped the fight and called for the doctor to examine me. The doctor, a Major and a paratrooper from the Army Medical Corps, climbed onto the ring, examined me carefully and pronounced me fit to continue the fight. The round continued. Perhaps by now I was a little tired because I failed to see his left arm swing to my head and I was once more knocked down to the canvas. I got back up on the count of nine and prepared to face Bosco again, when the bell once again came to my rescue and the second round came to an end.

Back at my corner, my second once more cautioned me about Bosco's left hand. But I knew it was of no avail. Bosco was too good. However, it had now become a clash of wills. Bosco was determined to knock me out and I was determined to not let that happen. If I could survive two rounds without being knocked out, then I could last one more?

I looked at Bosco. Was he tiring? It seemed so, or was it my imagination? I was no longer tired – only battered and badly bruised. I regained some confidence and felt I could last this round, if only I could avoid his left-handed knockout blow. His vest was also covered with blood. That reassured me further. Little did I know that the blood on his vest was mine!

The gong sounded for the third round and the frenzied cheering stopped. However, by now, half the crowd was cheering for me, seeing the determined fight that I was putting up.

I went in with more confidence and teased Bosco with a couple of body blows. He was getting increasingly impatient and irritated with me and seemed determined to bring this fight to a close. He kept swinging at me but following the advice of my second, I managed to duck out of his way. He tried an upper cut but I was not there. Finally, one of his blows struck me hard and I was on the canvas once more. I staggered back up on the count of seven. The referee sent me to my corner and asked my second to wipe the blood that was streaming from my nose. He was about to restart the fight when my Squadron Commander threw in the towel. He was concerned that the bashing that I was taking would render me unfit for the hockey finals, but I was concerned about my honour. If the fight was stopped at that point, I would have lost on a technical knockout but it would also mean that I had given up.

Luckily, the referee seemed to understand that I did not want to give up. There was a huge uproar and cadets were shouting for the fight to continue. He asked for silence and the shouting stopped. The referee called me up and asked me within everyone's hearing whether I would like to continue the fight. 'Yes,' I said. The fight continued. Half the crowd did not want to be cheated from watching me get knocked out but the other half wanted me to survive. Bosco did his best to keep up his record of winning all his fights by knockouts but it didn't happen. I lasted out the last round and to my relief the gong sounded the end of it. The referee collected the points from the judges, cralled us together and raising Bosco's arm, he said, 'Well fought Blue, Red the winner.'

Bosco had won but maybe he was not happy about having won on points and not by a knockout and although I had lost, I was quietly elated. There were some who felt cheated that they had not witnessed a knockout but I was glad I had vindicated the faith I had in myself. I had lost, but I felt that in some ways, I had also won. At the beginning of the bout most of the cadets were all for Bosco but by the end of it, many were supporting me. Perhaps it was the inclination to support the underdog! Once again, I was given the accolade of being a 'Good Loser' and my squadron notched up some more points for the inter-squadron boxing championship. We won the hockey finals in a closely contested match, and so, we won the Inter-Squadron Championship. My Squadron Commander was ecstatic. The fifth term had ended on a high note and I looked forward to my last term at the NDA.

Whilst on term break at home, I received a letter from the Academy informing me that I had been appointed as the Academy Cadet Captain (ACC) for the final term. I feel sure that besides the improvement in my academic performance and in games and sports, the boxing bout with Lebon Bosco played some part in my selection, and I would like to thank Bosco wherever he is.

I was asked to report a day earlier than the rest. On arrival, I was given a file that laid down what was expected of me as the ACC and also as the President of the Honour Code Committee.

However, there was a sequel to the story of the boxing bout with Lebon Bosco!

Many years later, my eldest son Sunith, who was commissioned into my regiment was serving on the staff in a brigade headquarter at Dalhousie and the formation was visited by the Army Chief, General S. Padmanabhan. Sunith, being the junior-most, was last in the lineup of the officers to meet him. When the Chief reached Sunith, he saw from his nameplate that he was a 'Cardozo' and the conversation ran something like this:

'Are you in any way related to General Ian Cardozo?'

'Yes sir.'

'Who is he to you?'

'He's my dad, sir.'

'Has he told you about the thrashing he got in the boxing ring at the NDA?'

'No sir.'

'Ask him. Tell him that I was part of the junior-most course at the NDA, sitting on the floor and watching him get the thrashing of his life. Tell him also, that I have never forgotten that fight and that I admire his guts.'

'Yes sir. I will,' said Sunith.

When Sunith came home on leave, he asked me about what the Chief had said and I was compelled to tell him the story of that fight.

The Honour Code was a bit of a problem – it required a cadet to report the misdemeanour of another cadet, if the cadet didn't own up on his own. I felt that it was dishonourable to report on someone else's wrongdoing – it turned us into informers. Most of us, when we were juniors, had broken every possible rule at the Academy. We smoked clandestinely. We choked on the smoke and did not enjoy the experience in the slightest but we smoked anyway, only because it was prohibited! The point was to challenge the establishment and not get caught and to do something that was prohibited. The challenge was the thing itself and the risk of being caught was exciting! Was this not what the army was all about? What about the risks in war? Would we not be required to do daring things in war and to challenge the enemy and to get the better of him? I am not suggesting that we should break the law but that's the way it was and that is what we believed to be true at that time.

I was asked my views about the Honour Code as the Academy Cadet Captain, and I recorded my views to say that some parts of it were not right, such as reporting to the authorities of what someone else had done amounted to snitching and that many of us found it unacceptable. I don't remember exactly what I said. All this happened over sixty years ago. I know however that my views exist in some file at the NDA because an Admiral of the Indian Navy told me a couple of years ago that he had seen my remarks on file. He did not say that he agreed with me, but he did say that he found my views remarkable because they were made by a cadet at such a young age.[13]

The concept of the 'Honour Code', in my opinion, needs to change. Cadets of the 1st Course apparently felt just as I did, and I think that it's about time that we modified our system, more in keeping with our own Indian values rather than imitating the West Point Honour Code. Brigadier Madhav Prasad of the 1st Course JSW states:

> It remains a moot point whether or not we should have an Honour Code as at West Point – the fact of the matter, however, is that, we as cadets, by and large, did practice an honourable way of life whilst at the Joint Services Wing, with the possibility of a few exceptions still proving the rule.[14]

The last term was very busy – a wrap up of all academic, military and outdoor subjects. There was also a final camp called 'Camp Torna' – Torna being one more of Chhatrapati Shivaji's strategic forts. We also had to notch up as many PT tests 1st Classes and Specials as we could. I was good at beam and rope work but not at vaulting over the wooden horse.

Swimming tests for me were easy, including the Life Guard test. Jumping from the 10-metre diving board was daunting for a few cadets because the swimming pool shrunk to the size of a match box when you looked at it from the diving board, 30 feet high, but like it or not, all of us did it!

After four terms of practice, riding was no longer a pain. I had got the hang of it and we learnt to ride bareback. It became a joy because we now rode outside of the equitation lines, galloping across the open space behind Sudan Block. It was exhilarating to ride like this with so many others. I imagined I was taking part in a cavalry charge and had to stop myself from yelling. But it was something else that made my sixth term unforgettably memorable.

Major Sekhon,[15] the Training Major, was responsible for all matters concerning army subjects. He was a hard taskmaster. He was lean and dark and had a tough exterior. With a sardonic sense of humour and a sharp pair of eyes, he never missed anything. He made it a point to know the names of every cadet and within the first six months he knew each of us like the back of his hand. If we cadets thought we were street smart, then he was smarter than all of us put together! We knew that we had met our match because he was always one step ahead of us. His commitment and dedication to make us the best officers of the Indian Army can never be questioned. Unfortunately, he rubbed everyone the wrong way. The cadets were in awe of him because we knew he could not be fooled. The officer instructors who were junior to him were subjected to the same hard, rigorous routine to which he himself adhered to, but for reasons unknown, he annoyed his immediate superior – the colonel who was Head of the Military Training Team. After he took charge, his camps were the toughest; so much so that 'Camp Chindit' which we did later on at the Indian Military Academy was a 'cakewalk'!

Major Sekhon's diction and expression however, was his weak spot and the cadets zeroed on this weakness to get back at him and he was frequently imitated behind his back. At one of the battalion socials, Major Sekhon was imitated by a cadet in front of the officers and their wives. His poor diction was exaggerated and led to a lot of laughter. Major Sekhon was an invitee and he sat through it all, feeling extremely humiliated. He stated as much, within my hearing, at one of the dinner nights and said that he would never, ever attend another social again.

I felt that the cadets were being unfair to Major Sekhon and the manner in which they were getting back at him was hitting him below the belt.

I responded to Major Sekhon's remark and said, 'Sir, as long as I am the Academy Cadet Captain, I will ensure that you will not be imitated again.' He looked at me with a bitter smile and said, 'Cardozo, never make a commitment that you will not be able to honour.' I said, 'No sir, I mean it.' Major Sekhon was right. I could never have imagined the consequences of my statement.

Towards the end of the term, we went on Camp Torna. Major Sekhon made sure that it was a tough camp; very, very tough. Map reading and night navigation were so difficult that many of us lost our way in the hills where Chhatrapati Shivaji and his guerrillas must have fought hundreds of years ago. Our food convoys were ambushed and we were without food and water for 24 hours. We learnt to live off the land and clawed our way back to our objectives. We learnt many lessons which would benefit us in time to come. But in those days and nights, Major Sekhon earned the displeasure of our course and also of the officers who worked on the camp under him. Major Sekhon must have been aware of the resentment against him but he could not care less. His aim was to bring our experience on the camp as close to the reality of war and I think he succeeded admirably. Finally, after ten days, tired and dishevelled, we reached the finishing point close to the Khadakvasla dam.

Upon reaching the finishing point, I had to resume my duties as the ACC and was told to organize a campfire. I was sitting with my coursemates Satish Shirinagesh and Tunku

Ahmed Nerang,[16] who were rehearsing an item that the two of them had decided to perform. One of the songs that was popular those days was '*The Green Door*' that was played repeatedly in the squadron ante-rooms. We had no musical instruments with us. Tunku was going to sing and Satish was to accompany him by making (what he thought) were musical noises blowing through a comb and tissue paper. We were laughing at their efforts when an officer came up to us and said that the Head of our Military Training Team, a senior colonel, had sent for me.

I wondered why the Head of the Military Training Team would want to see me. I handed over the responsibility of organizing the campfire to another cadet and went with the officer to meet the colonel. It was around one o'clock in the afternoon.

The Camp Officers' Mess was in a grove of trees and the officers seemed to be in high spirits, fostered perhaps by the beer that they were drinking. I was made to stand before the Colonel and he seemed to be on a high, laughing at something that I was not aware of. He had some sheets of paper in his hand from which he was reading and all who were present were laughing their heads off. I was totally ignored and I kept standing there for a few minutes after which I decided to break off. I came to attention and very properly broke off, however, without anybody's permission. I went and sat behind some bushes while the roars of laughter continued. When I had stood there, I had noticed that Major Sekhon was not present.

After a while, my exhaustion for not having slept adequately for two nights got the better of me, and I dozed off. I was woken up by the same officer who had brought me there and once more made to appear before the Colonel.

The Colonel now seemed to notice me for a change and said, 'You there! You Academy Thingamajig. Come here!'

I did not know what 'Thingamajig' meant but I knew that it could not be very complimentary. The mood of those assembled continued to be jocular but I resented the way he spoke to me.

He said, 'Now, look here you, Thingamajig, I have an item for you for your campfire. Here is the script. The item is about Major Sekhon. It is a follow-up on what was presented at the No. 3 Battalion Social.' Everyone present, including the Colonel, burst out laughing. The Colonel seemed to be enjoying himself and was red in the face with laughter.

The Colonel continued, 'The cadet from your course who imitated Maj or Sekhon the last time will continue to play that role and you will be the Mess Havildar.' Again, everyone burst out laughing. He then told someone to hand over the script to me and said, 'I want both of you to learn your parts well and to come here at three o'clock for a rehearsal.'

Major Sekhon's advice to not make commitments that I would not be able to honour came back to me then, but I also remembered the honour of a commitment made. Here was the Head of the Training Team ordering me to imitate Major Sekhon to whom I'd given my word that as long as I was the Academy Cadet Captain, I would ensure that he would not be made fun of.

I also knew that my future lay in the hands of this Colonel who was Head of the Military Training Team.

What was I to do? On one hand my future would be assured if I took the easy way out. On the other, if I did as I was ordered, it would be against all the values that I had learnt at home, at school, and at the Academy. Honour was important. How could I live with myself if I compromised all that I believed in? It was a tough call and I had to take it there and then!

I heard myself say, 'Sorry sir, this cannot be done. I have a deep respect for Major Sekhon and I have given him my word that he will not be imitated as long as I am the ACC.'

The Colonel was aghast! His expression changed. There was a palpable shift from the noise of loud laughter to tension and then to pin-drop silence. All those present wondered what would happen next.

Here, the Head of the Training Team of the NDA was being challenged by a mere cadet, that too in front of all his officers!

Understandably, the Colonel was extremely annoyed. The colour of his face changed from ruddy red to deep purple. I thought he was going to have a fit. A few minutes earlier he had this whole lot of officers hanging on to his every word and here was this mere cadet refusing to do as ordered. He started shouting at the top of his voice and was at his abusive best.

'You %#@*+[18], who do you think you are? I will relegate you, you %^#*+[18], I will have you withdrawn, I will destroy you and break you into little pieces and you will never be able to put yourself together again. Now f… off you little #@%^*+.'

I did not wait for the Colonel to carry out his threats and immediately took off. A couple of officers – a major and a captain came running after me and made me stop.

'Do you even realize what you have done? You have challenged and disobeyed a senior officer? Do you realize that this amounts to indiscipline, defiance and insubordination? Do you realize that your future lies in this Colonel's hands? Are you mad? Here take this script and come for the rehearsal at three o'clock if you know what's good for you.'

And thrusting the offending script into my hands, they walked back to the mess.

I was now painfully aware of the enormity of my refusal to do the bidding of the Head of the Training Team. The Colonel was third in the line of hierarchy at the NDA.

By refusing to be part of a skit to imitate Major Sekhon, was I guilty of a breach of discipline and could I legally be punished for it? And if it was legally not an offence, could the Head of the Training Team find other ways to punish me? He had lost face in front of the other officers and that must have hurt!

I was also very vulnerable in other ways. As the ACC, I was probably in line for one of the medals. At each passing out parade, one cadet was given the gold medal for being the best all-round cadet, one was given the silver medal for being first in order of merit and a bronze medal was given to the cadet who was second in order of merit.

All military subjects – army, navy and air force came under the control of the Colonel and he could punish me in more ways than one.

If I had said 'Yes' to the Colonel, I would not be in the shadow of all these imponderables but how would I face my conscience, the man in the mirror? This was a matter of moral courage. Again, I thought of my parents and my teachers at St. Xavier's School, the Jesuit school where I had studied. They had said: 'If you are true to yourself, you cannot be false to any man, therefore do what is right irrespective of the consequences.' I wished my parents were here to guide me but they weren't and I was not a child any more. They had done what needed to be done as parents. I was on my own now and I had to fight my own battles.

I also remembered the days of my first term and how I had admired the way the cadet appointments carried themselves and my resolve on that day, that if I ever became a permanent appointment, I would carry myself with the dignity and honour that the position bestowed upon me. This was now an obstacle that needed facing, but it was not an easy one.

As the ACC, I was used to being alone – but now I felt lonelier. I was on my own and I had to stand my ground.

At a few minutes to 3 p.m., a Flight Lieutenant from the air force asked if I was ready for the rehearsal.

I said, 'No sir. I am not coming for the rehearsal.'

I thought I saw a glimmer of respect in his eyes. However, he said, 'In that case, please hand over the script to me. I will convey your decision to the Head of the Training Team.'

After that I got busy with the arrangements for the campfire, but this whole episode hung over my head like the sword of Damocles and I began to get very apprehensive of the consequences of my action.

That day, a batch of NCC girls from Bombay had come to Khadakvasla and their camp was located above the dam, quite close to where we were having our campfire. The Deputy Commandant, a naval officer, a fine officer and gentleman, thought it would be good for our morale if the girls were invited for the campfire and so there they were, occupying the front rows waiting for it to begin. They were smart girls from Bombay and our course was delighted by their presence. There was not a single girl in the Academy in those days except one who happened to be the daughter of a civilian instructor. She used to catch a bus in front of the mess to go to college and the cadets used to be hanging out of the windows just to get a glimpse of her. And here, to our great pleasure, there were about forty young girls to look at. Did we stare at them? Of course we did! We could not get enough of the beautiful vision of so many girls at such close proximity.

And then disaster struck!

The Commandant was the last to arrive and then he saw the girls. I don't know whether he was in a bad mood or whether he believed the worst of us. 'Why are these girls here?' he asked. The Deputy Commandant said that he had invited them as they were camping in the vicinity, and he thought it would be a good idea to call them over for the campfire.

The Commandant said, 'Are you aware of what these monkeys are going to present at the campfire? They normally come up with vulgar jokes and we can't have these girls listening to all their rubbish. Ask the girls to leave.'

And so, the girls were asked to go. We felt bad. The girls must have felt bad too, but there was nothing we could do. Most of the cadets were looking forward to talking to them at the dinner after the campfire. Now that would not happen. The campfire dragged on and after it was over, we gratefully went for our camp dinner. Major Sekhon was there and he had made sure that the dinner was really good. Tipsy pudding,[17] an all-time favourite with all of us, was exceptionally good that day and while I was eating, a coursemate came to me and said that the Commandant wished to speak with me.

I looked beyond the campfire, still burning bright, and I could see the Commandant talking to the Head of the Military Training Team.

I realized that the Colonel had taken up the matter of my refusal to imitate Major Sekhon with the Commandant.

I went across to the Commandant. He looked upset.

Luckily for me, I had thought about how I would respond if I was hauled up before the Commandant and here was a God given opportunity to have my say in such a situation. Fortunately, the Colonel was standing there along with the Commandant.

The Commandant said, 'Cardozo, what is this I hear? I am told that you are afraid to imitate Major Sekhon. Do you not know that at events like these, you can imitate your instructors? If you are afraid to do a little thing like this because you might earn the displeasure of your seniors, how will you conduct yourself in times of war?'

Having rehearsed my response for exactly such a situation, I quickly replied, 'Sir, I personally have a very high regard for

Major Sekhon. He was recently imitated at a Battalion Social and felt most humiliated.

'I made a commitment to Major Sekhon that as long as I was the ACC, I would ensure that he would not be imitated. Major Sekhon, in fact, told me not to make a commitment that I would find difficult to honour.

'Sir, as far as being afraid is concerned, it is the Colonel who I should be afraid of. He has threatened to withdraw me from the Academy and to break me into pieces if I did not imitate Major Sekhon. I have nothing to gain from Major Sekhon but have everything to lose by failing to follow the wishes of the Colonel. So, who should I be afraid of sir, Major Sekhon or the Colonel?'

It was a cheeky statement, but I had nothing to lose and I was lucky that the Commandant had the patience to listen to my protracted answer. He was surprised at what I said and turning around to the Colonel, he said, 'Since when have you become the Head of the Board of Relegation and Withdrawal? I thought that was my job! Is Cardozo right in what he says?'

The Colonel kept silent and the Commandant had got his answer. He said, 'Run along now Cardozo and do what you have to do.'

I realized I was lucky that I could explain my position to the Commandant. If I had been marched up to him officially, there would have been no hope. Being put up on a charge meant that the matter had been thoroughly investigated and guilt confirmed. All that was left would be the quantum of punishment.

No ACC up to that time had ever been marched up on a charge and if I was marched up, I would most certainly have been punished and I would have been the first ACC in the history of the NDA to be de-tabbed. My situation was precarious. All my results of the military subjects lay in the hands of the Head of the Training Team. I knew that I had done well in these service subjects. If I was given poor marks, I would lose out on my overall ranking but there was nothing I could do about it.

It was just a few weeks before the end of term and we were practicing for the Passing out Parade. My parents had been invited and they had confirmed that they would come. So far, I continued to command the parade during the rehearsals, but one never knew.

And then it happened! During the final dress rehearsal, Regimental Sergeant Major Ayling ordered me to fall out and come to the Quarter Deck. A Battalion Cadet Captain (BCC) was ordered to take command of the parade. I doubled up to the Quarter Deck in a state of acute disappointment. This was the final dress rehearsal. No more rehearsals. The parade continued and I had to experience the mortification of watching someone else command the parade. During the rehearsal of the award ceremony, one cadet was awarded two medals.

'There goes my medal,' was my reaction. I was crushed. But I was once again asked to take charge of the parade and I marched the Academy off the parade ground.

Two days later, the passing out parade took place and it was reviewed by the Army Chief, General K.S. Thimayya DSO. I commanded the parade and my parents witnessed me getting the gold medal for being the best all-round cadet and the silver medal for being first in the order of merit. My parents were told that it was for the first time in the history of the NDA that a cadet had been awarded two medals.

I realized that the Head of the Military Training Team had been fair to me. He could have taken the opportunity to get back at me, if he wished to. But honour and justice were still alive after all and doing the right thing seemed to have eventually worked out well. It does not always happen, as I would learn later on, but that day it did.

. . .

Major Sekhon hosted a tea party that evening for the permanent appointments before we broke off. It was his way of saying goodbye to all of us. While everyone was leaving after thanking him, he said to me, 'Cardozo, please wait.'

After all the other cadet appointments had left, he placed his hands on my shoulders and said, 'I will never forget what you have done.'

I said, 'Sir, how did you come to know?'

He replied, 'Major Sekhon comes to know everything.'

I went on to the Indian Military Academy (IMA) but we kept in touch. Many years later, he became a friend of my family and used to spend the night in our home whenever he passed through Delhi when I was posted there. Strangely, whenever anyone in the family thought of him, he would make an appearance to be with us on that same day. My wife and sons loved to hear his stories and they still remember him with fondness and deep affection. He was a really good man, and I am sure that most of us remember him with fondness, notwithstanding the tough time that he gave us.

If the NDA with its academic content could be considered as a school of learning, then the IMA could be considered a college of military knowledge. In fact, from 1949 to the end of 1954, the Armed Forces Academy (AFA) consisted of the JSW and the Military Wing. It was only in January 1955 that the NDA in its present avatar took shape at Khadakvasla and the Military Wing went back to its title as the Indian Military Academy.

Our course, the 12th Course, was the last course at the JSW and we still like to call ourselves as 'The 12th J'. At the IMA, ours was the 21st Course which had the numerals of 12 reversed to 21. Our navy and air force coursemates went on their way to the Naval and Air Force academies for the final year of specialized training in their respective services. Later on, we fought shoulder to shoulder in the Sino–Indian War of 1962 and the Indo–Pak wars of 1965 and 1971, as Indian soldiers have fought in all the wars before and after Independence. In the 1971 war, it was Nanda Cariappa, my coursemate, who was one of the squadron commanders whose helicopters carried my battalion into Sylhet. I have coursemates who fought and died at Walong and Namkachu in 1962. As cadets of the NDA, we are proud to belong to the only military institution in the world that trains potential officers from all the three services – the army, navy and air force.

The names of 323 ex-NDA cadets who were killed in war and five who were missing-in-action are recorded in a book, placed in the *Hut of Remembrance* which, in fact, is a War Memorial. The first name in the list is of IC-8947 Captain G.S. Salaria, PVC, who was killed in action in Congo in December 1961.

The speeches made by General Thimayya and myself, at the inauguration of this war memorial, are on its walls. This memorial was built during our tenure at the NDA and we cadets helped in the making of it, through *shramdan*.

At the IMA we morphed from plain cadets to 'Gentlemen Cadets'. The emphasis lay on the term 'Gentleman', which laid down a high code of conduct characterized by the Chetwode motto:

> *'The safety, honour and welfare of your country comes*
> *first, always and every time.*
> *The honour, welfare and comfort of the men you*
> *command men come next.*
> *Your own ease, comfort and safety come last,*
> *always and every time.'*

The word 'Gentleman' emphasized all the qualities that

Hut of Remembrance – National Defence Academy.

characterized gentlemanliness – being a gentleman meant an honest person who would not steal, cheat or lie, a person with a sense of duty, who always gives others their due, is kind and considerate to the weak, polite and chivalrous towards women and who has principles and lives by them – a person who is loyal and trustworthy and puts the interests of others before himself.

The training at the IMA was more military in nature i.e., the emphasis was more on military subjects and less on academics and we had to prove ourselves within the short span of one year. The focus was on weapon training, tactics, physical training, studies of military campaigns, army organization, military law, ethics, customs and traditions of the army and its way of life. The academy was organized into six companies – Naushera, Sangro, Meiktila, Cassino, Zojila and Kohima. The names of the companies were of battles fought by the Indian Army during the Second World War and during the Indo–Pak War of 1947–48. The companies were part of three battalions. The Commandant was a Brigadier and the Deputy Commandant was a Colonel. The three battalions were commanded by Lieutenant Colonels, the companies by Majors and the platoons by Captains. Our instructors were from all regiments and corps of the Indian Army including the Army Education Corps, the Corps of Army Physical Training and the Remount and Veterinary Corps.

Drill at the IMA was a variation of what we did at the NDA. Here it was basically rifle drill; periods and periods of it at the same pace that drill was carried out at the NDA, except that this time it was with rifles. For drill, we had drill purpose (DP) rifles that had red and white stripes painted on the magazine to indicate that they could not be used for firing. They were of Second World War vintage or probably earlier and handed down through successive courses of Gentleman Cadets from the time that the Academy started. Some of them had barrels that were corroded or suffered from cord wear, which meant that however much we tried to clean them, the results were a foregone conclusion. Luckily, those of us who became Under Officers in our final term were required to do sword drill, which was much easier.

At the time, there were only two blocks with good accommodation – the Collin's Block and the Kingsley Block, and you only got there if you were the Champion Company or the runners-up at the end of each term. A term was of six months. The other four companies were accommodated in barracks like the ones at JSW Clement Town, and were located at what was called the East Block and the Dhobi Ghat Block.

The emphasis on sports was more on troop games – basketball, volleyball, football, hockey, swimming, boxing and athletics. Officer sports like tennis, squash, riding, polo, cycle polo, golf and cricket were also played, but you had to

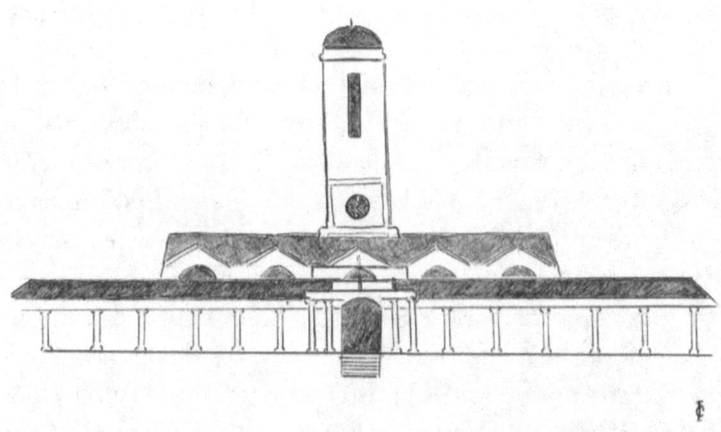

Chetwode Hall – Indian Military Academy

have a proven reputation to be good at these games to get an opportunity to participate in them.

During my first term, I pulled a muscle during an athletic meet and that muscle plagued me throughout my time at the IMA. I had been drafted into Naushera Company and we emerged as the Champion Company. So, in our final term we moved to the luxury of Collin's Block. Here, as a Senior Under Officer, I had a room to myself with an attached bathroom. In front of Collin's Block, we had a Spitfire[18] on the lawn and at a corner was a tank named *'The Curse of Scotland'*, that was a part of the Burma campaign.

Although I took part in most games, cycle polo and volleyball were new to me. I boxed, and played hockey for the Academy but my tenure at the IMA was not as dramatic as it was at the NDA.

At the beginning of the second term, I was appointed as the Senior Under Officer of my company. Unfortunately, our company commander, 'Nana' Thorat[19] was posted out and we got someone else who was peculiar, to say the least. The new company commander seemed to be unsure of himself and apparently wanted to brand us with his personality but seemed to have no idea of how to go about it.

During the first week of the new term, he sent for me. He was in his office and he kept me waiting outside for about fifteen minutes. Finally, he asked me to come in but seemed uneasy for reasons I could not fathom. He had no papers or file in front of him nor in the 'Out' tray nor was he making any telephone calls, so I don't know what he was doing during those fifteen minutes during which he had kept me waiting.

He looked at me for a while, cleared his throat and finally came to the point. He said that two of my Junior Under Officers (JUOs) were not disciplined enough and that they should be marched up to him. I asked him what the charges were, to which he said that one of their rifle barrels was corroded and the other did not have a bulb in his table lamp. I was shocked! I informed him that our rifles were handed down from generation to generation and that both charges were not serious enough to warrant being marched up on a charge. These were JUOs who had to lead their platoons in the conduct of all activities and that these charges would diminish company morale.

My company commander was outraged at my reply and shouted, 'Do as you are told or I will have you also marched up for insubordination. Now get out!'

Fortunately, I did not have to frame the charge sheets. He did so himself. I marched up the two JUOs to him the next day and since he did not have the power to punish them, he remanded them to the Battalion Commander. The following day, the two JUOs and I were lined up in front of the office of the Battalion Commander. The Battalion Commander was away at a conference and he walked in after we had been waiting for about twenty minutes. We were all standing outside his office when he walked in. He apologized for making us wait.

My company commander had been walking up and down the corridor all this while. He was asked to come into the office of the Battalion Commander. After a few minutes, I too was called in as I would have to march my JUOs in.

The Battalion Commander asked for the charge sheets. He put on his reading glasses, looked at the charges and was visibly taken aback. He asked me to leave his office and I was only too happy to get out of there.

The company commander received a tongue lashing from the Battalion Commander for wasting everyone's time.

He said, 'Not only are you wasting my time and yours but you do not seem to understand the basic duties of a company commander at the Academy. You are required to build the morale of your company and you seem to be bent on destroying it. Charges dismissed. You may leave.'

Unfortunately, we were standing outside and were witness to this whole performance and my company commander had lost face in front of his Under Officers. He got out of the Battalion Commander's office, red in the face, and hurried away without a word to us. Since we had no orders to break off, I took charge and broke off the two JUOs and we went to our classes. Unfortunately, the company commander appeared to hold me responsible for what happened instead of accepting blame.

He probably thought that by putting up the two JUOs to the Battalion Commander, he would project that he was in control of the company and knew his job. He never spoke to me after that, and we had to function without his guidance. Luckily though, we had good Platoon Commanders who stepped in when needed.

Towards the end of term, we paid a visit to the Bengal Engineer Group and Training Centre at Roorkee, not too far from Dehradun. The programme included the crossing of a canal and we were made part of the exercise. Vehicles were loaded on to rafts and groups of gentlemen cadets (GCs) embarked on the rafts along with the vehicles and we began moving slowly across the canal. The width of the canal was approximately 100 feet.

One of the rafts was apparently overloaded and started sinking. The GCs on that raft started jumping into the water and it became clear that some of them were finding it difficult to swim, encumbered as they were, with boots and uniform.

Three of us jumped in. Ravi Maira who was known as 'Jumbo' because of his height was one; Vimal Shingal known as 'Decimal' because of his diminutive size was another; and I was the third. Each of us did our bit to help those in difficulty to reach the safety of the canal bank.

After all the GCs had collected on the home bank of the canal, a head-count was ordered and it was found that two GCs were missing. Boats with outboard motors went up and down the canal looking for our missing coursemates but there was no sign of them. Their bodies were found two days later many miles downstream

The term ended in a pall of gloom with the news of the death of two of our coursemates casting a looming shadow. Two of them would now never be commissioned. This was difficult to accept because it was something that need not have happened. This incident made me understand that water must never be taken for granted and had to be handled with care. It was rumoured that the three of us would be awarded life-saving medals but that never happened.

Towards the end of term, senior cadets are evaluated for the sword of honour and for other awards. In this evaluation, company commanders have a major role to play. Apparently, I had no support whatsoever from my company commander.

I passed out seventh in order of merit and being from amongst the first twenty, I was permitted to choose my regiment. A team from Army Headquarters came to the Academy to allot us our regiments. I chose the 5th Gorkha Rifles (FF) because

I was impressed by one of our Platoon Commanders[20] who was from this regiment and by the conduct of the JCO and NCO instructors from this renowned regiment. The officer from Army Headquarters allowed me to choose from between two battalions that had vacancies and I chose the 1st Battalion to which I was finally posted. This would be the family that I would belong to for the rest of my life.

Notes

1. A class that existed at that time between Ist Class and IInd Class coaches.
2. Bombay was a large state created at the time of India's independence. On 1 May 1950, the state was divided into Maharashtra and Gujarat. Today it is the capital of Maharashtra. In 1995 its name was changed to Mumbai. It is the second most populous city in the world.
3. Equivalent to Sergeant.
4. Name changed.
5. A teacher or instructor.
6. Brigadier Madhav Prasad, 'Forging Warriors', as yet an unpublished account of his days as part of 1st Course Joint Services Wing 1949, p. 1.
7. A body of officers who are given the power to examine a situation, to adjudicate whether there was a default and to recommend a suitable punishment/penalty if necessary.
8. Brigadier Madhav Prasad, 'Forging Warriors', as yet an unpublished account of his days as part of 1st Course Joint Services Wing 1949, p. 2.
9. Nanda Cariappa and Satish Shirinagesh were the sons of former chiefs of the Indian Army.
10. 'Liberty' is a naval term that meant that a cadet was permitted to proceed from the environs of the Academy on an 'out pass'.
11. An award at the NDA and some universities worldwide for sports that signify a high level of accomplishment.

12. Major General E. Habibulla, the longest serving and most loved Commandant of the NDA. He commanded the NDA from January 1953 to December 1958. He introduced the right values and traditions in the NDA and gave cadets and cadet appointments sufficient space to grow and develop.

13. Vice Admiral Pradeep Kaushiva had been asked, some years earlier, to examine the aspect of the Honour Code and its relevance to the NDA and he said that he had come across my noting on files at the NDA. For his remarks, please see Appendix A, p. 381.

14. Brigadier Madhav Prasad, 'Forging Warriors', p. 1. An unpublished account of his days as part of the 1st Course at the JSW (NDA).

15. Name changed.

16. Tunku Abdul Nerang, also mentioned earlier, was a tall, slim and jovial cadet from Malaya who took the tough training at the NDA in his stride.

17. The Academy name for trifle pudding which is a confection of sponge cake with custard, jelly, jam, fruit, cream etc. It has always been a favourite with the cadets from the 1st Course onwards. I have had trifle pudding in many parts of the world but none of them were as good as the ones we had at the NDA.

18. A classic British fighter aircraft that played a decisive role in the Battle of Britain and in other war zones during the Second World War. The Spitfire that was located at the IMA belonged to a RIAF Spitfire squadron located in India. However, so great is the love for this aircraft by the Royal Air Force that it was taken back to the UK refurbished, and is now in flying condition after some remarkable aeronautical engineering.

19. An officer from the Maratha Light Infantry and brother of the Vice Chief of Army Staff, Lieutenant General S.P.P. Thorat, DSO.

20. Captain M.L. Chibber who later on rose to the rank of Lieutenant General and the appointment of Army Commander Northern Command.

CHAPTER TWO

The Gorkhas and Nepal

Kafar hunu banda, mornu ramro
(IT IS BETTER TO DIE THAN TO BE A COWARD –
MOTTO OF THE GORKHAS)

If anyone says he is not afraid,
he is either a liar or a Gorkha
FIELD MARSHAL SAM MANEKSHAW

Medium Machine Gun Detachment–1/5 GR (FF)

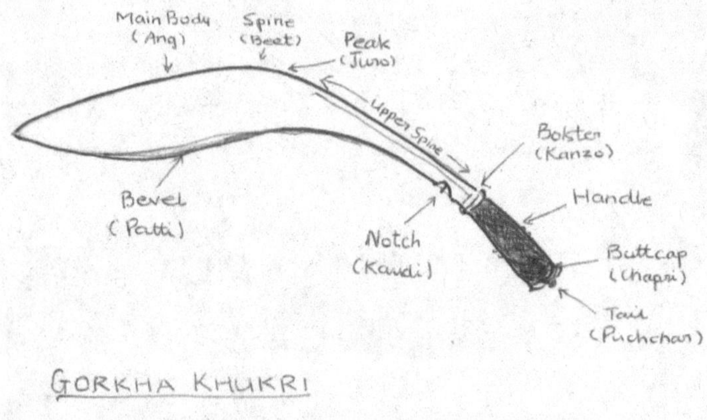

GORKHA KHUKRI

After four years of hard training at the NDA and IMA, we got that coveted pip on our shoulder. Not even 21 years of age, it was a matter of pride and satisfaction that we had been able to take whatever our training institutions could throw at us and were still able to survive! To me it meant that at last I was a part of the Indian Army and posted to an elite battalion of a famous Gorkha regiment.

Before leaving the IMA, on 9 June 1958, we were informed about the location of our units and issued with 'joining orders' and a railway warrant. My unit, the 1st Battalion of the 5th Gorkha Rifles (FF), was at Ambala. I had to join my unit there.

When I detrained at Ambala, I was met by Lieutenant Gurdip Singh Gill, the junior-most officer of the battalion, and a rifleman who was detailed as my batman. My batman met me with a huge smile, a smart salute and a firm handshake. He had a cherubic face and was about five feet tall. He had a gold tooth which became visible every time he smiled. I spoke to him in Hindi but he didn't seem to comprehend what I was saying. Lieutenant Gill smiled and said, 'His name is Tanaraj Pun. He does not know Hindi and that is why he has been selected to be your batman. He understands only Nepali. He will communicate with you in Nepali and that is how we hope you will learn the language.'

Gurdip said something to Tanaraj in Nepali and he beckoned to a coolie to pick up my baggage, which was the ubiquitous black trunk and hold-all that followed us from the NDA to the IMA and thereafter until we retired, except that by that time we had many more black boxes!

Tanaraj Pun and I got along reasonably well. When I spoke to him in Hindi his forehead would crease into a big frown and I could literally hear him working out what I had said. Then he would break into a big smile to convey that he understood and would say something in Nepali which I could not comprehend. In the beginning, neither of us understood each other but after a while we began to get the hang of what the other was trying to say. Nepali is the link language for all the tribes and communities in Nepal and the regimental language in all Gorkha regiments. The Puns are part of the Magar clan and are known for their cheerfulness and ability to be jovial in the most trying circumstances. I was lucky to have Tanaraj Pun as my first batman.

I had arrived at the battalion on a Saturday evening and was told that I had come when a change of the command of the battalion was taking place. The handing and taking over between the current and the next Commanding Officer (CO) was scheduled for Monday, after which the new CO would meet me.

Sunday was spent sprucing up my uniform so that I would be smartly turned out on my first day with the battalion when I would meet the CO, all officers, JCOs and men of the unit. Fortunately, the 5th Gorkha Rifles (FF) was the only rifle regiment that wore brown leather belts and boots[1] – all the rest wore black leather. So, I did not have to change my boots and belt, and Tanaraj gave them an extra shine.

Early on Monday morning, I was summoned to the office of the Adjutant, Captain Jagmohan Singh Rawat, a very smart officer from the NDA. He looked me up and down, stood up, shook my hand and welcomed me to the battalion. He did not ask me to sit down and I was thankful – those days our cotton uniforms were starched and if I sat down my uniform would have got crumpled. After confirming that I had settled down, he took me to the office of the second-in-command (2ic).

The 2ic was an officer from the Travancore State Forces. All four rifle company commanders were VCOs[2] who had been given what was in those days called the 'Thimayya Commission', a step taken by the Chief to promote VCOs to make up for the shortfall of officers in the army caused by the vacuum created when the British left India.

The only regular commissioned officers were the CO, the adjutant, the quartermaster, two subalterns of lieutenant rank, senior to me by one year and two years, respectively, and I. The CO was the only one who had a car – a black Hillman and that placed him in a special category.

The Adjutant took me back to his office, rang up 'Alpha' Company and asked for the Company 2ic to report to his office. In a short while Subedar Bhaktabahadur Gurung reported. He crashed into the office with the smartest of salutes that I had ever seen and said in Nepali, 'JC No. 2641 Subedar Bhaktabahadur Gurung, 2ic Alpha Company reporting.'

The Adjutant introduced me to the JCO and told him that I was being posted to Alpha Company as its Company Officer. Bhaktabahadur turned around and gave me another one of his lightning-like salutes. He was a very smart JCO with a round face and smiling eyes and two rows of Second World War campaign ribbons, which indicated that he had served with the 8th Army and that he was decorated with the Indian

Distinguished Service Medal (IDSM), a gallantry award. He welcomed me with a big smile. The Adjutant told him that he was to take me under his wing and to instruct me in the traditions, customs and history of the regiment and the Nepali language. For the next month I would join the *Umedwar*[3] cadre and learn all that a junior officer of the unit ought to know about the battalion, the regiment and my profession as an Infantry platoon commander. Bhaktabahadur did another smart about turn, saluted the Adjutant and speaking to me in English, said, 'Come along, Saab.'

Bhaktabahadur was a bundle of energy and jumped straight into action to carry out the directions of the Adjutant.

All of us bachelors shared a big bungalow hired by the Military Engineering Service (MES). The seniors had the bigger rooms and juniors got the smaller ones. Being the junior-most, I got the smallest room. The room could just about accommodate a bed, a chest of drawers and a chair. The bed was a charpoy with bamboos at either end to hold up a mosquito net. The room had no fan, so I slept outside in the open. Adjacent to this room was a smaller one which served as a bathroom. It had no tap. The tap was outside in the garden. There was no wash basin either but there was a metal bucket with a mug on a stool. There was a hole for water to go out and I was warned to be careful – it also served as a pathway for snakes to get in. There was also something which in the army is called a 'thunder box', akin to a primitive commode. Water was heated outside in an old tin can over a wood fire. The rent for the room was deducted from our monthly salary by the Controller of Defence Accounts (O). To the civil bureaucracy it did not matter whether you lived in a proper flat with all the modern amenities or a tent or the type of accommodation that we lived in – the rent that was debited from our salary was the same! That was the way it was, and no one cribbed or complained.

Early in the morning, Tanaraj would wake me up with a cup of tea that he would bring from the officer's mess in a thermos and would then run off for PT. When I came back from the mess after PT and breakfast, he would have prepared my uniform, polished my boots till they shone and heated water for my bath and would be off for training.

Tanaraj Pun loved being a soldier, loved the individual training that all soldiers had to undergo and he enjoyed all aspects of soldiering. The only parade that he missed, because he was my batman, was the first period after breakfast. Thereafter, I saw him only in the afternoon when he would prepare my uniform for the evening or the next day, bring my evening tea and then he would be off again for games.

In those early days the only means of transport we second lieutenants could afford, on a pay of Rs. 450 per month, was a cycle, which we would hire from the regimental contractor @ Rs. 10 per month. There is an allegorical story that before the contractor delivered the cycle, he would ask whether it should be fitted with a carrier or a stand. On asking why, he would answer, 'Saab, in the army you can either look after your career or take a stand!'

Thinking that I could reduce Tanaraj's exertions in walking to the mess in the afternoon sun to get my evening tea, I told him to use my cycle. At first, he declined. When I insisted, the inevitable frown appeared on his forehead but this time there was no smile. He dutifully took my cycle to the mess every day but I noticed that the time spent away was just the same. I chose not to say anything until Gurdip Gill, on his way back one afternoon, saw Tanaraj walking with my cycle with the thermos of tea slung on his shoulder. It was only then that I understood that Tanaraj did not know how to cycle! But he obeyed orders and dutifully walked along with my cycle to the mess and back every day. He must have thought I was daft for giving him such an order, but he carried it out because I had told him to do so.

Sometime later, when I was supervising firing on the firing range, I found one soldier repeatedly hitting the bullseye at 400 yards, a remarkable feat. I went to investigate and found it was none other than Tanaraj. He was thoroughly enjoying himself smacking one bull after another. When he saw me watching him, he gave me a huge grin with his glinting gold tooth, and went on to hit a few more bullseyes on his target.

My battalion was part of the famous 4th Infantry Division that had made a great name for itself during the Second World War. Although a large number of personnel from those war days had gone home on retirement, the unit still had a few JCOs and NCOs from that period and I was awestruck to see the rows of ribbons on their chests that included service with the 8th Army in Africa, Sicily and Italy.

Amongst the JCOs there was one with an Indian Order of Merit (IOM), two JCOs with Military Crosses and nine JCOs and NCOs with IDSMs, and one JCO and two NCOs with the Military Medal (MM). The Subedar Major was decorated with the IDSM and the MM. There were NCOs with Mahavir Chakras (MVCs) and Vir Chakras (VrCs) earned during the Indo–Pak war of 1947–48. The battalion had a huge number of gallantry awards and battle honours and it was wonderful to belong to such a gallant unit.

Gorkha soldiers are tough. Living in the hills of Nepal makes them strong and resilient and they can withstand the vicissitudes of war, climate and terrain better than most. Cheerful in disposition, nothing disturbs their equanimity. They are fiercely loyal and fearless in battle. No matter how bad the situation, they never complain. All these qualities make them among the best soldiers in the world and they are much sought after. Soldiering for them is a natural profession and the battalion had men of the same family who were fifth-generation soldiers.

The 5th Gorkhas recruit their soldiers from western and central Nepal and the men are mostly Gurungs and Magars, although there are a few Puns, Rais, Limbus and Chhetris. Magars and Gurungs are *parbatiyas* meaning that they come from the parbat (hilly part) of Nepal. They are the original speakers of what is today known as Nepali. The parbatiyas include the Brahmins, Thakurs, Chhetris and a few others. The Rais, Limbus and Tamangs are from eastern Nepal and are from the *Kiranti* tribes. The Gurungs and Magars form the largest tribes in Nepal and within the 5th Gorkhas, they are recruited in more or less equal proportion.

Subedar Bhaktabahadur took me under his wing. At that time in 1958, the 4th Indian Infantry Division was saddled with a Divisional Commander who had never seen action. Although he had started his career with an infantry regiment, he decided to take the softer option of transferring to the Army Service Corps. He had never commanded an infantry company, battalion or brigade but, in complete disregard of all rules and regulations, was promoted to Major General's rank and elevated to the command of this famous Infantry Division due to his political connections. Instead of using this opportunity to train soldiers for war, he used its manpower and resources to please his political masters by building houses in the infamous *Operation Amar* and reduced the personnel of this famous formation to a collection of brick layers, masons and overseers. This proved to be calamitous, as was seen later on. Subsequently, he was promoted still higher to command a corps in the Northeast during the Sino–Indian War with disastrous consequences.

Subedar Bhaktabahadur and I were often together on duty supervising the building of these houses. We had no expertise at all in this area of work but orders were orders and we had to be there to see that everyone was on time and to oversee the work. In between supervision of the construction work, Bhaktabahadur Saab would teach me Nepali and recount fragments of our history. During our conversations on those long mornings and afternoons, regimental history came alive when he told me stories of what happened during the regiment's early days, during the two world wars and in the Indo–Pak war of 1947–48.

Bhaktabahadur Saab advised me to go through the regimental history which I did and learnt that the battalion was at Abbottabad when the Second World War commenced on 3 September 1939. This war led to the Indian Army contributing over two million men in arms to assist the Allies. This constituted the largest volunteer army in military history.

Initially, the battalion, as part of 8th Infantry Division, was located in Persia to protect the oil refineries but was later moved to Africa and then to Sicily and Italy to take on the Germans and Italians.

The battalion fought its way up the Italian peninsula across a series of rivers directly across the Allied advance – the Sinello, the Sangro, the Moro, the Arielli, the Gari, the Volturno, the Grande, the Arno, the Senio, the Santerno, the Po, the Adigetto and the Adige rivers. The Germans had built their defences on these rivers using them as formidable obstacles. Battles involving river crossing operations were fought at Atessa, Mozzagrogna, Moro River, San Angelo, Ripa Ridge, Rocca D'Arce, Patella, Femina Morta, Monte San Bartolo, Santerno and the Adige River.

These battles started with the Battle of Attesa on 12 November 1943 and ended with the battle on the Adige River when the German armies in Italy surrendered unconditionally to the Allies on 2 May 1945.

During the Battle of Atessa, Bhaktabahadur Gurung was a Lance Naik commanding a Section which took part in a silent attack launched by two of our rifle companies against the Germans. The companies moved forward quietly at night and reached the German posts that were holding them up on the outskirts of Atessa undiscovered. They went in with khukri and grenade, surprising and killing the German defenders. Some of the German machine gun posts tried to react but it was too late and they were overrun before they could respond.

The Germans launched a series of strong counter-attacks to recapture the ground that they had lost but were beaten back with heavy casualties. However, after a while, the ammunition of the Gorkhas had run very low and the situation had become critical when the Germans launched one more counter-attack. At that juncture, Lance Naik Bhaktabahadur's section was almost down to their last round! He allowed the Germans to come within 20 yards from his post and launched a khukri attack. Hand-to-hand, the German bayonet was no match for the Gorkha khukri. The German attack broke and the Germans fled. Lance Naik Bhaktabahadur's Section followed them some way downhill shouting their war cry of '*Ayo Gorkhali*' and overran another German machine gun post. Okel Gurung, a rifleman from Bhaktabahadur's section, picked up the machine gun left behind by the Germans and turned it on the retreating Germans. The Germans left behind a number of bodies including that of an officer who had been decorated with the Iron Cross.

Okel Gurung went on to greater exploits as the war progressed. At the Battle of Patella, Okel, now a Lance Naik, he destroyed three German posts for which he was awarded the IOM. Bhaktabahadur Saab, however, shared that Okel had told him that he would one day be awarded the Victoria Cross, Britain's highest award for valour in the face of the enemy. Okel Gurung was undoubtedly a very brave soldier and his promotion to Lance Naik and Naik and the awards of the IOM, the MM and the mention-in-dispatches in quick succession were a testimony to his courage, but the Victoria Cross eluded him. He was killed in an assault on a German position at the Santerno River. Ironically, the Victoria Cross was won instead by Thaman Gurung, a rifleman of the same company, a few weeks later, at the Battle of Monte San Bartolo. Thaman was also killed while executing an amazing act of courage.[4]

One of the accounts records that during the Second World War at the Battle of Patella, one Lance Naik Raman Singh Rana, while tackling a German post single-handedly, buried his khukri in the skull of a German machine gunner and was unable to withdraw it. He thereafter picked up a German shovel and despatched the other two survivors with this unorthodox but effective weapon for which he was awarded the IDSM.

The capture of Atessa opened the way towards the Sangro River and the regimental history records an enthralling account of the Battle of Mozzagrogna. After this battle, the CO selected a house for his headquarters and gave orders for the removal and burial of nine German bodies that were lying in the cellar. A party of Gurkhas carried the bodies up on a ladder and dumped them into a shell-hole. They had disposed of eight and were about to carry up the ninth when the 'corpse' jumped to his feet with a scream of terror. Khukris were drawn and the hapless German was about to be dispatched when some British anti-aircraft gunners who were with the Gurkhas said, 'Hey, Johnny, you can't kill him like that.' The typical reply of remorseless Gurkha logic was, 'But we were ordered to bury nine dead Germans. Surely you don't expect us to bury this one alive!'

The battalion continued to fight its way up the Italian peninsula, one battle after another across a series of rivers. During an attack on a German position at Arielli in January

1944, CQMH[5] Lachiman Rana, who was commanding a platoon realized that our artillery could not do much damage to the German position that they had to capture – the position was under the lip of a ravine. After the artillery bombardment, his platoon would have to negotiate a hundred-foot hill covered by German machine gun fire. The NCO decided that there were times when a strict adherence to orders might not be advisable. He did not wait for the appointed zero hour. Instead, calling on his own platoon and the next one to follow him, he led them through the exploding shells of our own artillery and fell upon the Germans who were crouched in their trenches waiting for the bombardment to lift. The surprise was complete, and the blood-curdling yells of '*Ayo Gorkhali*' were too much for the Germans. They fled in wild disorder, abandoning position after position until 'C' Company secured not only its own objective but also the objectives for a later attack by the 1st Royal Fusiliers, the second battalion of the brigade.

Gorkhas are inveterate hunters and are skilled in stalking their prey. The word for meat in the battalion even today is 'shikar' because in the hills the only meat they consume is what they can kill by hunting. Bhaktabahadur had many more anecdotes up his sleeve – of how when the opportunity presented itself, selected men from the battalion who were skilled at stalking were often sent across 'no man's land' to stalk and kill German sentries at night. On one occasion, he said a two-man party went across into the German defences at night, silently entered a trench, decapitated two Germans and let the remainder two off so that they would tell the grisly story about the Gorkha ghosts who walk by night and make heads roll, contributing to the terror that the Gurkha and his khukri inspired – an example of psychological warfare at its best, even before such warfare was even conceived of and taught.

The battalion served twenty months in Italy and lost over a thousand men. In addition to the Victoria Cross won by Rifleman Thaman Gurung, officers and men of the battalion earned two DSOs, five IOMs, one OBE, three MBEs, seventeen MCs, twenty-seven IDSMs, six MMs, an American Silver Star and a Bronze Star. Some of these awards adorn the walls of our Officers' Mess even today.

In those days, we had what was called the 'Retention Exam'. It required young second lieutenants like me to be tested in the regimental language, regimental history, tactics and administration at Section and Platoon level. We were required to pass this exam within the first six months of service. Without meaning to, Bhaktabahadur Saab had prepared me for these subjects seamlessly.

I don't think anybody ever failed the Retention Exam. It was a redundant test anyway, probably meant to be taken by British officers who did not know the language or the Indian soldier, and after a few years it was scrapped. But there were other exams like Part 'A', 'B', 'C' and 'D' that determined our promotion to captain and major's rank and one had to prepare seriously for these exams in order to be promoted.

Describing the early days of the battalion, Bhaktabahadur Saab told me about the Afghan wars and the Battle of Peiwar Kotal on 2 December 1878, where the battalion won its first battle honour and the first of its four Victoria Crosses. We were told that the painting of this battle by Vereker Hamilton, the brother of General Sir Ian Hamilton, hangs on a wall of the dining hall of the military academy at Sandhurst. Peiwar Kotal was a great battle, but Lord Roberts, our first Colonel of the regiment, recounted that the Battle of Charasia was of greater significance. An extract of the description of the battle by General Sir Ian Hamilton says:

The battle of Charasia, on 6 September 1879, furnished history with one of those spectacles which adorns the galleries of a soldiers' retrospect and makes him feel that it is better to have lived and fought than never to have fought at all… All at once, in a long line of scattered groups, our infantry left the cover of their rocks and began to scramble the last 150 yards to the ridge. There was a lull in the firing. The smoke cloud lifted and down came the Afghan regulars! Right on top of the Gurkhas they charged. Our lives – everyone's lives hung upon the conduct of this battalion. They stood firm… and the gallant 5th never faltered, but stood their ground like bricks and shot the Afghan counter-attack to pieces. If the Gurkhas had given way, no one would have gone back to India. Lord Roberts himself always said that this battle was the most touch-and-go affair of his career. The tops of the mountains overlooking Charasia were literally white with masses of armed tribesman watching to see which way the struggle would turn… the penalty of defeat, or even a repulse, would have been annihilation.

Based on these two battles and the conduct of the battalion throughout the Afghan campaign, Lord Roberts, when appointed Commander-in-Chief of the Indian Army, chose a 5th Gurkha soldier to be part of his coat of arms.

Another amazing incident took place soon after the Battle of Charasia. On 7 October 1879, the Kabul Field Force entered Kabul and on 12 October, the battalion was given the duty of guarding the magazine in the Bala Hissar Fort. On 16 October, a fire was reported in the fort. The fire alarm was sounded and preparations were made to evacuate the arsenal. The guard commander was ordered to leave his post with the guard party, but this he refused to do, until according to orders given to him by the Adjutant, he was properly relieved.

In consequence, the entire guard of 22 men was wiped out when the magazine exploded. This incident was only one of many which exemplified the extent to which Gurkha soldiers will go in the execution of duty and the carrying out of orders once given.

The regiment subsequently served for many years in Afghanistan. It became the most famous and the most decorated of all the Gurkha regiments and in due course its officers and men won seven Victoria Crosses. It was the only Gurkha regiment to be designated as 'Royal' and permitted to add 'Frontier Force' to its title.

In 1924, the first battalion of this regiment, the 1st Battalion the 5th Gurkha Rifles (FF) was declared to be the best battalion in the British Empire and today it is the only infantry battalion in the Indian Army that has been awarded the Unit Citation[6] four times for its performance against terrorists, insurgents and for its performance on the Siachen Glacier.

Gorkhas normally have the word 'Bahadur' appended to their names, like Bhaktabahadur Gurung, Bir Bahadur Thapa, Jagat Bahadur Ghale, Jit Bahadur Pun. To get around this problem of avoiding long names, the names are reduced by shortening a Nar Bahadur to 'Nare', a Dhan Bahadur to 'Dhane', a Jit Bahadur to 'Jithe'. However, zeroing on the right individual would continue to be a problem because in each company there could be a number of 'Jithes', 'Bhaktes' 'Nares' etc. So, in the battalion, as in every other Gorkha regiment of the Indian Army, every individual has the last one or two numbers of his regimental number appended to his name, e.g. a Narbahadur whose last two digits of his regimental number is 11 would be known as 'Gyara Nare' to distinguish him from the other 'Nares' in the battalion and this applied equally to the 'Dhanes', 'Bires', and 'Bhaktes'. Gorkha women generally do not call their husband by their names, so they too are beneficiaries of this system – the wife of a JCO, whose last two digits of the number are 37, for instance, would refer to her husband as 'Saithees Saab'.

Gorkha parents also do not call their children by name but by terms that indicate the order in which they were born – Jetha (eldest), Maila (second eldest), Saila (third eldest), Raila (fourth eldest), Thaila (fifth eldest) and so on ending with Kancha (youngest).

The battalion also had some excellent customs and traditions. One of them was that when an officer was commissioned, he did not go home on his first leave. Instead, he spent it in Nepal in the homes of his men. The young officer would be accompanied by a soldier who was due to proceed on leave, who took him to his own home, where he spent two to three days and then he would be handed over to the next family and the next, and so on, until all the families of his men were visited and it was time to return to the battalion.

In this manner, the young officer got to know the families of his men, their language, dialects, customs, culture and traditions, and the difficulties they faced in those mountainous areas of Nepal where most of the travelling was done on foot. The fathers and grandfathers of his men told him stories of battles fought in faraway lands and the history of the battalion would come alive. By the time he returned to the battalion, he would have met and known every member of his men's families and strong bonds would form between the officer and the men he commanded, which would last a lifetime.

So closely do the men's families associate with the unit, that family honour and the honour of the battalion become synonymous and generation after generation of soldiers continue to serve with the unit. It becomes a matter of honour to ensure that the link between family and battalion never breaks. When I joined the battalion, the unit had soldiers of the fifth generation serving in its ranks. Family, clan, tribe, district and village come to be closely linked with the battalion.

In one instance, a third-generation soldier of the battalion was killed in Sri Lanka. It was the custom of the unit at the time that when a soldier died in war, every individual of the unit right from the CO down to the junior-most rifleman contributed the equivalent of one day's salary, which was put together and sent to the family to tide over the period till the family pension started arriving. This money was sent to the soldier's home through a JCO or an NCO who lived closest to the home of the soldier who had been killed. In this case, a JCO from a nearby village was sent, both villages being remote hamlets on the Nepal–Tibet border.

When the JCO arrived at the village, he met the dead soldier's mother and was surprised to see that she was already in mourning. Perplexed at how she could have known of her son's death, he sat quietly by her side. After a while, the mother whose husband belonged to the same unit said, 'It is good of the Commanding Officer saab to send you to meet me, but how did he know that my husband had died?'

The JCO now realized that she had not only lost her son but also her husband around the same time, that she was unaware of the loss of her son and that he now had the unfortunate task of informing the lady that her son had also died. Nevertheless, he did what he had to do and gave her the news. She was speechless for a while. She sat in silent sorrow and except for the tears that rolled down her weather-beaten face, she did not give way to the emotions that churned her inner being. They sat in silence for quite a while.

'How did he die?' she finally asked. 'Did he die like a good soldier?' On being told that he had died a hero's death, she was relieved. Then she said that they had only two sons. The elder was sent to the battalion in keeping with the tradition of sons following fathers into the regiment, and the younger one had remained at home to work the homestead.

Just then, the second son returned from the forest where he had gone to collect wood. She sat him down and told him about his brother's demise. Pointing at her younger son, to the JCO she said, 'It is not right that the battalion is not represented by our family. Our line must not break. Take him back with you.' To honour his mother's wishes, the boy was duly recruited and joined the battalion where his brother, father and grandfather had served. The line did not break. The boy now has a son and the battalion awaits his coming of age so that he could be the fourth in line of that family. It is this principle of the 'cause' being larger than 'self' that is the ultimate arbiter – it decides how men and women of the forces live and act in peace and teaches them how to fight and die in war. I had visited this family on my first visit to Nepal and later on, when I heard about what had happened, wrote a poem about the incident.

Gorkhas are never intimidated by senior officers or persons in high office and are egalitarian in their approach to every level of society. They are as comfortable with kings as with commoners. They are obedient but never obsequious. They are loyal but never servile. They are cheerful in adversity and never complain. During Dashera we would be drinking and dancing the night away but never would any soldier take advantage of the closeness with his officers thereafter.

The festival of Dashera is very special to the Gorkhas. It commemorates the triumph of good over evil and the victory of Goddess Durga over the demon king Mahishasura, and animal sacrifices are made in her honour. It is also a test for the junior-most officer to use the khukri – a sort of initiation into the art of war-fighting. The head of the animal has to be sliced off in one clean cut to kill it instantly. If that does not happen, then the blood of the animal is rubbed on the hapless officer's face in order to avoid bad luck in a future war.

Lieutenant Colonel Ralph Turner, MC who had served with the 3rd Gurkha Rifles during the First World War, wrote this moving tribute to them in the introduction to the *Dictionary of the Nepali Language* which encapsulates the typical Gorkha soldier. He says:

My thoughts turn to you who were my comrades, the stubborn and indomitable peasants of Nepal. Once more I hear the laughter with which you greeted every hardship. Once more I see you in your bivouacs or about your fires, on forced marches or in trenches, now shivering with wet and cold, now scorched by a pitiless and burning sun. Uncomplaining you endure hunger and thirst and wounds; and at the last your unwavering lines disappear in the smoke and wrath of battle. Bravest of the brave, most generous of the generous ----

These words echo the manner in which the Gorkha soldiers fought during the First World War. Over 200,000 fought in this war of which 20,000 became casualties.

By the time the war ended, the Gorkhas had distinguished themselves in every theatre and their reputation for courage, steadfastness and competence proved difficult to match.

The Second World War saw India providing over two million men, the largest volunteer army in military history. Of these, many battalions of Gorkhas participated in every campaign in Asia, Africa and Europe. Once again, their courage and competence proved proverbial. Battalions of my regiment fought in Iraq, Egypt, Italy, Burma, Malaya, Siam and Indonesia in one of the most destructive wars in human history. The Gorkhas, as usual, won a huge number of gallantry awards and battle honours. Of the twenty-eight

Victoria Crosses (VC) awarded to the Indian Army during the Second World War, ten were awarded to Gorkha soldiers. Of these four were awarded to soldiers of my regiment. Of these, one was awarded to Thaman Gurung of 'First Five' and the rest to Gaje Ghale, Agan Sing Rai and Netrabahadur Thapa of Second Five. Subedar Netrabahadur Thapa and Agan Sing Rai won their VCs on the same day and Second Five is the only battalion of the Indian Army which has won two VCs on the same day – the battalion is known as 'VC *Paltan*'.[7]

The words Gorkha and Nepal have become synonymous, although the origin of the word Gorkha arises from the name of the Gorkha district in Central Nepal, northwest of Kathmandu. It is from here that in 1742, its king, Prithvi Narain Shah sallied forth to conquer the small kingdoms of the Kathmandu Valley and established the foundation of the present state of Nepal. Prithvi Narain belonged to the Shah dynasty and had Rajput roots that traced back to Rajasthan.

The conquests continued to spread till they threatened the interests of the British East India Company. An inevitable confrontation took place that resulted in the three Anglo–Nepal wars. Strangely these wars, instead of exacerbating relations between the opponents, gradually resulted in an increasing admiration and appreciation of each other's fighting skills, attitude and behaviour. At the battle of Kalunga – 31 October to 30 November 1814, the Gorkha army led by Bal Bahadur Thapa displayed extraordinary courage and inflicted heavy casualties on the British force. Major General Robert Rollo Gillespie was killed during this battle. At the battle at Malaun, in 1815, David Ochterlony who led the British forces, allowed Amar Singh Thapa, the defeated Gorkha general to march out from the fort at Malaun without surrendering his weapons and with his honour intact in recognition of the courage with which they had fought.

Nepal, however, had to sue for peace and by the Treaty of

Sugauli, had to give up their conquests and so, the kingdom's boundaries shrunk to what they are today. The treaty also gave the British the right to recruit soldiers from Nepal for the British Indian Army. The Treaty of Sugauli was signed on 2 December 1815 but ratified by Nepal only on 4 May 1816. However, the mutual respect and admiration between the British and the Gorkhas continued to grow since then.

On 24 April 1815, the Governor-General authorized the raising of the first Gurkha battalion which entered into service with the East India Company and the first battalions, the *'Nasiri' (Friendly)* paltans came into being. The 1st Battalion the 1st Gorkha Rifles is known as the Nasiri Paltan even today. The number of battalions continued to grow, and by the First World War, the Indian Army had ten Gorkha regiments, each with varying number of battalions. At the end of the war, the regiments were reduced to two battalions each.

After the Second World War, Britain could not afford to hold on to all ten Gorkha regiments and a Tripartite Conference took place between India, Nepal and Britain where it was decided that Britain would hold on to just four regiments and six would become part of the Indian Army. A referendum took place and the regiments as well as the soldiers were given the freedom to join either the British or the Indian armies. The 2nd, 6th, 7th and the 10th regiments went to Britain and the 1st, 3rd, 4th, 5th, 8th, and 9th came to India. The basis on which Britain decided to choose to retain the 2nd, 6th, 7th and 10th regiments is still unknown. The 2nd and the 6th comprised mainly of Gurungs and Magars, and the 7th and 10th were basically Rais and Limbus. However, a large number of Rais and Limbus from the 7th and the 10th who did not opt to join the British army formed a separate new regiment and that is how the 11th Gorkha Regiment of the Indian Army was born.

Although the divisions took place amicably enough, it was not without some amount of rancour. So far, the account of this separation has been narrated only by British officers from Gurkha[8] regiments and the Indian side of the story has never been told. However, this is not the place to tell it. It will find place in another book about the Gorkhas of the Indian Army, which I hope to write one day.

■ ■ ■

By January 1959, I had completed seven months at Ambala and I applied for my first leave. The leave was sanctioned but I was told that I couldn't go home, but I could go to Nepal. The Quartermaster, Captain Vishwanath Rao also wanted to go, so we decided to go together. At that time, the first and only road that linked India with Nepal was built by Indian Army engineers to Kathmandu, which lies more or less in the centre of Nepal. The road started from Raxaul in Bihar and went via Bhimpedi onwards to Kathmandu. The officer in charge of building this road was Colonel Jaganathan, a strong and colourful personality from an Indian Army engineer regiment, who finds mention in the book *The Mountain is Young* by Hans Suyin.[9]

On the invitation of Captain Ronald Pereira, an officer from the battalion, we chose to visit a place called Dang, close to the Indo–Nepal border, where his wife's family, descendants of indigo planters, lived. They had a farm there, close to Champaran in Bihar where Mahatma Gandhi started his first satyagraha movement in 1917. We thought it would be an interesting prelude to our journey to Nepal. We had to travel approximately 200 kilometres by train and bus from Dang to Sunauli in Uttar Pradesh, our entry point to Nepal.

Captain Rao and I decided to enter Nepal on foot by a route frequented by our soldiers. We walked on a track along the Andhi Khola river that runs down western Nepal. This track was used by veterans to collect their pension from

Kunraghat in Gorakhpur and we chose it with an intent to meet as many of our pensioners as possible. In order to enable them to recognize us, we travelled in uniform with our red 'royal' lanyard clearly visible.

Before entering Nepal, we also decided to visit the Gorkha Recruiting Depot at Kunraghat to get a close look at the recruiting process.

Although by the Treaty of Sugauli, Gurkhas were permitted to join the British Indian Army, British officers were not permitted to enter Nepal for the purpose of recruiting. So, the British resorted to sending their NCOs to recruit soldiers from their villages and the best way to do it was for the NCOs to bring them along while returning from leave. In this manner, links began to be established between families, villages, communities, districts and the regiments. Sons followed fathers into the regiments and soldiers came to understand that good conduct in the regiment brought a good name to their family, village and tribe. Soldiering became an honourable profession and added to one's individual status amongst their peers in the village.

Another approach was to hire persons, mostly retired JCOs/NCOs capable of bringing good boys from the villages. These were called 'Gallas' and the group of young men who entered the Recruiting Depot together as a group belonged to a group that was called a 'Galla Party'. Subsequently it became synonymous for groups who entered into service with a battalion at the same time or even a group of soldiers from the same village.

Gorkha soldiers were recruited between the ages of seventeen to nineteen with an average height of five feet two inches. They are tested on their physical abilities, along with a medical test to rule out diseases like tuberculosis and deformities. Considering that employment in Nepal had its limitations, getting recruited into an Indian or a British regiment was a windfall. When the potential recruit came to the depot he would have long hair, would be barefoot and not very clean because water is a scarce commodity in the hills except for the rivers down below. After recruitment, however, the Gorkha soldier learns to be scrupulously clean and anything within his reach is regularly washed. He takes to discipline as a duck takes to water and is neat, tidy and smart in his appearance. He also takes to drill very quickly and his movements are easy like clockwork. Once trained, he can be relied upon to carry out necessary actions exactly as he has been taught, even to the point of death. He is never in a hurry and is usually unflappable.

Disciplinary problems at the Recruiting Centre or in the battalions are rare. Gorkhas do not consider any situation worth shouting over and find abuse unacceptable. This is a major issue that officers who came in from other regiments had to understand. Gorkhas feel that if they do something wrong then they are liable to be punished and they accept their punishment with equanimity. They also like to be treated fairly and justly and recognize the importance of merit as the yardstick for reward.

It is these same recruits, raw, uneducated and inexperienced in the ways of the so-called developed world, who by good training, strict discipline and a value system that is fair and just, become the finest infantrymen in the world. However, to say that Gorkhas have no limitations would be false. Some of them are inveterate gamblers and their drinking and gambling have to be strictly controlled.

■ ■ ■

We entered Nepal at a place called Butwal and before we could enter the valley of the Andhi Khola we had to climb a hill called the Masiem Danhra. At the top of the saddle of this hill, one track goes towards Gulmi and Bharse and the other descends into the valley of the Andhi Khola. We had hired two *bharias,* or load carriers to carry our baggage. Gorkhas carry heavy loads with the help of a headband called the *namlo*. This headband is attached to the load and the entire weight is taken on the forehead. It is in this manner that cars, pianos, and heavy furniture were taken across the intervening hill range to Kathmandu, the capital of Nepal, before roads or airstrips were built. Generally, heavy loads were broken up into smaller loads and reassembled at Kathmandu.

The route via the Andhi Khola was picturesque and we met a number of soldiers from our regiment. It was a big advantage that we were in uniform. Although the soldiers did not know us, we were easily recognized by our distinctive Gorkha hat and the red lanyard, and they were delighted to meet us. Many pleasant hours were spent with them, chatting about the 'old days' spent in various parts of the world.

There were small places along the Andhi Khola called *bhattis* where we could spend the night. These little temporary habitations provided shelter for the night to pensioners and other travellers. One could spend the night for six Nepali rupees and a hot meal cost a similar amount. An equal amount was spent on the *bharias* with an additional two rupees for a tot of *rakshi*[10] for each of them.

At that time, in 1959, the Indian rupee was called the '*Company ka rupiya*', a legacy of the East India Company and the rate of exchange was one hundred and sixty Nepali rupees for every hundred Indian rupees. The women manning the bhattis were *Thakalnis* as they hailed from a place called Thakola, located close to Manang Bhot at the foot of the Annapurna range of the Gorkha Himal.

They addressed us as *Lahures,* a term used from the time when Gorkhas served in the army of Maharaja Ranjit Singh of the Sikh Empire. Returning to their homeland, the Gorkha soldiers were asked where they were coming from and the answer 'Lahore' resulted in their being called '*Lahures*'. The name has stuck and is used even today when one addresses a Gorkha soldier when you do not know his name. We spent a week along the Andhi Khola skirting past the villages of Walling, Putli Keth, Phedi Khola and Phule Bhatti. At Phedi Khola we spent time with Bhobisor Gurung, an NCO from the battalion. He was delighted to see us and insisted that we stay with him. He also sent word to the pensioners from all the villages in the vicinity and a procession of them trickled in to meet us and to hear news of the battalion. Though we could not stay the night with them, I can never forget the warmth in their welcome, the affection and generous hospitality that is proverbial of these simple people from the hills. After two days of walking, we stopped at a junction where the road branches off to Tansen Palpa on one side and to Payung on the other – it was here that we would meet a large number of our soldiers travelling along these roads.

While we were visiting these villages, we learnt that the king of Nepal – Maharaja Adhiraja Mahendra Bir Bikram Shah, Panch Sarkar, was travelling around his kingdom dressed in the uniform of the Nepal Army, similar to what we were wearing. As a result, many Nepalese citizens presumed that we were part of the Royal entourage and came to us with their petitions.

Colonel Rana of the king's party heard that we were walking across Nepal visiting our soldiers. He met us and invited us to a dinner at Ramdi Pul to meet the king. The ambience was 'royal' in every sense of the term with a huge marquee with sofas and giant braziers of coal fire to keep the king and his guests warm on that cold February evening. Beautiful Nepali girls danced to please the king and it was an evening to remember. We were introduced to the king and he very kindly asked us what we were doing, where we were going and whether we were having an enjoyable visit to his country. The next day we carried on towards Pokhra and met our Police Havildar Budhibahadur Gurung, MM, who was on leave, at a place where the road winds down to the Pokhra Valley. He insisted that we visit his home for a cup of tea, which we happily did. I asked him whether he would like to present his MM to the battalion, and generous soul that he was, he without any hesitation offered his medal. We told him that this was better done at a Battalion Durbar[11] where it could be formally presented. His medal lies today amongst the vast array of gallantry awards that adorn our Officers' Mess.

At Pokhra, we stayed at the Pokhra Pension camp and met pensioners from the battalion including many who had taken part in the Second World War. Lance Naik Amarbahadur Gurung, who had retired from the battalion only two years ago, was very happy to meet us. He was from Lamjung district and was keen on us visiting Simi Tanje, his village on the Nepal–Tibet border. We left Pokhra and trekked up to Kuncha and spent the night in the office of the District Soldiers' Welfare Board, thanks to the kindness of the veteran in-charge. We were amazed to see the walls of his office lined with pigeonholes containing medals of soldiers dating back to the First World War, which had not been collected by the recipients, most of whom had passed away. Twenty-four years later when I visited Kuncha again, I found that the medals were no longer there.

To reach Simi Tanje, we had to cross the Seti Gandaki over a high wire suspension bridge and undertake a tough climb. Fifty feet below, the river frothed over rocks and boulders and that's why it was called the Seti (White) Gandaki. It had begun to snow during our climb and we were glad to reach Amarbahadur's home, which had a cheerful fire burning to keep out the cold. We had brought bottles of rum, which Amarbahadur gratefully accepted.

The next day we visited the home of Naib Subedar Panchu Ghale MC from our Second Battalion who was the senior most pensioner of the village. We also trekked to the other villages where our pensioners lived. The villages were quite far from each other and wild animals roamed freely in these hills. Most families have big Bhutia dogs who are more than a match for the panthers and leopards that are found in these areas.

We returned via Pokhra and took a flight to Kathmandu. During those days Pokhra just had a grassy airstrip and a tin shed that served as its airport. The airline that connected Pokhra with Kathmandu was the Royal Nepal Airline which had a fleet of Dakotas that were relics of the Second World War.

At Kathmandu, we attended the ceremony at the Hanuman Dhoka when eminent jurists from the Governments of India and Britain presented to Nepal its Constitution. We were lucky to be invited to witness this important event in 1959 when King Mahendra Bir Bikram Shah, Maharaj Adhiraja Panch Sarkar received the Constitution on behalf of his

Sketch of temples at Kathmandu

country. Colonel Rana was also here and he was delighted to see us. At the tea, after the presentation of the Constitution, Colonel Rana took us to the king who remembered us and asked us how we were getting along and whether we were enjoying our visit to Nepal.

The Hanuman Dhoka is infamous for the massacre that took place within its walls on 14 September 1846 due to the intrigues led by the queens from the House of Thapa against the House of Ranas. Also called the 'Kot Massacre', it allowed the emergence of Jang Bahadur Rana as the most powerful prime minister in the history of Nepal. It sidelined the weak monarchy and Jang Bahadur Rana's descendants ruled Nepal until February 1951.

Our sojourn in Nepal was coming to an end. Although Captain V.N. Rao and I spent a month in Nepal and met many of the 'old and bold' of the battalion, there were many villages that we were not able to visit and we resolved to return. We realized that we had seen only part of the beauty of this great little country and its generous people. We returned to India via the road built by our army engineers with a firm resolve to visit Baglung, the home of the village of Tanaraj Pun, my first batman and Thako la and the villages close to the Annapurna range. That unfortunately never happened. Can I still go? Of course, I can. Let us see how soon I can make this happen.

Notes

1. All rifle regiments wore black leather boots and belts except the 5th Gorkha Rifles (FF).
2. Viceroy Commissioned Officer, a predecessor to the nomenclature of JCO.
3. Literally means 'hopeful/aspirant'. It is the first level of training to prepare a Rifleman for a test that will determine whether he is

fit for promotion to Lance Naik – the junior most appointment in an Infantry Unit.

4. For Thaman Gurung's citation for the Victoria Cross, please see Appendix 'B', p. 383.

5. CQMH – Company Quartermaster Havildar. He was probably given command of a platoon due to shortage of VCOs due to heavy casualties.

6. Unit Citation is an award which is akin to a battle honour and is given these days to a unit for outstanding performance against terrorists or insurgents or in actions against the enemy like on the Siachen Glacier in situations when war has not been declared.

7. Paltan is a colloquial word for a battalion.

8. Initially 'Gurkha' was the spelling used by the British. After Independence, the Indian Army spelt it as 'Gorkha', which is phonetically more accurate. Whenever the term is used as belonging to the period prior to India's independence, the word is spelt as 'Gurkha'.

9. Also the author of *Love is a Many Splendoured Thing*, an eminent love story that was made into a film and brought her international acclaim and success as a writer

10. Rakshi is a local brew distilled from fermented rice. However, today in Gorkha regiments it has also come to mean rum.

11. Durbar is a meeting called for by the CO of all ranks of the battalion where he speaks to the men on important matters and also listens to any issues raised by them. This meeting in now called a 'Sainik Sammelan'.

CHAPTER THREE

NEFA and the Sino–Indian War of 1962

We learn little from victory, much from defeat.
JAPANESE PROVERB

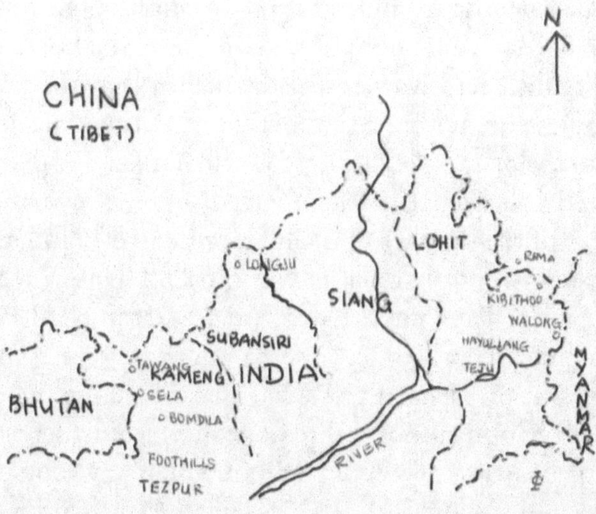

Map of North East Frontier Agency

When India gained independence in 1947, she inherited land boundaries with China, which were marked on maps but not demarcated on the ground and worse still, not ratified by China. China's occupation of Tibet in 1950 led to tensions with India and India moved forward to secure its borders against Chinese ingression and brought Tawang, near the eastern Bhutan border, in Arunachal Pradesh, firmly under its administrative control in 1951.

In 1958, when the 4th Infantry Division was building houses at Ambala as part of 'Operation Amar', China had already begun its incursions across the Sino–Indian border in the area of the Aksai Chin of Ladakh and the North East Frontier Agency (NEFA).[1] These provocations resulted in clashes with Indian security forces guarding our borders, and many Indian soldiers were killed in these skirmishes.

Despite indicators of aggression and hostility, Pandit Jawaharlal Nehru, India's first prime minister, refused to accept that China was following an expansionist policy; that her aggressive actions on the Sino–Indian border were inimical towards us and that our reaction could only result in war. Sardar Vallabhbhai Patel, who was the home minister and a realist, had warned Pandit Nehru that the actions of the Chinese on our border were that of a potential enemy. His letter to the prime minister dated 7 November 1950[2] explicitly analyzed the events of that period and warned the prime minister of the dangers that China presented to India. Nehru, however, insisted that China was a friend. Unfortunately for India, Sardar Patel passed away on 15 December 1950. With his passing, there was no one to counter Nehru on China. In addition to Sardar Patel's warning on China, he outlined future developments and threats from our northern, western and northeastern neighbours, all of which have come true.

Notwithstanding the views of the prime minister, it was important that areas this side of what constituted the international boundary, should be effectively administered – sanction was obtained to establish the North East Frontier Agency, or NEFA. The administrative control was extended over the tribal districts of Kameng, Subansiri, Siang and Lohit frontier divisions of NEFA. These districts were administered by the Frontier Administrative Service, an excellent service that did a great job in very difficult circumstances duly acknowledged by Pandit Nehru. It was later amalgamated with the Indian Administrative Service (IAS).

The incursions by China, however, continued to escalate. In Tibet, the situation had reached such a tipping point that the Dalai Lama had to escape to India in May 1959. The news of the Chinese attack on our post at Longju made the headlines of Indian newspapers on 28 August 1959 and for the first time, Prime Minister Nehru had no option but to explain to the members of the Lok Sabha that the situation between India and China had indeed worsened. The Indian public now began clamouring for action.

In order to assuage Indian public opinion, the Government of India decided to send the 4th Infantry Division towards the end of 1959, to take over the operational control of NEFA. My battalion, the 1st Battalion the 5th Gorkha Rifles (FF), a part of the division, was moved out of Ambala by a special train for Missamari in Assam, located in the region of the foothills of NEFA.

Our military special steamed into Rangapara North. A representative from the division had not yet arrived and the platform was deserted except for a man and his dog. Our Second-in-Command, Major S.S. Jog, alighted from the military special and was met by this lone man. Major Jog seemed to know him and said, 'How kind of you to come to meet the battalion.' To his surprise, he replied, 'Thank you Sardanand but I have not come to meet the battalion. I have come to meet Second Lieutenant Cardozo.'

I was called for and produced before the officer who happened to be none other than Lieutenant Colonel Sekhon,[3] who I had last met at the NDA in 1957. He had not forgotten me. He had kept tabs of my posting to 'First Five' and when he had heard that the division was moving to Assam, he followed the move of my battalion and came to meet me at the station.

I now learnt that Lieutenant Colonel Sekhon was on deputation to 5 Assam Rifles, which was headquartered at Lokhra in Assam. He asked permission from Major Jog to take me away for a few hours.

The two of us had lunch at his Battalion Officers' Mess. Although he did not drink, he made sure that cold beer was on hand for me. We talked of events past and present – a Lieutenant Colonel and a Second Lieutenant! Seniority wise, many years separated us, but we were bound by the incident at the NDA, which he had not forgotten! His penetrating eyes had the same spark and he had not lost his sense of sardonic humour.

The 4th Infantry Division had, in the meanwhile, set up its headquarter at Tezpur and had given orders outlining the responsibilities of the brigades. 11 Infantry Brigade was made responsible for the Lohit frontier district of NEFA, 5 Infantry Brigade which was ours, was given charge of the Subansiri and Siang frontier districts and 7 Infantry Brigade was given charge of Kameng frontier district. Our battalion was subsequently deployed at a place called Daporijo in the Subansiri district. 2 Madras, another battalion of our brigade, was deployed at Along in the Siang district and 2 Rajput at Walong in the Lohit frontier district. I had coursemates in each of the frontier districts. The 5th and the 9th Assam Rifles had small outposts on the Sino–Indian border across the whole of NEFA.

After lunch, Colonel Sekhon dropped me at the Rangapara

North Railway Station and wished me the best of luck. The men were busy unloading the train and I joined my company. We had been informed that there was no accommodation for the battalion, so we had brought our tentage along. A tented camp was set up along the Bhareli River at a place called Siloni Ghat. Within a matter of hours, our camp was ready with tents in perfect dressing with a Quarter Guard, cook houses, officers and JCOs messes, living areas for the men, lavatories, a small mandir etc. Just as in civvy-street where persons are careful to build their homes in accordance with Vaastu shastra,[4] we in the army have our Standing Orders which cater for setting up camp to provide for matters such as security, the direction of the wind, movement of men and vehicles, the effect of sun and rain, the location of the mandir, living accommodation, cook houses, and lavatories.

The Officers' Mess tents were along the river bank and we slept under the stars to the sound of the river gurgling by. I was glad that the river was between us and the forest on the opposite bank because we were told that wild animals roamed there. Sometimes we would hear the sound of drums at night from a village not very far away. I would have loved to have gone there to watch the villagers singing and dancing but permission was denied. After a month of waiting, 'B' Company received orders to go across the Inner-Line[5] to a place called Ziro which was where the Political Officer of the Frontier Administrative Service of the Subansiri Division was located. It was accessible by road.

The rest of the battalion received warning orders to move to Jorhat and then across the Brahmaputra and the Inner Line to Daporijo. The move from Jorhat to Daporijo had to be made by air as there was no connecting road.

'B' Company Commander, Major R.C. Dutta, asked for a young officer to be sent to his company at Ziro to carry out a long-range patrol and I was deputed to carry out this task. To reach Ziro, one had to travel across the plains of Assam past an abundance of tea gardens to a place called Kimin in the foothills. The tea gardens were a beautiful sight. They looked like patchwork quilts in different hues of green as far as the eye could see and had musical names like Hatigarh, Kakajan, Dilipadong, Kellyden, Doolahat and Mangaldai. The Inner Line ran along the foothills just beyond Kimin and no civilian was allowed to cross the Inner Line without a pass. From here the hill road built by our army engineers commenced and the journey to Ziro took about six hours. One had to spend the night at the Battalion Headquarters of the Assam Rifles at Kimin. This was the headquarters of the 9th Assam Rifles. Officers of the Indian Army were deputed to command Assam Rifle battalions and the CO at that time was Lieutenant Colonel Claude Nambiar of the Parachute Regiment.

After reaching Kimin, I made my way to the Officers' Mess and met the CO. He seemed a friendly person and after introducing ourselves, he invited me to join him at the bar for a drink. Leaning against the wall near the bar was a .275 rifle. After he downed his drink, he picked up the rifle. I asked him where he was going. 'To shoot a tiger,' he said. I asked him whether I could come along. He answered, 'No way!' I was dejected but he was right. One cannot have persons uninitiated in the skill of hunting messing around when hunting a tiger. And so, I sat alone in the mess, as all the officers were at their posts in forward areas. Kimin was a beautiful location bang in the middle of a forest.

While I sat in a gazebo outside the mess, I could hear the sounds of elephants and other animals as the sun set below the tree line. As darkness took over, the forest settled down and one could only hear the crickets and the myriad insects that proliferate in these areas. The moon had not yet risen and fire-flies vied with the stars to provide some light on a dark night.

The mess staff was Nepali, as the Assam Rifles had a large number of Gorkhas and they were happy to talk with me in Nepali. I not only spoke Nepali well, but had also learnt a bit of Gurung khura, one of the dialects.

After a while, I heard the sound of a barking deer – initially far away and then louder as it came closer; probably a warning that a beast of prey was on the move. Then there was the sound of a gun – two shots and then silence. It was a couple of hours later that Colonel Nambiar returned in a jeep with a trailer and sprawled across the trailer was a magnificent tiger. He must have been 10 feet between pegs and had a glorious coat. After spending at least ten minutes looking with wonder at this beautiful beast, we went back into the mess and had a couple of drinks.

Colonel Nambiar told me that over the past few months this tiger had killed a number of cattle of the village folk, mauled and killed a man and there was fear that he would turn into a man-eater and then prey on the villagers. The Assistant Political Officer had requested him to see if he could do something to solve the problem.

The previous night, the tiger had killed a bullock and dragged it into a clearing in the forest and after eating his fill, had pushed the remnants of the bullock between two trees to hide it from vultures and other birds of prey. The villagers who went looking for the bullock were able to locate it due to the drag marks on the ground. Colonel Nambiar was informed about the location of the kill. The Colonel, who was a *shikari* (hunter) of repute, had selected a tree that overlooked the kill and had a machan erected on it. Knowing that the tiger would return to the kill only at night, he had moved to the machan at dusk after I had met him, and lay in wait for the tiger. He had two crack shots from his unit on trees in the vicinity with orders to shoot, only if something went wrong.

The tiger came from the direction that Colonel Nambiar had anticipated. Colonel Nambiar waited until the tiger had pulled out the bullock from between the trees. A perfect head shot followed by another was all that was required. It was unfortunate that a beautiful beast like this had to be killed. It was we who had trespassed into his area and not the other way around. However, in the existing circumstances there seemed to be no other option.

The next morning, I set off for Ziro hoping to see wild animals but saw nothing. I reached Ziro around 2 p.m. and Major R.C. Datta was waiting to welcome me. The Assam Rifle accommodation consisted of wooden huts on stilts five feet above the ground. I spent a very comfortable night and went out the next morning to explore Ziro. It was a broad valley inhabited by the Apatani tribe.

The Apatanis were a peaceful tribe whose main occupation was agriculture. The men were not too tall and had their long hair pulled up into a knot with something like a knitting needle pushed into it. With tattoos on the forehead above their eyebrows and below the lower lip, they wore no clothes as such, except for something around their loins. Their bodies were not overly muscular but they were lithe and fit and browned due to their work in the sun. The women were very pretty and topless. They were fairer than the men and the younger ones had perfect bodies due to their hard work in the fields. Unfortunately, their faces were disfigured by wooden plugs pushed into the sides of their nostrils, probably to render them unattractive to the warlike tribes that inhabited the dense forest areas outside the valley and who raided the Apatani homesteads to carry away their women.

The Apatani village was a huge collection of bamboo huts, all of them built on stilts high above the ground to protect them from marauding animals and reptiles. Each hut was about 50 feet long and 15 feet wide. The number of cooking fires in a hut indicated the number of wives a man had, and the number of *mithuns*[6] that he possessed indicated how wealthy he was.

Although the reach of the administration extended up to the Sino–Indian border, the jungle beyond the valley was the hunting ground of the Tagins and the Daflas – the tribes who lived in the forests. They were hunters and lived by what they killed. The men were naked except for a bamboo sheath to cover frontal nudity. Their hair was long and tied up into a knot like the Apatani men. Most wore cane helmets adorned with tiger claws, animal skins or bird beaks. Each was armed with a sword in a bamboo scabbard and some had bows and arrows in a bamboo quiver slung along their backs.

All the men had knives of varying lengths stuck into cane belts around their waists. On their cane belts they also had a pouch that carried what looked like tobacco and igneous stones to start a fire. The arrows were tipped by a dangerous poison, probably aconite, which made an arrow wound fatal. Walking into this area was like walking backwards into time and into the era of the Iron Age.

It was into this fragment of time and space that the men of my patrol and I walked, towards the end of 1959. I had been tasked to recce a route to a place called Tamen on the banks of the Kamla Nadi. The aim of this patrol was to gather information on the terrain so that a road could be built to link Along, which was the headquarters of the Siang Division, to Ziro, the headquarters of the Subansiri Division. The Kamla Nadi was a tributary of the Subansiri. My patrol consisted of ten men, all volunteers. My 2ic was Naik Padambahadur Limbu. In addition, we had ten porters from the Apatani village. Each of us carried our own loads consisting of our second set of clothes, our rations, our weapons and equipment, groundsheet and blanket and the porters carried the wireless set and the charging engine, batteries and additional rations for all of us. We also had a guide and interpreter, Bini Hiru from the Miri tribe. Bini Hiru knew some Hindi and was knowledgeable about the tribes in this area. A few years earlier, a patrol of the Assam Rifles had been massacred by the Daflas in the same area that we were entering, and I was glad to have him with me.

Major Dutta was worried for our safety because of the previous incident but I told him that we could take care of ourselves. I was asked to meet the political officer who would brief me on the prevailing political conditions. I met him a day before our departure, when he briefed me about what had happened a few years earlier. It was known as the RD Singh incident.

It was in October 1953 when a patrol from the Assam Rifles, led by Major Ripu Daman Singh, had gone some distance on the route we were about to take. They could not find a suitable campsite alongside the Kamla Nadi and kept asking for guidance from the tribals. These tribes were aggressive by nature and attitude and perceived the entry of the patrol into their area as a threat. The Assam Rifles patrol apparently did not take the threat of the tribals seriously. After some days of hard marching, they found a shingled beach on the banks of the river and decided to set up camp. They made the crucial mistake of not placing a sentry to guard the weapons and stores. The Daflas followed the patrol for some distance. They were after the magical weapons of the soldiers 'that shout and kill'. When the patrol was washing their clothes and bathing in the river, the tribals descended in their hordes and killed the officer and soldiers mercilessly with their knives and swords and threw their bodies into the river. The soldiers did not have a chance and the river Kamla and its banks were stained red with their blood.

A patrol led by Lieutenant A.K. Moorthy, who was on deputation to the Assam Rifles was sent to recover the bodies and to carry out the last rites of those who were killed. The only body that was recovered was the body of Major Ripu Daman Singh, which was found caught in the roots of a tree on the bank of the river. Lieutenant Moorthy cremated the body and carried out the last rites according to the religious customs and traditions of the Sikhs.

After the attack, the marauding tribesmen disappeared into the interiors with their booty. Troops were dispatched to recover the lost weapons and ammunition but only a few tribesmen were caught and a few weapons were recovered.

It was the task of the political administration to befriend the tribes and to bring them within administrative control through development and education but this incident was a setback to all the good work that had been done in previous years. The political officer stationed at Ziro, Major Duggal, advised me to be careful and act in a balanced and mature manner in case of a conflict. I thanked him for his advice and briefed my patrol accordingly. The Frontier Administrative Service consisted of volunteers from the Indian Army and the IAS.

After a couple of days of hard marching, we reached the Kamla Nadi and marched along its east bank, noting all the data that I thought would be useful to the engineers who would follow and build the road. Once we reached Tamen, we were to return by the same route.

We reached Tamen after about two days, but found that it was on the other side of the river. It meant that we would now have to cross the river and return by the west bank, collecting information about the route all over again in order to give the engineers the option of choosing the better route to take. However, the problem was crossing the turbulent Kamla Nadi, which had no bridge.

I discussed the matter with Naik Padambahadur Limbu who suggested that he could make a raft out of the bamboo trees that grew in the jungle alongside the river. We would, however, have to camp for a couple of days as it would take time to cut bamboo, haul them to the bank, make the raft and then effect the crossing. I thought it was a brilliant idea. But there was no place along the river to accommodate twenty people, so I sent out a patrol to explore the river bank and they found a small beach where we could camp.

We decided to see the place for ourselves and the whole patrol moved forward. The beach was exactly as reported. This was the only place we saw where we could set up a camp.

The porters, however, were murmuring amongst themselves and I asked Bini Hiru to find out what the matter was. It turned out that this, probably, was the same place where the earlier incident had taken place. But as there was no other suitable place we decided to camp there anyway, determined that we would not make the same mistakes.

The bamboos were cut and hauled up to the riverbank and construction of the raft commenced. The porters offered to help and their help was most welcome. What Gorkhas can do with their khukris is pure magic and by evening of the second day the raft was shipshape and ready. Bini Hiru reminded me that the porters with us wanted to leave this area as soon as possible and return to Ziro. We decided to attempt the crossing the next day.

Throughout the two days and nights that we were at this location we had posted double sentries by day and by night. It was tough for a small patrol to have to do this in addition to their other work, but we had no other option. I asked Bini Hiru to also get the porters to be alert and to have at least one porter awake at night to report on any unusual activity.

At night, Padambahadur Limbu had a fire going with dry wood, which was in plentiful supply, to keep away wild animals.

I chose a resting place behind a big rock that sheltered me

from the wind that blew from the mountains ahead of us and also gave me a good vantage point to see both our sentries and the fire.

We posted one sentry on a high rock that gave him total observation of the camp and both sides of the river. We were very tired the first night but we needed to be alert. Padambahadur was more than equal to the task and he had made a schedule for the sentries and explained the danger to the men. Bini Hiru did the same for the porters. I don't know whether Padambahadur ever slept because whenever I awoke at any hour of the night, I would see him moving around, checking on the sentries.

A few hours past midnight, the wind from the mountains grew in intensity and came howling down the river causing a great rustling of the trees on both banks of the river. Along with the noise of the wind, there were animal calls in the vicinity of the camp. I woke up and found Padambahadur and Bini Hiru awake and alert. The noise of the wind and the screaming abated after an hour and this was followed by animal calls on both sides of the river. Were these animals calling or were these the calls of marauding tribals signalling to each other? We did not know but it kept us on our toes and after an hour I fell into a fitful sleep and awoke when dawn broke.

On the second day, the men and the porters worked with a will to ready the raft. The porters and the men believed that the area was infested by spirits and the sooner we got out the better. The raft was completed only by the evening of the second day, and it meant spending a third night on the beach.

That evening we had the best meal in a long time. Gorkhas are not only great hunters but also great fishermen. I have seen them catching fish with their bare hands and this is just what they did that day. Along with the fish that they had caught, they also made a pickle from the tender parts of the bamboos that had been cut.

After a nice, hearty meal we prepared ourselves for a third night at this haunted site. The porters were once again briefed about the situation and that they should be extra alert. Darkness falls early in the mountains and by 5 p.m. it was totally dark. After two hours a crescent moon rose above the trees. It did not give much light but there was sufficient light from the stars to see clearly up to a distance of about 50 metres. The night sentries were posted and I decided to sleep early in case the activities of the previous night were repeated.

I got up some time after dawn had broken. Padambahadur was busy organizing the break-up of the camp and preparations to launch the raft. The porters had told Padambahadur what we already suspected, that the camp site was haunted by restless spirits.

After a quick breakfast, we started to prepare for the crossing. Double sentries were posted to ensure that we were not attacked during our attempts to cross the river.

Padambahadur, Bini Hiru, five porters, five soldiers and the charging engine and batteries went across in the first crossing. The raft seemed to be stable but it was still carried downstream for quite some distance.

Padambahadur was alone on the raft on its return to the home bank. Due to the absence of any load, the raft was carried swiftly downstream bobbing up and down and it was only by skillful handling that he managed to stop the errant raft onto a rocky ledge projecting into the river.

Five more porters, five soldiers, some weapons and ammunition, the remaining baggage, Padambahadur and I were left to do the second crossing. We directed the party that was across the river to post sentries so that we were not caught unawares and I told Bini Hiru to also keep watch. Having loaded the raft, we pushed the raft away from the home bank.

Half way across the river, there was an ominous groaning and creaking as the bamboos began to part. The raft began to sink. Probably the pushing and tugging was more than the raft could stand. Knowing that desperate measures were needed, I jumped into the river to try to hold the raft together. Padambahadur, Nandlal Gurung and Hirabahadur Thapa also jumped in. With a great deal of herculean effort, we managed to hold the raft together and to ground it on the far bank. Bini Hiru kept shouting to the porters not to panic, because if they did, then the raft would have surely sunk. Fed by the snow of the mountains, the water was ice-cold and we spent an hour drying ourselves in the sun. Some time was spent cleaning wet weapons so that they would be ready to fire if need be. Loads were re-distributed and we started our return journey on foot after an hour and a half.

I led the patrol from the front with four soldiers, kept Bini Hiru with the porters in the middle and Naik Padambahadur brought up the rear with three soldiers. Two soldiers were appointed as scouts who moved ahead of all of us – one on the track and one above the track. Jumbahadur, my batman, was the scout moving above the track. It was difficult going because the track was overgrown with vegetation and brambles and some amount of hacking had to be done specially by Jumbahadur who was moving above the track. Bini Hiru also warned us that we were not far from the habitation of the Daflas and that we needed to be careful.

Keeping the political officer's advice in mind, the men were repeatedly warned not to fire without grave provocation and that if anyone had to fire it would be me.

The going was tough. For most of the distance, the route climbed up and down with a steep fall towards the river and the other side was thick jungle.

We reached Ziro without incident and made our reports to both the military and civil authorities.

A few days after the return of the patrol, I was recalled to the battalion which was still at Silonighat. The battalion had received orders to move to Daporijo and preparations were under way for the move to Jorhat, the Staging Camp for the airlift. The airfield at Daporijo could take Dakota and Otter aircraft. Due to the vagaries of the weather, it took a couple of months for the battalion to be fully inducted into Daporijo. Meanwhile, Tibetans escaping from the Chinese depredations in Tibet started trickling into Daporijo and permission had to be obtained to airlift them in aircraft returning to Jorhat.

Forest areas close to the landing ground had to be cleared for barracks for our troops and gradually a bamboo township came up along the banks of the Subansiri. Since there was no restriction on land at that time, we soon had a long range and a mortar range for training and playing fields for games.

Two young officers joined us during this period – Second Lieutenant Emanuel Dewan whose father had commanded the battalion many years earlier, and Second Lieutenant Harpal Singh, who was commissioned as an officer after serving in the ranks of the armoured corps.

In order to get familiar with the terrain and the logistical problems they threw up, long range patrols (LRPs) commenced to Limeking, Taksing and Maja, the Assam Rifle posts on the Sino–Indian border. The marching distances to these posts extended from eighteen to twenty days each way. An LRP to Limeking was undertaken by Lieutenant Colonel KJS Chhatwal, the CO, and was code named 'Champagne Glass'. LRPs led by Gurdip Gill and Harpal followed.

One evening, after a game of basketball, Harpal suggested that we take a walk along the river and we walked a couple of miles towards a cane bridge over the Subansiri River. We stood on the bridge which swayed under our weight as we watched the river tumbling downstream. The bridge had been made by the tribals at the narrowest and deepest part of the river. I mentioned to Harpal that I was fascinated by water and had always had an irresistible urge to jump into water bodies.

Harpal looked at me and said, 'Even a turbulent river like this?'

'Yes,' I said.

'Well, what's stopping you?'

I took it as a challenge. With the foolhardiness of a twenty-two-year-old and without a second thought, I clambered over the cane bridge and jumped into the river. It was a 20-foot drop and the water was ice-cold and I went deep down into its depths. I learned later that there were huge rocks beneath the surface of the river and I could have been seriously hurt and also that the Subansiri was a very dangerous river that took many lives every year. Fortunately, I landed in a deep part of the river and was propelled downstream by a choppy, fast moving current. It was dusk and the men were washing their hands in the river after their evening meal, when I sped past. An alarm was apparently raised that 'Cartoos Saab'[7] had fallen into the river.

Meanwhile I was speeding down the river and trying to reach the nearest bank. I considered myself to be a powerful swimmer but I found it impossible to get close to the bank. The current was apparently pushing against the near bank and returning and propelling me towards the middle of the river. It was now getting dark. About a couple of miles downstream, the river broadened out, and the pace of the current reduced. With great difficulty, I was able to swim to the bank and managed to crawl ashore, very cold and tired. It was dark and beyond the river bank were dense forests. Fortunately, there was enough star light to see the direction in which I had to head for the battalion location. I realized that I had lost my canvas shoes in the water. Walking barefoot was not easy.

After I had walked for about an hour; I saw a number of lighted *mashals*[8] heading in my direction. It was a search party from the battalion looking for me. They were shouting out for me. I could see their mashals but they could not see me. I tried shouting out in reply but all I could do was merely croak. After about another thirty minutes we were able to meet. Was I glad to see them! They too, were happy to find me. Harpal was there looking most relieved and I was embarrassed to see that Major Jog was also there, welcoming me back like a prodigal son.

The Subansiri was cheated of a life and all were glad that I survived. We retraced our steps back to the Paltan and someone started singing a *Jaunre*.[9]

I shall always remember that walk back to the battalion lines with the burning mashals and the men singing verses made up on the spur of the moment that 'Cardozo Saab' had fallen into the river but had come back, the chorus of which ran something like this:

> *'Cartoos Saab khola ma poryo*
> *Bhan ko bato ma.'*[10]

My feet were cut and blistered. Captain Rawat, the Adjutant, however, learnt that I had not fallen into the river but had jumped and that was not taken lightly. I had to pay for it by having to do 'Duty Officer' for six weeks thereafter with a strict warning not to be so stupidly impetuous and that I was setting a bad example to the men.

This episode, however, had an unfortunate sequel. Sometime later, I think it was in 1961, Harpal went on an LRP to Taksing. Somewhere along the way, he told the patrol 2ic, Naib Subedar Uman Singh Gurung that he was going to wash his face in the river. Harpal however failed to return. An extensive search was carried out but he could not be found. The Subansiri River had deceptively claimed one more victim.

After an intensive and fruitless search, the patrol reported the loss of the officer over the wireless. The patrol was ordered to continue its mission and to make its report on its return. The incident left a pall of gloom over the battalion. Loss of a life in the army is not taken lightly. Although Harpal was the leader of the patrol, he was a Second Lieutenant and JCOs acted as mentors to young officers. Naib Subedar Uman Singh Gurung, an excellent JCO, was never promoted thereafter.

Very recently, Brigadier R.V. Singh, an officer of the battalion shared with me that when he was on a tour of Nepal some years ago, he met a JCO from an Assam Rifles Battalion who on learning that RV was from the 5th Gorkha Rifles, recounted that he was at a post along the Subansiri River around 1961 and that he had seen a corpse floating in the river close to his post. The floating body had epaulets that indicated that he was an officer of the 5th Gorkha Rifles. The body had decomposed badly and could not be retrieved. The Subansiri is an unforgiving river and I realized that I was lucky to have survived my misadventure.

Sometime later, in the latter part of 1961, I was sent to a place called Taliha, a three to four days' march from Daporijo. Taliha was a different experience. The post was constructed by Major Burathoki,[11] who at that time was the company commander of Charlie Company. I was appointed as his Company Officer. The post was maintained by air and the Dropping Zone (DZ) was way down below the post and it was a strange sight to see Dakotas flying many hundreds of feet below us.

Road building in the Subansiri Division moved at a snail's pace. From 1959 to 1962, the road had reached just a few miles beyond Daporijo to a place called Sipi. It appeared that India was still taking the Chinese threat lightly. Another explanation for the slow pace of road-building could be that Daporijo was not connected by road and heavy road building equipment could not be ferried by aircraft.

The Chinese had, however, not wasted any time. After the annexation of Tibet by the Chinese in 1950, they built an extensive network of roads right up to the frontier. This was not difficult for them – their side of the border was a flat plateau. In contrast, our side of the border in the Subansiri Division was heavily forested by thick jungle with a single track that climbed up and down razor-like ridges that ran perpendicular to the border. Our Assam Rifles outposts at Longju, Limeking, Taksing and Maja were about twenty days, march from Daporijo. These jungles were inhabited by hostile tribes, wild animals and every imaginable insect from the time of the creation of the world.

■ ■ ■

In April 1962, I was detailed to go on the Regimental Signals Officer's course at Mhow. While on the course, I met Priscilla for the first time at the annual fair of the Mhow Cantonment. I was introduced to her by a friend who was an officer from the Corps of Signals. I found her very attractive but she did not indicate a more than cursory interest in me and I could not pursue the matter further. However, I could not get her out of my mind and thought of her often in lonely moments at the border outposts.

Meanwhile, our battalion that had had three years' experience in those areas was de-inducted in July 1962, a few months before the Sino–Indian war. So dismal was our intelligence system! Pandit Nehru still failed to accept that the Chinese were hostile to us and continued with his policy of *'Hindi Chini Bhai Bhai!'*[12]

After de-induction from NEFA, the battalion was posted

to a delightful place called Palampur in district Kangra in the state of Himachal Pradesh. From our Officers' Mess we had a beautiful view of the Kangra Valley. Our Commander in Palampur, Brigadier Sartaj Singh, GM was one of the very few Indian recipients of the George Medal and was a fiery character. Many were afraid of him. In later years he rose to the rank of an Army Commander.

Although the strategy and deployment of the Indian Army was a military matter, Pandit Nehru preferred to hand over the evolution of a strategy for the defence of the Sino–Indian border to the Intelligence Bureau (IB). 'The Thorat Plan', which was the Indian Army's strategic plan for the defence of India against China, conceived by Lieutenant General SPP Thorat, the Vice Chief of Army Staff, was junked by Prime Minister Nehru in favour of the 'Forward Policy' conceived by B.N. Mullick, a police officer who headed the IB at that time.

The Forward Policy of 1960 of B.N. Mullick required small posts to be established by India on, or as close to, the claimed borders as possible, with an intention to block probable Chinese lines of advance and to interpose themselves between existing Chinese posts and our posts to deny them control of the area. This policy was based on an assessment by the IB that the Chinese would not go to war and attack Indian positions. As part of this policy, army units were moved into Ladakh during 1961 and 1962 and a number of such posts were established there. The Chinese protested and in July 1962 the Chinese surrounded one of our posts in the Galwan Valley in Ladakh. The troops stood firm and after a tense stand-off, the Chinese withdrew. This seemed to reinforce the view of the IB and Prime Minister Nehru that the Chinese would not attack Indian posts. As a consequence, the army in NEFA was ordered to replicate the Forward Policy in the East and to establish twenty-four small posts along the McMahon Line.

The McMahon Line demarcated the boundary between India and Tibet. This boundary was accepted by the British representative, Henry McMahon, the Chinese delegate Chen I-fan and the chief Tibetan representative, the Lonchen Shatra, but was not ratified by China at a conference held at Simla in 1914.[13]

At that time NEFA came under the operational control of 33 Corps. The Corps Commander, Lieutenant General Umrao Singh was not in favour of this policy but he was overruled by Army Headquarters. It was because of the Forward Policy that small posts were established along the Namka Chu that had no tactical significance whatsoever. In fact, it was totally dominated by the Chinese positions on the Thagla Ridge. These posts were to become the spark that would ignite the Sino–Indian war that broke out between India and China in October 1962.

Lieutenant General Umrao Singh protested at the establishing of posts without artillery and administrative support and so it was decided by the government that a corps commander more willing to implement the Forward Policy should take on the task of defending NEFA. Orders were issued for the raising of 4 Corps and Lieutenant General B.M. Kaul was appointed as the Corps Commander of this new corps, which was given the responsibility of the defence of the whole of NEFA. He assumed the appointment of GOC 4 Corps on 4 October 1962.

Intrusions by the Chinese and resultant clashes continued to take place. Fed up with India's failure to stand up to China's bullying tactics, public anger continued to mount, and demands were made to free Indian territory from Chinese occupation. On 12 October 1962, Prime Minister Nehru left for Ceylon for a three-day conference. He was met at the airport by newspaper reporters and the meeting developed into an impromptu press conference. In answer to questions by the media, Nehru stated that instructions had been given to the security forces to free Indian territory and added that there did not appear to be any chance of talks. The Indian press, ever ready to be sensational, reported that 'the Indian Armed Forces had been ordered to throw the Chinese aggressors out of NEFA'. This was just the excuse that the Chinese were looking for. On 20 October, the Chinese launched attacks against Tawang and Walong in the East and Ladakh in the West.

The war was being reported on the radio and in the newspapers. Far away in Palampur, we were glued to our radio sets listening to the news. Places familiar to us while we were in NEFA now became battlegrounds where the war was being fought. We despaired when we heard that our troops were outgunned, outmaneuvered and outfought at Namka Chu, Khenzemane, Tawang, Bumla, Bomdila, Sela, Walong and Jang. Prime Minister Nehru now realized the folly of his own perceptions and the ill-advised counsel of Krishna Menon, his arrogant and supercilious defence minister, and Mullick who headed the IB. But by then it was too late! The Indian Army had to pay the price for the denial of critical weapons and equipment that it so badly needed and an unworkable strategy devised by a policeman of the IB rather than qualified, competent army generals.

The Indian Army, however, was not entirely without blame. After the retirement of General Thimayya and General Thorat, the supine military hierarchy that succeeded these brave and competent officers, allowed the Indian Army to become a toothless image of its former self. An officer like General B.G. Kaul who had never commanded a rifle company, battalion or brigade was propelled to the rank of a corps commander due to his political linkages and was given charge of the defence of the entire NEFA. Worse still, he was never present at the place and moment of decision, when a firm order during the Battle of Sela may have tipped the balance. But he was in Delhi, instead of his headquarters at Tezpur. A useless strategy, an incompetent general, a dubious defence minister and an arrogant but fearful prime minister helped the Chinese no end and we were subjected to a disastrous defeat.

Heads now began to roll. The Army Chief General P.N. Thapar, General B.G. Kaul and the Defence Minister Krishna Menon were removed from office but the damage had already been done!

I had coursemates and friends with battalions that were fighting the Chinese and I wondered what had happened to them. Mahabir Singh Mangat and Pramod Mehta were at Namka Chu, PPS Bains (Pips) was somewhere between Jang and Sela, and Girish Bhatnagar was at Walong.

The war until then was being fought by Eastern Command and part of Western Command and we wondered when we would be called to take our place to stem the onslaught, as it was obvious that reinforcements were urgently needed.

Then late one evening, in the fourth week of October 1962, the battalion was told to be ready to move by early next morning. I learnt about the move and as the 2ic of Support Company, quickly called the platoon commanders. I gave them the warning order for the move and discussed what we needed to take and what to leave behind. We also worked out the details of what the CO Lieutenant Colonel S.S. Jog would ask for and in anticipation of his orders, made our contingency plans. This happened exactly as I had anticipated.

Early next morning, the vehicles were lined up and the battalion moved out without fuss or fanfare. The officers' families collected at a place on the side of the road to say goodbye. We would not see them again for many years.

The convoy reached Adampur airfield that evening. At

that point of time, we were not aware whether we were moving to NEFA or Ladakh. No one was telling us anything. Early next morning, we learnt that we were headed for NEFA and the biggest airlift in Indian military history began when our infantry division was airlifted to its area of operations by a variety of service and civilian aircraft all the way from Adampur in Punjab to Tezpur in Assam. Sleepy Gorkhas were disappointed when told that they could not carry *dauro*[14] with them as there would be plenty of firewood where we would be going.

On arrival at Tezpur, our brigade was immediately deployed to check the Chinese advance that had reached Chaku in the foothills of the mountain ranges ahead of us. We dug trenches, built bunkers and foxholes, and laid barbed wire in record time. Meanwhile, while I was out on a patrol, the Brigade Commander, Brigadier Sartaj Singh, passed by in his jeep. He stopped and said that he had been informed that a huge dump of explosives was reported at a Border Road Camp, at a place called Balukpong, and that I should go and destroy it so that it did not fall in the hands of the Chinese.

He gave me the grid reference of the site and said that an NCO from a Sapper unit would meet me where I was, along with a patrol from 4/9 Gorkha Rifles. My patrol was sent back because we were neither equipped nor rationed for the number of days that we would be away. I waited alone for six hours in the dark on a deserted road until the patrol from 4/9 Gorkha Rifles arrived along with the Sapper NCO in the early hours of the morning.

We proceeded to Balukpong and I was astonished to see a huge camp filled with engineer stores of every category, abandoned by Border Road personnel. We found the dump of explosives and the Sapper NCO took nearly two hours to prepare for the blow up. After he had wired up the explosives we quickly hurried away from the site. What followed was a colossal explosion that shook the ground we were standing on and great plumes of smoke arose from the site. This explosion was heard as far away as Tezpur.

. . .

In order to understand what had occurred up to this time we will need to go back a little in time. In accordance with the Forward Policy, the battalions of 7 Infantry Brigade, responsible for the defence of the Kameng frontier division, were moved forward in the second week of September towards the Namka Chu which was a five days march from Lumpu, the location of the Brigade Headquarters. 2 Rajput and 9 Punjab were strung along the river with 1/9 Gorkha Rifles and 4 Grenadiers in depth.

A one-ton track had been built by the Border Roads up to Tawang. All movement forward of Tawang was by mules and on foot. The positions along the Namka Chu were indefensible. The Brigade Commander, Brigadier John Dalvi requested for permission to redeploy his battalions to a more defensible position to the rear, but permission was denied probably because the Forward Policy had been approved by the highest authority in the land.

From 8 October 1962 onwards, Chinese forces had begun probing Indian positions and by 15 October, the Chinese build up for the attack on Thagla Ridge was clearly visible. The Namka Chu defences held by the Indians were totally dominated by the Chinese positions at Thagla, both by observation and by fire. On 19 October, Brigadier John Dalvi made one last attempt to get permission to withdraw from the indefensible positions along the Namka Chu but his request was once again turned down. At 5 a.m. on 20 October, Chinese guns and heavy mortars opened fire on the Indian positions. After a bombardment which lasted for over an hour, the Chinese attacked in a series of waves. The Rajputs, Punjabis, Gorkhas and Grenadiers fought valiantly but without any artillery support, there was little that they could do against the overwhelming Chinese hordes. 2 Rajput suffered the most. Their strength was 513. Of these, 282 were killed, 161 including 81 wounded were taken as prisoners, and 60 were able to escape. By 12.30 p.m., 7 Brigade ceased to exist as an organized force. My coursemate Mahabir Singh Mangat, of 2 Rajput was amongst those who were killed. What was left of the Punjabis, Gorkhas and Grenadiers withdrew through Bhutan. Brigadier Dalvi and his party lost their way and were captured by the Chinese on 22 October. Neville Maxwell in his book *India's China War* writes about John Dalvi and his brigade:

> Thus, the Indian Army lost an outstanding officer, perhaps it had better compensation in the account he gave of the Namkachu in his book under the apt title 'The Himalayan Blunder' epitomizing the predicament of an officer under orders which he knows will lead to the destruction of his command.

■ ■ ■

Mahabir Singh Mangat was a close friend. He was passionately keen to join the Armoured Corps and was hoping for an old armoured regiment. However, there were few armoured regiments at that time, and the vacancies in these regiments went to those who passed out amongst the first twenty in the order of merit or to those who had a family claim.[15]

Unfortunately, Mangat had no such claim like that of his friends Himmat Singh Gill whose father commanded Hodson's Horse, or Balwant Singh who had a family claim or like Surinder Grewal and Ravi Maira who had passed out high in the order of merit. Mangat was then prepared to settle for a newly raised armoured regiment but that was not to be. He was commissioned into 2 Rajput, a battalion of an old, brave and distinguished regiment, which he grew to love fiercely over a period of time. Both our battalions were part of 4th Infantry Division. We used to meet in the summer of 1960 at the Staging Camp at Jorhat from where we had to move forward to our respective battalions located at Daporijo and Walong.

During those long, hot sultry days at Jorhat, in the summer of 1960, we had to sometimes wait for days for the weather to clear so that our aircraft could land us on difficult airfields in the forward areas. It was while waiting that Mangat, a few others and I used to have long discussions on a variety of topics. One of them was who amongst us would be the first to see action and who would be the first one to get married! Love marriages and arranged marriages was another topic that we discussed. Mangat had told me that his parents had selected a girl for him and he wondered how it would turn out.

We went to our respective locations and were busy following our paths to our own independent destinies. By July 1962, moves commenced to de-induct some battalions from our brigade and neighbouring brigades to peace time locations. Whereas 1/5 Gorkha Rifles had reached Palampur in Himachal Pradesh, 2 Rajput and 1/9 Gorkha Rifles were still at Missamari when the forward movement of large Chinese forces was noticed and they were sent back to the border but into areas that they were not familiar with. 2 Rajput was moved forward and dug defensive positions along the Namka Chu in accordance with the misconceived strategy of the 'Forward Policy'.

Those of us in operational areas were each entitled to use Forces Letters – five in a month. It was pink on the outside and blue inside. One such letter came to me from Mangat. It was written a few days before he was killed and it reached me many weeks after the Battle of Namka Chu. In it he said:

Dear Cardi,

Where are you? I am sure you must be hearing about what is happening out here. Do you remember our discussions on who would be the first to see action? Well, it appears that I will beat you to it. The balloon is going to go up any time now and the enemy is gathering on the hills above us. Let us see what happens.

I can't say more as all letters are censored but I am sure that you must be aware of the situation we are in!

Wish me the best of luck. I will need it and also your prayers. Let us hope we can meet and exchange notes after all of this is over.

With best wishes.

Your friend
Mahabir

We could never meet. He died fighting at Namka Chu. The Chinese suffered heavy casualties at the battles of Jang and Bumla; however, overwhelming forces, superior weapons and better leadership took their toll at those locations and at Namka Chu the Indian forces were overrun and demolished.

A similar situation developed at Walong when the Chinese attacked Indian positions held by 4 Sikh and 6 Kumaon on the night of 20/21 October. The initial attacks were beaten back but as the pressure increased our battalions had to fall back to positions north of Walong. After 23 October, the Walong Sector was placed under command of 11th Infantry Brigade and the newly raised 2nd Infantry Division and the strength of the brigade was brought up to three battalions with the induction of 3/3 Gorkha Rifles. The Kumaonis and the Sikhs launched counter-attacks but failed to recapture positions that were lost. After a lull in battle, the Chinese launched coordinated attacks once more, in overwhelming strength on both sides of the Lohit River and by 11 a.m. on 16 November, the Brigade Commander had to order a withdrawal.

The Chinese did not advance into the Subansiri sector as they were aware that the terrain was too tough. In the Siang Division they attacked the positions held by 2 Madras who suffered heavy casualties.

While we were on the move to reinforce 4th Infantry Division, the battle at Walong was reaching its final stages. Girish Bhatnagar, another coursemate of mine, was directing artillery fire against the Chinese to cover the withdrawal of the troops of 11 Infantry Brigade when he was killed. So was Captain Baba Adam, a Parsi officer from 3/3 Gorkha Rifles who did the Weapons Course with me.

The tragedy of the war on the Eastern Front need not have taken place. Despite the fact that the troops of 4th Infantry Division were badly deployed, were without artillery support, and that many of the troops had never seen the areas they were thrown into, we could have still beaten back the Chinese hordes.

The trump card that we had in our hands was that our air force bases were within striking distance of the battleground. The Chinese air bases in Tibet were beyond the range of the area of conflict. Even if they were within range, they had no fuel for their aircraft. We could have destroyed the Chinese forces on the ground and turned the tide of the battle.

The Indian Air Force, through detailed reconnaissance, had collected ample evidence that we could use our aircraft and the Chinese couldn't. Yet, once again, we failed our troops on the ground. Prime Minister Nehru instead of considering the evidence on the ground collected by air reconnaissance by our pilots, preferred to take counsel of his fears. He preferred to listen to the American ambassador Kenneth Galbraith, who warned of a non-existent threat to Indian cities by the Chinese air force. Menon, the defence minister and a Communist by inclination, also warned the prime minister that the Chinese had a huge air force of over 2,000 aircraft but we do not[16] know whether he knew that the Chinese air force was devoid of fuel.

In effect, although we had the means to beat the Chinese offensive, we threw away that monumental advantage. We preferred to take council of our fears and Prime Minister Nehru instead sent requests for help to the American president when there was no reason to do so.

The Chinese invasion in 1962 was meticulously planned and not something that was a reaction to India's troop movement along the McMahon Line, as Neville Maxwell and some Western authors have tried to project.

The Chinese had conceived their strategy for the war and conducted it according to a well-conceived and coordinated plan, in keeping with the philosophy enunciated by Sun Tzu and Mao Tse Tung. Sleeper fifth columnists had been inducted years in advance. Many Chinese soldiers spoke perfect Hindi and that includes doctors and nurses of the Chinese Army.

These Chinese agents knew exactly where the Indian positions were located and all the tracks and paths by which our positions could be by-passed. Many of their informants were the porters that worked for our troops before the war started and it was they who guided the Chinese troops to outflank our troops again and again.

China had pushed India in accordance with a well-contrived plan knowing that when 'push came to shove', India would react and give them just the excuse that they were waiting for.

The Sino–Indian War highlighted the inability of India's political masters to distinguish between facts and fabricated fiction. It had become obvious that the military leadership had lost its spine and were unable to stand up against blatant wrong orders of the government, that the political hierarchy placed greater reliance on advice from persons unqualified in the area of military strategy, and that interference in the promotion of a senior army officer to a critically important appointment based on political connections was uncalled for. These were factors predicated to military defeat.

These are factors we need to remember.

Postscript

The version on the internet of the R.D. Singh incident is different from what I saw. It narrates a story of a place called Aichangmori where it states that this incident took place. Aichangmori must have been a Dafla habitation. This version, however, does not explain how the body of Major Ripu Daman Singh was found entangled in the roots of a tree on the banks of the Kamla Nadi. The porters who accompanied my patrol appeared to be quite clear, right from the beginning, that our campsite on the banks of the Kamla Nadi was the scene of the massacre. I have met Colonel A.K. Moorthy who found the body of Major Singh and he confirmed that he did find the body in the Kamla Nadi.

Notes

1. Originally known as the North East Frontier Agency (NEFA), the region was initially under the administrative control of the Ministry of External Affairs. It later came to be known as Arunachal Pradesh and its administration was transferred to the Ministry of Home Affairs.

2. Please see Appendix 'C' (p. 387) for Sardar Patel's letter to Prime Minister Jawaharlal Nehru on this issue.

3. Name changed. Please see Chapter 1, Cradles of Leadership.

4. An ancient science that is a guide to the construction of dwelling and working places in harmony with nature and the environment leading to order and wellbeing.

5. Inner Line: A boundary across which no foreigner or unauthorized person was allowed to cross for fear of destroying the culture and way of life of the tribals who lived across the line. It was probably also a matter of security.

6. A cross between a cow and a bison.

7. 'Cartoos Saab' was the name given to me by the Gorkha soldiers of my battalion who probably found 'Cardozo' difficult to pronounce.

8. A torch of fire made by setting fire to a piece of wood.

9. Nepali song and dance.

10. The words of the chorus meant that 'Cartoos Saab' had fallen into a river that ran along a jungle path.

11. Major Burathoki later on commanded the battalion. His father Hony Captain and Subedar Major Giriprasad Burathoki, of the 2nd Battalion the 5th Gorkha Rifles on retirement was elected and appointed as the Defence Minister of Nepal. Later, on a visit to India, he was met by the Indian Defence Minister and the three Service Chiefs with all the protocol and deference that his position demanded. He was a very dignified person and a grand old man. Lieutenant Colonel Burathoki himself was also elected as a minister in the Nepal Government some years after he retired.

12. Indians and Chinese are brothers.

13. Shiv Kunal Verma, *1962 The War that Wasn't*, Aleph Book Company, New Delhi, 2016, p. 101.

14. Nepali word for firewood.

15. Family claim: If your father had commanded the regiment or if your father had been decorated or had been wounded in war with that regiment then that constituted a 'family claim'.

16. Please see Appendix 'D' (p. 395) for articles by eminent writers
    who accept that had we used the Air Force, the outcome of the
    war would have been different.

'Four Five' and the 1965 War

*It is better to deserve honours and not have them
than have them and not deserve them.*
Mark Twain

The debacle of the Sino–Indian War of 1962 forced the
Government of India to acknowledge that a major overhaul
of the Indian armed forces was in order and that the forces
had to be reorganized, revamped and equipped, if they were
to effectively carry out their duty to safeguard the country.
TIME magazine when reporting on the Sino–Indian War of
1962 declared, 'the Indian Army needs almost everything
except courage.'

As a result of this realization, the raising of more infantry
battalions was ordered. One more battalion of our regiment
was ordered to be raised at our Regimental Centre at
Dehradun as our fourth battalion, with effect from 1 January
1963. Actually, the 4th Battalion was a unit that had been

raised during the Second World War and had distinguished itself in the fighting in Burma. Being a war-raised battalion, and the junior most battalion in the regiment at that time, it was disbanded after the war. It was now being given an opportunity to distinguish itself once again.

Three officers from the 1st Battalion, the 5th Gorkha Rifles were posted to the new battalion – the CO, Colonel S.S. Jog, the Adjutant Captain J.S. Rawat and me. I was a Captain at that time with service of almost five years. A number of JCOs and NCOs and other men of the battalion were also posted to the new battalion. Knowing how emotionally difficult it was for officers and men to leave what one considered as 'one's home for life', the orders stated that the move was to be executed within 48 hours and that no representations would be entertained.

In the meantime, China declared a unilateral ceasefire. They perhaps understood that only part of the Indian Army had been utilized against them, or that they would not be able to administer their troops across extremely difficult and extended lines of communication. Perhaps, they also knew that we would eventually wake up to the fact that they could not use their air force against us, whereas we could very much do so.

General B.M. Kaul, now sacked, tried to justify his conduct and behaviour in his autobiography, *The Untold Story* but it cut no ice with anyone. His promotion and appointment to a key position prior to the Sino–Indian War was a reminder to the government as to what happens when it interferes with army promotions and appointments and when political connections override merit and when perfectly competent officers are superseded on grounds that are politically motivated.

General Sam Manekshaw's promotion had been held up for eighteen months due to a case allegedly instigated by

General Kaul. It was finally cleared after the sacking of Krishna Menon. On 2 December 1962, General Manekshaw was promoted to the rank of Lieutenant General and ironically, took over 4 Corps from General Kaul. The first 'Order of the Day' passed by Sam in his own characteristic manner was brief and to the point. It stated: 'From now onwards there will be no withdrawals except on my personal orders which will not be given. We shall stand and fight where we dig in. Remember we are all expendable; the reputation of the army is not, nor is the honour of the country.'[1]

Coming back to the battalion, officers from every battalion of the regiment had been posted to make up the strength of the new battalion. We had, however, not been able to shake off our emotional links with our previous units. When anything was discussed, each of us had the habit of referring to our previous unit, and conversations invariably ran like this: 'In my battalion…' This did not help in fostering unity and team spirit for consolidating the identity of the new unit. So, it was decided that if any one of us referred to our previous unit again in this manner, he would have to present a bottle of Scotch whisky to the Officers' Mess. This way, we were able to discourage officers to brag about their old units and to establish the battalion's own ethos and at the same time collect a sizeable cache of liquor for our mess!

Some of us deliberately trapped one another into talking about previous units and the CO, Lieutenant Colonel Madan Bhatia was the one who contributed the most to our horde of whisky. So, with much laughter we finally got rid of our hang up of referring to our old units as 'in my battalion…' and we began to identify with 'Four Five', at first haltingly, but before long, totally and irrevocably.

We worked hard to get the battalion into shape and within six months were declared 'fit for war' and the battalion was posted to hold a sector of the Cease Fire Line (CFL) in

Jammu & Kashmir (J&K). The 'Pakis', by close observation of movement across the CFL, usually find out when a change of units takes place and often used ingenious methods to test the competence and alertness of the new unit. Warned about this, we decided to give them a run for their money. Heavy firing by them was responded to with silence from us. They did not know what to make of it!

After a number of days when we did not respond, they decided to raid one of our picquets to check whether we were sleeping. We waited for them and held our fire till they came close and then we let them have it. The message was not lost on them and thereafter they treated us with respect. However, somewhere around the fourth week of November 1964, Pakistani saboteurs crossed the CFL and laid mines on a track to one of our picquets and one of our soldiers was killed. A flag meeting was held and we conveyed to them that it was a cowardly act and that they would pay for it. Predictably, they denied complicity, but they knew we meant business. For the next one month they were extraordinarily alert. We waited for them to relax a bit and then launched a raid across the CFL, in what is nowadays euphemistically called a 'surgical strike'. The raid was led by me and Major MMP Kala. We caused sufficient damage to convey to them that such actions would not be tolerated. The weapons we had captured were handed over to the brigade.

Around July 1965, the battalion had done two years on the CFL but we had never had the opportunity to do 'Collective Training'[2] since we were raised. We requested that permission be granted to have us withdrawn from the CFL to train. Permission was given and we came down from our picquets and set up camp south of Rajauri in the first few days of August. However, it appeared that the opportunity for the battalion to train was jinxed.

Pakistan's obsession to take Jammu & Kashmir by force

tempted her around the first week of August 1965 to replicate her earlier failed attempt of 1947–48.

The military hierarchy of Pakistan was of the opinion that India had not yet got over the debacle of the 1962 Sino–Indian war and that reorganization of her forces had not yet been completed. Significant economic assistance and massive military aid had been received by Pakistan from the United States of America amounting to more than 1.5 billion dollars. This included 200 Patton tanks, one squadron of Supersonic Starfighters, four squadrons of Sabre jet fighters, and two squadrons of B-57 bombers. In addition, they had been given enough medium and heavy guns to raise several heavy and medium artillery regiments and equipment to revamp their signal communication system. All this completely upset the relative military balance between India and Pakistan.

At this time, Pakistani President General Ayub Khan, who had come to power through a military coup, felt that the opportunity was ripe to attempt once again to take Jammu & Kashmir by force. After the death of Pandit Nehru on 27 May 1964, India's political leadership was perceived by Pakistan to be found wanting, that this was the right time to strike because such an opportunity in favour of Pakistan might never come again.

Pakistan's military planners conceived a series of military operations to achieve her aim. The first was 'Operation Desert Hawk' in the Rann of Kutch, to take a measure of India's political and military leadership, to test her competence to handle her newly acquired arms and lull us away from the focus on Jammu & Kashmir. Once this was done, Pakistan planned to launch 'Operation Gibraltar', which involved the crossing over of a large force of guerrillas across the Line of Control (LoC) to create anarchy in the hinterland of Jammu & Kashmir and initiate a civil uprising. Pakistan's trump card, however, was 'Operation Grand Slam', which planned to sandwich the Indian troops on the LoC between a division sized force attacking from the front and the guerrillas attacking from the rear.

Operation Desert Hawk was fairly successful because at that time we had no military presence on the border with Pakistan in Gujarat. All we had were police outposts to check smuggling and by the time an Indian force was sent, they had made considerable ingress into Indian territory. A ceasefire brokered by Harold Wilson, the Prime Minister of England, brought this operation to a close and both sides returned to their original positions. The ceasefire agreement clearly specified that both armies would return to their original positions and that force would not be used by either country to settle bi-lateral problems.

Pakistan, however, had learnt all the wrong lessons from Operation Desert Hawk. They wrongly concluded that with the passing away of Pandit Nehru, India's political decision-making had lost its efficacy, that the Pakistani armed forces had acquired mastery over the American equipment given to them and that they had lulled us into complacency over the issue of Jammu & Kashmir.

Despite agreeing to refrain from using force to settle bilateral issues, Pakistan commenced immediately to launch Operation Gibraltar – a meticulously planned operation. However, they had not reckoned with the response from the Indian Army. The guerrillas were hunted down and destroyed, the remnants dispersed and forced to withdraw across the CFL. 'Operation Grand Slam' was also well planned and executed but checkmated by Lal Bahadur Shastri, the new Indian Prime Minister who though short in stature, had a big heart. He reasoned that an attack on Jammu & Kashmir was an attack on India and allowed the opening of a second front in Punjab. This put the Pakistanis on the back foot and they had to withdraw their forces from the Akhnur front

and move them post haste to the areas newly threatened in
the Punjab.

. . .

Coming back to the battalion, as soon we came down from
the picquets, the CO, Lieutenant Colonel Bhatia, who had
not had a break ever since he had assumed command of the
battalion, decided to go on leave and Major Prem Das, the 2ic
assumed command as the Officiating CO.

We had just about established a tented camp for our
proposed training and were busy planning a schedule, when
we heard shots fired by one of our outlying picquets that were
guarding our camp. This was followed by heavy firing. On
investigation, we found that an infiltrating enemy guerrilla
column had hit our picquet which killed a few guerrillas.

Apparently, our battalion was one of the first units
to encounter one of the infiltrating guerrilla columns.
Interrogation of captured guerillas by division and higher
headquarters, revealed that a large force of guerrillas
organized into ten columns had crossed over the CFL between
Ladakh and Jammu as part of Operation Gibraltar. They also
revealed that the plans for Operation Gibraltar were made
in May 1965. Pakistan, unsurprisingly, denied complicity
and attempted to pass it off as an uprising by the citizens
of Jammu & Kashmir. However, clear evidence of Pakistan's
involvement was reported by the UN Military Observer
Group and shared as such by the UN Secretary General U.
Thant at the Security Council on 3 September 1965. Further,
it was also revealed that General Ayub Khan had himself
addressed the Force Commanders of the Gibraltar Force in
the second week of July 1965 at Murree in Pakistan.

Further north in the divisional sector, shepherds reported
that a strange group of armed men had taken shelter in a

forest close to our Brigade Headquarters. Captain C.N. Singh, a young officer from the Garhwal Rifles posted to the Brigade Headquarters took a patrol to investigate and was ambushed and killed. The guerrilla force withdrew and moved elsewhere, probably to the vicinity of Bhimber Galli.

At this juncture, our battalion was the only unit in the division that was not holding ground and so willy-nilly we became the Divisional Reserve.[3]

My company, Alpha Company, was ordered to shift to the Brigade Headquarters and we were moved post haste. Subsequently, the rest of the battalion closed up and established itself adjacently. A day after reaching the Brigade Headquarters, I was told that a guerrilla column had established itself at Pir Kalewa. I recalled that this was a high hill feature where we had fought a battle with the invading Pakistani forces during the Indo–Pak War of 1947–48. Alpha Company was tasked to deal with them.

We left well before daybreak, as Pir Kalewa was a long way off and a stiff climb was involved. The ridge line, of which Pir Kalewa was a part, was covered with dense forests of fir trees. We finally reached an adjoining knoll on the same ridge line and had a magnificent view of the surrounding area. It was evident that the feature was occupied because wisps of smoke were emanating from between the tops of the trees. The guerrilla column was preparing their afternoon meal. Subedar Bhimbahadur Rana and I were discussing how to attack the feature when all of a sudden, artillery rounds crashed onto the feature. We could hear cries of alarm and the guerrillas left in a hurry taking what they could with them. We later learnt that it was Major Premdas, the second-in-command and the officiating CO, who had organized the artillery fire on the hill feature.

We rushed to the feature but surprise had been lost. The fires were still warm. We put them out to prevent a forest fire and carried out a search of the area – we found items of clothing, equipment and ammunition of no use to us. We looked for the guerrillas on the next feature and the one beyond that, but they had disappeared so we decided to return to base.

We had come down from the higher reaches of the fir forests and were now in the pine tree line. Range upon range of pine-covered ridges extended as far as the eye could see. Suddenly we saw two fighter air craft in the distance, attacking a feature which was hidden from our view. We could faintly hear the sound of the jets and their guns firing and wondered what they were firing at.

We reached the brigade location after about six hours of hard marching to learn to our consternation that it was our battalion location that was the target of the Pakistani Sabre jets!

Apparently, an Army Service Corps (ASC) convoy seeing our battalion on the verge of the road stopped and took a break. Two Pakistani Sabre jets were on the prowl, it was too lucrative a target to ignore. After using their cannons

Pakistani Sabre jets prowling over the Indian battalion location

during their initial circuit over the area, they followed up with napalm bombs.[4] Though napalm bombs are banned by the Geneva Convention, such aspects mattered little to the Pakistani armed forces.

Napalm bombs create great walls of fire that burn everything to cinders. Unfortunately, Major Premdas who was trying to disperse the troops, after the first attack, got caught in the fire wall of the bombs and was burnt to death. He was the first 2ic of 'Four Five' to die. Seven more were to become casualties in the years that followed. But that is another story, part of which will unravel as my story moves forward.

Getting back to the 1965 war, in addition to providing protection to the Brigade Headquarters, my company was also tasked with convoy protection duty between Pathankot and Poonch. Knowing that the more threatened area was between Rajauri and Poonch, I detailed my Company Officer, Second Lieutenant Dinesh Singh Rana to escort the convoy from Pathankot to Rajauri, and I took on the responsibility between Rajauri and Poonch.

Information had been received that convoys to Poonch had been ambushed by the guerrillas and the drivers had been tied to trees, bayoneted and set on fire. As a consequence, no convoy could get through and Poonch remained cut off for about ten days. Since I had been tasked with taking a huge convoy of over 250 vehicles to Poonch, I visited the Division Headquarters and requested for light vehicles with which I could move my detachment of mortars and medium machine guns (MMGs) up and down the convoy to the place of decision, in the event of our being ambushed. The GSO1 (Ops) was not available, so I went to the AQ (Ops) with my request. Instead of heeding my request, the AQ gave me a long lecture for making what he considered to be unreasonable demands and sent me away. On my way out, I met the Commander

Artillery, who asked me what I was doing at the Divisional Headquarters. I explained my need and that the AQ had turned down my request. He said, 'I will see what I can do by providing you with artillery cover. You will need a Forward Observation Officer with a wireless set to communicate with the guns. It's not a promise, but I will try.'

Early next morning, I briefed the ASC JCO who was the Convoy Commander and the drivers. The ASC JCO was from Assam and came across as a person with a positive attitude. I was very happy to have him with me. It was a long convoy of over 250 vehicles. We had to keep a distance of 25 metres between vehicles. This meant that my convoy of vehicles would be 5-kilometres long. To protect the convoy, I had a platoon of less than thirty men. I briefed them on how they would be organized, and the action that they should take in the event of an ambush. I had a jeep from my unit but the detachments of mortars and MMGs were mounted on 15 cwt Chevrolet vehicles which were called 'Ulloo[5] Trucks' because of their flat bonnets which gave them an 'owlish' look. They were slower than the Dodge 1 ton, perhaps another reason why they were given that name.

The first vehicle was a 3 ton vehicle with a light machine gun (LMG) tied to the superstructure. The first section was mounted in this vehicle along with my 2ic, Subedar Bhimbahadur Rana, whose number was JC-11111 and was thus called 'Ek Saab'.

Subedar Bhimbahadur was deeply religious and was the only one in the battalion who had his head shaved except for a 'top knot'.[6] He was morally, mentally and physically very tough. An excellent company 2ic, he was intense and passionate about his duties.

Since I had only a platoon to protect such a huge convoy, I placed one section in the leading 3 ton, one section in the middle of the convoy and the third section at the rear of the column. Subedar Bhimbahadur was in the leading vehicle sitting next to the driver. I was somewhere in the middle of the convoy with the mortar and MMG detachments close behind me in their *Ulloo* trucks.

The road from Bhimber Galli to Poonch runs for 55 kilometres along a ridge which is about 1,000 feet high. The ridge was covered with clumps of pine trees interspersed with maize plantations and walnut trees and had a gradient of thirty to forty degrees.

On our way to Poonch, a few miles beyond Bhimber Galli, we came across a group of 20-30 guerrillas digging up the road. They were trying to create a road block. On the ridge above there were masses of them holding the ridge line. We dispersed those who were on the road with a burst from an LMG and followed up with some more bursts as the guerrillas ran up the hillside.

Subedar Bhimbahadur had collected the first section with the intention of chasing the guerrillas. I explained to him that our primary responsibility was the safety of the convoy – we needed to ensure that it got safely into Poonch, as quickly as possible. He reluctantly agreed and we proceeded to Poonch without further incident. At Poonch we were received like heroes. We had no idea that the situation was that bad. I told the ASC JCO to liaise with the staff at the Brigade Headquarters and have the vehicles unloaded and to use the next day for maintenance of their vehicles because I did not want any breakdown of a vehicle on the way back.

I had just finished briefing the convoy commander and my company 2ic, when I received a message that the Brigade Commander wanted to see me. After congratulating me for bringing the convoy safely into Poonch, he told me that there were over 200 vehicles stranded at Poonch and that he wanted them out the next day along with the vehicles that I had brought with me.

He added that there was not enough place to park so many vehicles in the Poonch garrison, the only location was the airfield which was under observation and shelling from enemy guns. It was essential that all these vehicles left Poonch as early as possible.

I explained to the Brigade Commander that I had broken an ambush in the vicinity of Bhimber Galli on my way up to Poonch and that I had seen at least 200 to 300 guerrillas on the ridge above. I was certain that they would be waiting for the convoy to return. It would not be possible for me with just 30 men to protect a convoy of 450 vehicles which would extend to a column of nearly 10 kilometres – we would be sitting ducks for the guerillas, and a lucrative target.

The Brigade Commander, who by now was getting irritated, said, 'This is war and I am giving you an order. Do it or face the consequences.'

'Sir, I do not come under your command. I come directly under the Divisional Commander. I suggest you speak with him before insisting on my taking the convoy back tomorrow,' I shot back.

The Brigade Commander was visibly annoyed but decided to do as I said. He rang up the division and asked to speak with the GOC. After listening to the Brigade Commander's complaint, the GOC asked, 'Have you asked Major Cardozo what he wants in order to carry out your orders?'[7]

'No sir,' said the Brigade Commander.

'Ask him,' said the GOC.

The Brigade Commander glared at me and said, 'What do you want?'

I said, 'Two infantry companies to protect the convoy or have the ridge line between Kalai Bridge and Bhimber Galli picqueted half way by your brigade and half way by my brigade and I will take the convoy through.'

'Why did you not say this in the beginning?'

'Because you did not ask me and because the drivers need rest and the vehicles need maintenance.'

'All right, I will have the ridge line held. Plan to leave by 9.30 tomorrow morning and that's an order.'

'Okay sir. However, the drivers would not have had enough sleep and no time for vehicle maintenance.'

The Brigade Commander did not say anything and I left. Fortunately, the JCO in charge of the convoy and Subedar Bhimbahadur were awake and I explained what was required to be done the next morning.

The next day at 8 in the morning I briefed all the drivers as to what I expected of them in the event of an ambush. Basically, all that they were required to do was to move at a steady speed keeping the inter-vehicle space to a reasonable 25 metres; and to keep to the left side of the road so as to give me road space to take my mortars and MMGs up or down the convoy. I briefed Subedar Bhimbahadur, the ASC JCO and my platoon separately.

As directed by the Brigade Commander the convoy moved out of Poonch at 9.30 a.m. There were also three busloads of civilians who needed to get out of Poonch. This was not part of my assignment but I accepted it as an exigency of war and placed them at the tail end of the convoy.

I waited at Kalai Bridge, which was the starting point, until the last vehicle left and proceeded to move up the convoy. This was just to make sure that the convoy had generally closed up and that the drivers had got into the habit of leaving enough space on the right of the road for me to move up and down with my *Ulloo* trucks, which carried my mortars and MMGs.

After about an hour and a half when I had reached closer to the middle of the convoy, I heard a loud explosion at a distance and the chattering of machine guns. I raced forward in my jeep. I was accompanied by my runner Girbahadur, a curly-haired young soldier and my driver. For my weapon, I carried a Mk 4 rifle. It was a .303 rifle with a smaller stock and lighter than the unwieldy .303 Mk 3 rifle. I never carried a sten-machine carbine because it was an unreliable weapon with a history of stoppages.

When we reached the initial part of the ambush site, Girbahadur and I clambered up the embankment and we saw in front of us a whole line of guerrillas firing onto the convoy. With my rifle, I fired at the LMG group closest to us, hardly 50 feet away. I dropped the Pakistani who was manning the LMG, reloaded and shot the second Pakistani soldier when a Pakistani NCO saw us and started shouting, '*Kafir ka Major – zinda pakro! zinda pakro!*' (An enemy (unbeliever) Major! Catch him alive.) There was no point staying there any longer.

I ascertained quickly that the only way to save the situation was to use the mortars and MMGs and that getting into a fire-fight with just Girbahadur and me against this horde of guerrillas would be pointless. My task was to save the convoy; so Girbahadur and I jumped on to the road and ran down the road looking for the *Ulloo* trucks.

After about 800 metres I found the mortar vehicle but the mortars and the mortar crew were missing. 'Tekbahadur!' I yelled, wondering what had happened to the mortar detachment commander with the full realization that without the mortars, the situation would be impossible. I was relieved to hear an answer: '*Yahan chha Saab. Mo Ayo.*' (I am here Saab. I am coming.)

'Where are you and what are you doing?' I shouted.

He said, 'I have climbed to the top of this ridge and I have seen the location of the ambush site and have laid the mortars accordingly.'

'Why have you not started firing?' I asked.

'I don't know where our boys are,' he said in Nepali.

I ordered him to open fire. Tekbahadur opened fire with his mortars and at the same time I saw Havildar Karnabahadur

Gurung and the middle section on the skyline hurrying towards the ambush site.

I told Havildar Tekbahadur to keep locating and firing at the guerrillas and I climbed up to where Havildar Karnabahadur had taken position and was firing at the enemy who had moved en masse to the reverse slope of the ridge due to the mortar fire. The Pakistani JCOs and NCOs were beating the guerrillas with lathis (sticks) in an effort to get them back to the top of the ridge.

I made Karnabahadur keep shifting the location of his LMG in an attempt to confuse the Pakistanis and to make them think that we were a platoon and not just a section. Meanwhile, Havildar Tekbahadur managed to drop a few mortar bombs where the Pakistanis had gathered. This was too much for them; the guerrillas scattered; and the Pakistani NCOs could not get them back.

I ran down the ridge to the convoy and saw that some ASC drivers had been killed or wounded. Luckily, I came across a Gorkha Naik from 11 GR on deputation to the Corps of Military Police. He was going on leave. I told him to look for 'second drivers' and civilians from the buses who could drive and to get them to drive the driverless trucks and to get the convoy moving because I wanted them out of this area before last light. He managed to do what I said and after I saw that the convoy had started to move, I hurried towards the front to see how Subedar Bhimbahadur and the first section had fared.

What I saw devastated me. Subedar Bhimbahadur was dead. He had decapitated the Pakistani soldier who had fired a rocket at our convoy and his khukri was buried in the head of the number two of the Pakistani RL team. His body was riddled with bullets but he had a peaceful smile on his face as though he had achieved what he had wanted all along.

The scene at the leading 3 ton too, was gruesome. The

tailboard was down and the floorboard was awash with blood. The rocket fired by the Pakistanis had taken off the heads of Naiks Dilijang and another jawan and what remained of their bodies lay in a heap on the floor of the truck. Four others who had continued to man the LMG had been badly wounded and were being evacuated.

By now my CO and about two companies had arrived from the Brigade Headquarters at Galuthi. They had apparently received a message from the Poonch Brigade that they should move and hold part of the ridge line but there was no transport and they had to move on foot. By the time they arrived, it was too late.

By this time, I was furious. It had become clear that I was wrongly informed that I could move the convoy from Poonch, when the ridge line had in fact not been held. Havildar Karnabahadur had confirmed to me that he had not seen anyone from the Poonch Brigade in his move on the ridge line in that part of the sector and in our part of the sector there were only the Pakistani guerrillas.

Meanwhile, the convoy had moved on its way and I was busy at the Galuthi TCP evacuating the wounded when I received a call from the Brigade Major 'Tiger' Tyagraja. The Brigade Commander wished to speak with me. I am afraid I was rude and said that I was busy evacuating my casualties, and if he wished to speak with me, he could come up to where I was and that in any case, I would be requesting for a Court of Inquiry to determine why this had happened.

The Brigade Commander complained to my CO that I was misbehaving and I was given a 'shut up call' by the CO.

I was miserable and restless and did not know what to do. I had lost my company 2ic, my best NCOs and men, all because I had worked on trust. The next few days were spent in cremating those who had died and the follow-up actions that were required to be completed before we were launched on the next operation. My company's strength needed to be made up from the other companies. However, all the companies were below strength and all that I got was Naib Subedar Prem Singh, the newly promoted MT (Military Transport) Havildar to fill in the vacancy caused by the death of Subedar Bhimbahadur.

Gorkhas are generally cheerful with a positive attitude. Although I was angry and hurt, I realized that I could not pass on my discomfort to the rest of my company and so during a brief period of rest, I organized a basketball match and joined them at their evening meal at the langar (community kitchen). We talked about what we needed to do in future operations.

The next day a mountain artillery regiment joined us at the Brigade Headquarters. The CO of the regiment was 'Bobby Sihota' – a cheerful officer who was a friend of my CO, Colonel Bhatia. His presence was instrumental in helping us overcome, to a great degree, the anguish of the past few days.

The battalion now received information that two to three companies of guerrillas, involved in the ambush, had occupied a defensive position at a place called Gajna that overlooked Bhimber Galli and the Rajauri-Poonch road. Our battalion was tasked to attack Gajna and destroy them. It was uncharacteristic of guerrillas to hold ground but it appeared that this group either lacked imagination or they had nowhere else to go.

The next morning the CO assembled his 'O' group[8] at a vantage point from where we could see our objective, the Gajna feature. Just as I was leaving for the CO's orders, my Company Havildar Major came to me and said that Jumbahadur, my batman, who had been wounded in an earlier engagement, had returned from hospital and wanted to resume his job of being my batman as he considered this to be his duty. I assented and hurried off to attend the CO's orders.

Gajna was the highest feature on the skyline. From its

peak emanated several ridgelines or spurs. Two of these ridge lines were central to the peak and descended down into the valley below us and then climbed back up to where we were. The other spurs were further away and were not tactically relevant to the Gajna operation.

The CO intended to attack along the left central spur. That meant that we had to descend into the valley and climb up the spur. There was no cover on either of the spurs. Since Alpha Company had suffered many casualties in the ambush and was under strength, it was placed in reserve and last in the order of march.

After the CO had given his orders for the attack, he asked if there were any questions.

I pointed out that the other spur that ran more or less parallel to the spur along which we were to approach the objective offered an excellent opportunity to the enemy to bring fire on us, if it was not held. The CO saw the point and told the Battery Commander, to register the parallel ridge as a target.

The company commanders were as follows: 'A' Company self, 'B' Company Captain Sunit Dogra, 'C' Company Major Ashok Mehta and 'D' Company Lieutenant Bikram Chand. The Battery Commander was Major Wagh. 'A' Company was in reserve.

Ashok Mehta and I were the senior company commanders. Ashok was six months senior to me and by this time I had seven years of service. Sunit had approximately three to four years of service and Bikram Katoch had joined the battalion on raising and so he must have had about two and a half years of service.

We descended into the valley and the leading company began the climb up the spur when, just as I had anticipated, the enemy opened up with two MMGs from the parallel ridge and Major Wagh couldn't get through to the guns.

The leading company stopped and took what little cover was available. Our advance had hit a wall. I was part of the CO's 'O' Group. I wondered what I would do if I was in the CO's place. But he did not give me time to ponder further and said to me in Nepali, '*Cardi, kasto hola?*' Translated, he wanted to know whether I could take on the assault.

I didn't think I had an option. Early that morning, the Company Havildar Major had given me the parade state and reported that the strength of the company was just about sixty men, excluding me and two JCOs. I told Jumbahadur, who was my batman as well as runner, to inform Havildar Major to bring our company up and as soon as they arrived, we began clambering up the slope.

The fire from the enemy MMGs was intense and bullets were whizzing all around us, kicking up the dust and ricocheting off the rocks. Lance Naik Jitbahadur, my signaler, told me in a matter-of-fact tone, that his wireless set had been hit and we were out of communication. We continued to move uphill. Jumbahadur, who was at my side, got hit and fell. He was bleeding from the mouth which meant that he had probably been hit on the chest. I was in a dilemma. If I stopped and attended to Jumbahadur, there was risk of more casualties as we were in the open and I had to move on to capture the objective. I remembered what my Platoon Commander had once said when I was in the IMA: 'Your duty comes first, your personal emotions come last always and every time.' So, I left Jumbahadur in the shadow of a rock and carried on.

Short of the objective, the ground morphed into terraced fields and came down the slope in steps. These terraced fields were partly covered by maize plants which afforded the enemy adequate cover but there was no cover whatsoever in the area that we had reached. The enemy could see us but we could not see them. They seemed to have the latest weapons and lots of LMGs. Since the boys were observing the enemy with the head above the terraced fields, many of them were hit on their heads. I asked Naib Subedar Prem Singh, who was next to me where the fire was coming from. He was indicating the direction when there was sudden silence. I looked at him and to my disbelief, saw that he was shot in the head. The enemy was also lobbing grenades at us and they were bouncing down the slopes. Naib Subedar Narbahadur Gurung, one of my Platoon Commanders seemed to be unfazed and was throwing back the grenades that the guerrillas were throwing at us.

Suddenly there was a major movement in the maize field and we could see them massing for a rush down the slope. But our boys held firm and shot the attack to pieces with cries of '*Ayo Gorkhali*' and the guerrillas went back dragging their dead and wounded.

I took stock of the situation. We had suffered quite a few casualties and our strength had dwindled even further. In the meantime, the enemy had gathered for another rush at us from their position of vantage. We decided to charge at them before they could. With calls of '*Ayo Gorkhali*' we charged at them, sending them back helter-skelter. Once again, we had beaten back a force far superior in numbers but our charge was more noise than force. I realized that I neither had the strength to capture the objective nor would I be able to withstand another counter-attack. The dead and wounded were lying all around us.

Unfortunately, I had no communication with the battalion because my wireless set had been damaged. With my batman killed, the only answer was to charge the enemy but by now we were too few. I sent Lance Naik Jitbahadur, my wireless operator, with a message to the CO asking for reinforcements. I told him to tell the CO that we had beaten back two counter-attacks, and needed reinforcements quickly.

Luckily, Ashok Mehta came up with Charlie Company just as the third counter-attack by the enemy was under way and the enemy was forced to retreat. If I am alive today it is because of Ashok and 'C' Company.

The rest of the battalion thereafter came up and built up on Alpha and Charlie Companies and consolidated on the slope. True to the nature of guerrilla warfare, to disappear when faced by a strong force, they melted away into the night when they saw we were now in strength. When Charlie Company launched an attack the next morning, the guerrillas were gone.

The battalion thereafter continued to be used by the division like a fire brigade to put out fires as and when they occurred in the divisional sector. The next day we were sent to the Mendhar Sector. One of the picquets was in danger of being captured and needed to be reinforced.

A force comprising 'A' and 'D' Companies led by the CO was ordered to prevent the picquet from being overrun. We climbed up to the post and found it in bad shape. It was commanded by a JCO who had stuck to his post despite the repeated attacks by the enemy. On the way up, we found that the water point had bloated bodies of dead soldiers floating in the pond being fed by a spring. The water was undrinkable.

The beleaguered force welcomed us like conquering heroes. Discipline wavered and the difference between officers and men melted away as they hugged us like long-lost relatives. The enemy got the message that the post had been reinforced and resorted to heavy shelling with artillery fire.

Attacking a post is tough, but if you ask me, nothing could be worse than sitting in defence and being subjected to incessant artillery shelling for hours on end and not being able to do anything about it. In fact, all we could do was to punish the enemy with our own artillery but we had no

Forward Observation Officer, nor were we in communication with our guns. We could do nothing except sit it out while enemy artillery rounds crashed around us non-stop.

The next day we received orders to move to Mandi because a troop of our guns was under threat.

Just below this picquet was a hill which was not occupied by us. We saw Pakistani soldiers digging defences on the hill. This was a dangerous development and we asked permission to roll down and do away with this threat on our way down. However, we were told to come down immediately and move to Mandi – the guns were more important.

We did as we were told.

When we reached the Divisional Headquarters, we were told that the threat to the guns had evaporated and we were now not required to go to Mandi. But the post that was being built by the enemy in Mendhar soon developed into a very strong position that became the infamous 'OP Hill'! It required a brigade attack to capture it and many lives were lost.

These I suppose are the imponderables of war. One of the lessons to be learnt from the 'Op Hill' incident is that it is essential to be able to correctly evaluate threats and to be able to use reserves judiciously and at the right time. My experience of the ambush forced me to ponder on accepting orders without verifying facts. This was bad, because in the army, one works on trust. I had accepted blindly that the ridge line would be held and I could move the convoy at 9.30 a.m. but had been let down badly.

Pakistan's Operation Gibraltar did not meet with the success that was anticipated and with its failure, Pakistan now launched 'Operation Grand Slam'. This operation aimed at the capture of Akhnur and cutting the line of communication between Jammu and Poonch with a strong force of a Pakistani infantry division and an armoured brigade supported by their entire corps artillery, including heavy artillery.

All that we had, to face this strong enemy force, in the area of Chamb–Jaurian was an infantry brigade of two infantry battalions and a squadron of armour. The third battalion of this brigade was holding the hill sector.

India's patience was now pushed beyond the restraint which she has always maintained when dealing with Pakistan and she decided to launch operations across the International Border in areas of her own choosing. A second front was opened in Punjab which took Pakistan by surprise and forced her to withdraw some of her forces near Akhnur and move them to Punjab. Prime Minister Shastri's reasoning was that 'an attack on J&K is an attack on India.'

This pushed the war from within the boundaries of Jammu & Kashmir to an all-out war.

To carry out our plans to cross the border in areas of our own choosing, the Indian Army's 11 Corps was given the task of securing the line of the Ichhogil Canal by establishing bridgeheads across the canal and to pose a threat to Lahore. It was anticipated that Pakistani forces would react violently and provide 11 Corps the opportunity to destroy them. It was decided that Asal Uttar would be a suitable place to cover an enemy offensive rather than Khem Karan which could be bypassed. Asal Uttar covered both, the Khem Karan–Amritsar axis as well as the Khem Karan–Patti axis.

The Pakistani Armoured Division attacked exactly as anticipated on 10 September 1965 and attempted to break through. First, they tried to overrun the 4 Grenadiers' position. This battalion held out with great determination and gallantry against heavy pressure by the enemy. In this action, Company Quartermaster Havildar Abdul Hamid was awarded a posthumous Param Vir Chakra for destroying seven Patton tanks with his recoil-less gun before being killed. Indian armour had been so sited in the area of Khem Karan, Asal Uttar and Patti that the Pakistanis were unable to make any headway and they lost 97 Patton tanks of which 32 were in good running condition. The Pakistani General Officer Commanding the Armoured Division narrowly escaped capture and his Commander Artillery was killed.

The Pakistani offensive ground to a dismal halt and having lost the ability to continue the offensive any further, the Pakistani Commander-in-Chief had to call off the offensive and had to pull out the remnants of Pakistan's 1st Armoured Division to meet the threat of India's 1 Corps offensive in the north, which planned to isolate Sialkot from Lahore. The capture of Chawinda was part of this operation and it was here that Lieutenant Colonel Adi Tarapore was awarded the Param Vir Chakra.

To stop further infiltration and to cut off those who had already come across, operations were launched to secure the bases and routes of infiltration in the Kargil, Tithwal and Poonch sectors. A major operation was launched by Brigadier 'Zoru' Bakshi PVSM, MVC, AVSM, VrC, VSM of my regiment to secure the Haji Pir Pass and to clear the Haji Pir bulge, the major ingress routes for the infiltrators into the Kashmir Valley. Haji Pir was captured in a brilliant attack led by Major (later Lieutenant General) Ranjit Singh Dayal MVC of 1 Para and with its capture, Pakistan's ability to infiltrate into the Valley was curtailed.

Although many have tried to state that the result of the 1965 was a stalemate, it would be more appropriate to say that it was Pakistan who lost the war for the following reasons. Pakistan initiated the war with the express purpose of annexing the state of J&K. In this she failed miserably. In addition, Indian armour and infantry destroyed most of her Patton tanks numbering approximately 97 in the Asal Uttar area alone and another 64 in the Sialkot sector. This meant that out of the 200 Patton tanks gifted to Pakistan by the USA, approximately 161 were destroyed. Destruction of

Pakistani armour is a good indicator of victory in land battle.

One of the factors that Pakistan considered in the timing of the war was that India was still in the process of reorganization after the 1962 war. Many of the raisings were inexperienced and raw. India's strategic philosophy during this period was 'offensive defence' and Pakistan's appreciation that India was not quite ready for war was partially correct.

The experience of our battalion, the Fourth Battalion the 5th Gorkha Rifles (FF) is a case in point. We were sent to hold a sector along the CFL in J&K within just six months of raising. We were still deficient of items of arms and equipment and except for the initial training of the first batch of recruits, we had not done any worthwhile training. This must have been true of many newly raised units, formations and formation headquarters. Considering all this, we did quite well. Of course, in the process we learnt that Pakistan could not be trusted, that co-operation between the army and the air force needed radical improvement, that the performance of the intelligence services was a national weakness and that the armed forces continued to be woefully poor in its weapon and equipment profile.

The UN intervened on 22 September calling for a ceasefire. Many felt that a few more days was all that was required to deal with Pakistan more decisively but since the Government of India had accepted the ceasefire, nothing more could be said. The ceasefire came into effect from 3.30 p.m. on 23 September 1965.

The next few years of the 1960s were used to learn from the lessons of 1962 and 1965 operations and by the time of the start of the 1971 Indo–Pak War, India was ready and prepared.

Meanwhile, an uneasy peace prevailed along the CFL punctuated by the ceaseless chatter of machine gun fire as the Pakistani picquets fired their weapons at night at imaginary threats. Our Brigade Commander was court-martialed and relieved of his command due to incompetent handling of the brigade during the war. He was relieved by another Brigadier who had done well during the war in another sector. Apparently, the sacked Brigade Commander blamed the battalions for his removal. With his departure, apparently all citations for awards for the good work done by the battalions were binned!

The battalion had reverted to its role of holding defences along the CFL and we held picquets south of Rajauri. I was still in command of Alpha Company holding a company post in our new location. Colonel Bhatia had established his Tactical Headquarters (Tac HQ) below the picquet line and one day I got a call from him to come down to the Tac HQ to meet the new 2ic who was on his way up.

It was a lovely afternoon and the Tac HQ located at a lower height in a grove of pine trees was quiet and peaceful. The CO was in a good mood, probably because he was getting a 2ic who could take the load of the battalion's administration off his shoulders.

We sat in cane basket chairs in the mild afternoon sun waiting for Major M.C. Pol to come up. We could see him climbing up when he suddenly fell. We watched and waited for him to get up, but he never did. He passed away due to a heart attack.

MS Branch in their search for a 2ic for the battalion had found Major Pol in faraway Khadki. He had just two years left to retire and was not in good health. Like a good soldier he moved as ordered and passed away before he could proceed on retirement. The battalion had lost its second 2ic within a period of two months.

It was essential that a battalion holding a defended area on the CFL was posted with a 2ic. So, MS Branch now found a major, RO Thompson who was posted at Lucknow to assume the appointment of 2ic. He reached the battalion sometime in November 1965 and after a month of being properly acclimatized and oriented, he asked for a few days' leave to spend Christmas at home. Leave was granted but he never came back. He was run over by a bus at Lucknow and his leg had to be amputated. The battalion had lost its third 2ic within four months.

Word started getting around that the appointment of 2ic of 'Four Five' was jinxed, but we did not believe that until Subedar Major reported to the CO and said that he wished to speak to him about the battalion 2ics.

The Subedar Major is the senior most JCO of the unit, the right-hand man of the CO in all matters regarding the morale and welfare of the personnel of the unit. Matters concerning officers did not come under his purview unless, in his opinion, it affected the morale of the unit. The Subedar Major apparently decided that it was time to speak to the CO on this matter. The CO understood that the matter was serious and instead of keeping him standing as was typical when he gave his official report, asked him to take off his cap, sit down and talk. The Subedar Major informed the CO that during the Second World War when 'Four Five' was in Burma, two 2ics were killed in action as well as two commanding officers who had assumed command of the battalion after doing 2ic.

He continued that within the locality of 'Charlie' Company at Pir Badeshar, there was a thousand-year-old temple and close by was a pir's[9] *mazar*, or grave. The pir, he said granted favours to those who prayed at his *mazar*, and people came from distant villages to seek his favours.

The battalion looked after the maintenance of both the temple as well as the pir's grave. He said that it was the opinion of the JCOs that the next 2ic should pray at the temple and the pir's grave and the problem would be resolved.

The CO accepted his advice and since there was no

2ic, he asked the Adjutant to pass orders that the next 2ic and subsequent ones would be required to offer prayers for their own safety. The next two 2ics did as ordered, and both survived and went on to higher ranks – the first being promoted in due course to Brigadier's rank and the next one eventually to become a Lieutenant General.

■ ■ ■

Meanwhile, my relationship with Priscilla had moved forward over two years from mere friendship to a close relationship. We had got engaged before the 1965 war and had decided to get married in April 1966.*

I had applied for leave to make arrangements for my wedding and I was told that although my leave had been sanctioned, the Brigade Commander had decided to visit the battalion and so my leave was postponed.

A few days later, the Brigade Commander arrived at my picquet. It was a tough climb and after a brief rest and a mug of hot tea, he said he was ready to be briefed. My post had an excellent view of the Pakistani landscape and all VIPs who had to be briefed came to my post for briefing.

Far away to the left, one could see a Pakistani Supply Point at which some vehicles were being loaded. The Brigade Commander gave me the 'go ahead' and I started briefing him about the enemy strengths and dispositions and the pattern of operations in this sector but he seemed fascinated with the Supply Point, which he was viewing through a pair of binoculars. I finished after a while but didn't know how much he had heard. I was irritated – my leave had been cancelled because of his visit and he had not paid much attention to my briefing.

---

*See chapter 8.

When he realized that I had finished, he turned to me and said, 'Young man, you raid that Supply Point and I will give you a Maha Vir Chakra.'

The task was a mission impossible! It involved breaking through the enemy line of picquets opposite us, advancing approximately 20 kilometres in enemy held territory, raiding the Supply Point and returning once again through enemy held ground and infiltrating back to our positions. I wondered if he realized the impossibility of such a task. Also, no action had been taken by him or his predecessor to follow up on the citations for gallantry by personnel of the battalion for the good work that we had done during the war.

The Commander was waiting for my answer. 'Did you hear me?' He asked. Unfortunately, my answer was not one that a senior officer would have expected. I said, 'Sir, give me the task and it will be done. My battalion does not work for awards.'

The Brigade Commander turned around to the CO and said, 'You have a very cheeky company commander here, Madan. Do all your officers talk like this to their seniors?'

The CO was standing behind and puffing away at his pipe. He answered, 'Sorry sir, but you had asked for it.'

The Brigade Commander was visibly annoyed. He turned around to me and said, 'I want your plans for a raid on the picquet opposite you within a week. Do you hear me?'

'Yes sir,' I said contritely, realizing that my leave had now been further postponed due to my answer.

'What next?' he asked the CO.

'Would you like to talk to the men?' suggested the CO.

There were not too many men – some were detailed on duty at their posts and two patrols were out holding key areas because of the Brigade Commander's visit. The Brigade Commander was not too pleased at having to address just a handful of men. He too was from the Gorkhas, but from another regiment and he spoke to the men in Nepali. After he finished, the CO asked the Brigade Commander to have lunch. But he appeared to be in a huff and said, 'No thank you. I will go back.'

Both the CO and I were upset with ourselves. We could have handled the visit better. This was an opportunity to build bridges with the new Commander and instead we had antagonized him.

The CO had lunch with us and when leaving he said, 'You better work on your plan and come to me if you have any queries.'

'Yes sir,' I said as he left.

The next few days were spent looking at the enemy post from various vantage points but the pine trees blocked our view. The men had nicknamed this enemy post as '*Badmash*[10] *Post*' because their razakars[11] used to come across to our villages across the CFL to trouble our villagers.

The map did not help much except to indicate that the enemy post was on a spur that ran perpendicular to our ridge and that the post was on a knoll at the end of this spur. Out of seven, only three days were left and I did not have enough information to make a good plan.

Early in the morning of the fifth day, I was with my forward post of the picquet at 'Stand to', which is the period when the darkness of the night turns to the greyness of dawn and all posts are on extra high alert. While we were watching our front, the forward platoon commander alerted me, pointing to a group of Pakistani soldiers moving on their side of the CFL. They were about a dozen of them wearing their greatcoats which indicated that they had been on an all-night patrol. They had probably laid an ambush and were now returning to their post. Appearing tired and sleepy, they were going back in single file on a track close to the CFL.

While at the IMA I remembered being told something

about 'shadow patrols' – that if an opportunity presented itself, one could follow an enemy patrol into their own area of operations to get more information in order to launch a subsequent attack.

I was in dire need of information about the enemy post *Badmash* and an opportunity was unfolding itself in front of me. I felt it would be foolish to ignore it. I shared my intention to follow the enemy patrol into their area with Naib Subedar Narbahadur Gurung, the man known for throwing back enemy grenades at the Battle at Gajna. He readily agreed to come with me. Naik Kharkabahadur, a good NCO was listening to my plan and I told Narbahadur Saab to take him along. I tried talking to the CO on the telephone but the signal exchange replied that the CO was not answering.

Meanwhile, the enemy patrol had come closer. We counted them; they were ten soldiers, all fully armed. I quickly got hold of a sten machine carbine and some magazines and the three of us moved towards the CFL. We took shelter behind a big rock on the CFL itself and waited for the Pakistani patrol to pass. We could hear the crunch of their boots on the track as they came closer. The slightest noise would have given us away. They were ten and we were only three. I could hear the beating of my heart not quite in rhythm with the steady tramp of their feet. They came close to us and veered towards their post from where we were waiting.

They appeared to be very tired and must have been thinking about the mug of hot masala chai that awaited them at the post as they trudged past. After they had gone some distance, we followed in their footsteps to ensure that we would not step on any of their mines or booby traps.

We crossed the CFL, moved across into enemy territory, past their barbed wire, past their mine field, into their post and stopped just about twenty feet short of their *langar*. Fortunately, there was no sentry at the entry to the post and luckily, there was a low wall behind which we could take cover. The enemy soldiers leaned their weapons against the wall of the langar and began to have their tea talking among themselves, oblivious of our presence. We were quite comfortable because there was no sentry at the entry point to the post so the area behind us was clear.

We were able to get a clear view of the layout of the post and the approaches from the rear and the sides. Narbahadur and I discussed how we would approach the post and where we would place our machine guns to give us covering fire.

Suddenly an alarm was raised. We were discovered!

Unknown to us, a *razakar* who was cutting grass below the track we had used, had reached the top and had seen the three of us sitting inside their post and thinking there might be many more, started shouting '*Dushman aa gaya! Dushman aa gaya! Hamla ho raha hai!*' (The enemy has come, the enemy has come, we are under attack) and ran back down the slope he had come. He had a rifle in one hand and khurpi[12] in the other. If he had taken a stand with his rifle, we would have had a major problem dealing with him on one side and the enemy patrol on the other.

The Indian Army wears olive green uniforms and the Pakis wear khaki so we were clearly recognized as the enemy! The three of us jumped up and looked at the patrol – the main source of danger. Their eyes were open wide in horror. They could not believe what they were seeing! They threw away their mugs of tea and reached for their weapons.

We had our weapons with us and their weapons were still leaning against the wall of the langar. We had the advantage of surprise and if we opened fire, we could have caused a lot of damage. The aim, however, was to acquire information and not to have an encounter. We decided that it was time to leave. After all, a UN ceasefire had been enforced and we had agreed to abide by it.

The Pakis had no such inhibitions. However, to give them their due, they were under threat. They had no way of knowing there were only three of us. They opened up with their rifles, when they spotted us as we headed back, then with their light and medium machine guns, then with their mortars and finally with their artillery. Strangely, we were not followed.

By the time we had reached close to our picquet, artillery rounds were falling around us setting off our mines and throwing up great mounds of earth and rocks. There was smoke and fire and the Johnnies were waiting anxiously for our return. All our company posts were now being plastered by enemy artillery fire.

The CO was having breakfast down below at the Battalion Headquarters when the sounds of the enemy artillery reached him. He hurried to his bunker and put in multiple calls to all the company commanders. They all confirmed that their posts were under enemy artillery fire. On being asked why the enemy was firing, they all said that they did not know. The CO asked for me. I was not there to take his call. My company 2ic however answered.

The CO asked him where I was. He told the CO that company commander Saab had gone inside *Badmash Post* and had not yet returned. The CO could not believe what he was hearing.

'Why has he gone there?' the CO asked.

'I don't know,' replied my company 2ic.

The CO left instructions that I was to call him as soon as I got back.

Meanwhile, the Brigade Commander had gone for his morning walk, when he heard the sound of the guns. He hurried to his headquarters and was met by the Brigade Major.

'What's the matter? Who is firing and why?'

'The Pakis are firing, sir. Don't know why! Heavy artillery firing in the sector of the Gorkhas.'

'Are our guns in position and all units alert for any counter action?'

'Yes sir.'

'What is the cause? Put me through to the CO of the Gorkhas.'

'I have tried to speak to the CO Sir. He is busy dealing with the situation but I will have you put through to him as soon as I can.'

After I returned, I was put through to the CO and I explained the whole situation to him.

'Why did you not take my permission before you did something as stupid as this?' he asked.

'Tried to get through to you sir, but there was no response and I could not wait.'

'Are you aware that our Prime Minister is in Russia negotiating a peace agreement with Pakistan. And here you are starting another war?'

'No sir. I did not know sir. Sorry sir.'

In the meantime, the Brigade Commander had got through to the CO, who explained to him what had happened.

'Has your company commander gone mad? The whole division sector has come alive. Questions are pouring in from the division, corps, command and the UN Observer Group. What do I tell them? All that is left is for the Chief to call and ask me whether I am starting another war! Are you aware that the Prime Minister is in Tashkent negotiating a Cease Fire Agreement with the Pakistanis?'

'Where is Cardozo now? What did he do to start this incident? Did he raid the Pakistani post? Are there any casualties? Any evidence left behind?'

'He is back sir. No evidence left behind. The artillery firing has stopped. No casualties so far. However, I will check again.'

'Anyway, why did he go across in the first place?'

'Well sir, he says that he needed information about the approaches to the Pakistani picquet to make the plan you had ordered him to submit by this weekend.'

The Brigade Commander was aghast.

'What?' He shouted. 'Is he blaming me?'

'No sir. He is not blaming you. He is just saying that he could not get enough information about the approaches to the Pakistani post, so he decided to go across to get it.'

'Has the world gone mad? Send him to me immediately. How much time will he take to reach me?'

'About two hours, sir.'

'Send him to me at once.'

The CO called and asked me to come down immediately. He was sending an officer to take command of my post, but that in the meantime, I should hand over to my 2ic.

What we did not know at that time was that the Brigade Commander was due for promotion. He had done well in the war in command of another brigade and was sent specifically to command this brigade after his predecessor had been removed. This incident would show him in poor light, particularly if it was discovered that he was the one who ordered me to make plans to raid the Pakistani post in question and it was this order that had prompted me to go across. If this incident gained momentum, then somebody's head would roll and it could be his and all of us down the line!

I was in my overalls and had no time to change. I put on a belt and a beret and hurried down to the Battalion Base. A jeep was standing by and I was bundled into it. The CO said, 'I can't imagine why you did such a stupid thing. However, tell the truth and take the consequences like a man. I will see what I can do to reduce the enormity of your foolishness. Now go!'

I felt reassured that the CO would do something to mitigate the situation. During the drive to the Brigade Headquarters, in my mind I went over the events of the past three hours. What seemed to me like a brilliant idea had climaxed into a complex situation with international ramifications. Now the Brigade Commander had willy-nilly got involved and was hitting the ceiling.

Meanwhile the CO had rung up the Commander Artillery. He reminded him of the two occasions the divisional artillery had failed to come to my assistance. The first time, when I had asked for help from the division before the ambush took place and the second time when we were attacking Gajna and the guns failed to support our attack. He said that as the Commander Artillery, he would probably be aware of the good work done by the battalion during the war despite the lack of artillery support and that it would be useful if he could do something to mitigate the consequences of the present situation.

By this time, I had reached the Brigade Headquarters. 'Tiger' Tyagraja the Brigade Major (BM) met me with a big smile. He was from a parachute battalion and never lost his cool.

He said, 'The Commander has asked me to march you in, but I'm not going to do that because although I am senior to you, we are of the same rank. He is walking up and down in his office like a caged tiger. He is very upset… Are you aware that the Prime Minister is in Tashkent with the Russians and Pakistanis negotiating a Peace Agreement?'

With that, he opened the door and let me in.

The Commander was not walking up and down like a caged tiger. He had finished with that and he was now sitting behind his desk ready to eat me up!

'May I come in sir?' I asked.

'You stupid fool. Did you ask the Pakistanis that when you walked into their post?'

'No sir.'

'Then why did you go across the Cease Fire Line and enter an enemy post without anyone's permission?'

I kept quiet.

'I asked you a question and I demand an answer. Answer me.'

'I just wanted more information to make a good plan, sir.'

'What plan?'

'The plan you asked me to make, sir.'

The Commander nearly hit the ceiling. He seemed terribly agitated.

'You blithering idiot,' he shouted. 'Did I ask you to cross the Cease Fire Line? Did I ask you to enter an enemy post?'

'No, sir.'

'Then why did you do such a stupid thing? Are you aware that the Prime Minister of India and the President of Pakistan are in Tashkent negotiating a Peace Agreement? What do I do with idiots like you in my brigade?'

At that moment there was a knock on the door and the BM entered and said, 'Sir, the Commander Artillery from the division is here. He would like to talk with you.'

'Tell him to come in and move that chair here, next to me.'

The Commander Artillery walked in and sat next to the Commander.

The Commander began to tell the Commander Artillery about what had happened. The Commander Artillery interrupted him and addressing him by his first name said that he knew all about what had happened and that the GOC had asked him to intervene and carry out 'damage control'.

'Can I ask this young man some questions?'

'Go ahead,' said the Commander. 'Maybe you can make some sense of his story because I can't.'

Brigadier Freidal (for that was his name) said. 'Now listen carefully to my questions and answer me truthfully.'

'Did you kill or wound any Pakistani soldier?'

'No sir.'

'Did you fire any weapon?'

'No sir.'

'Did anyone from your picquet fire any weapon to cover your return?'

'No sir. No weapon of any kind was fired.'

'Good. Did you leave any evidence of any kind inside the Pakistani post to prove that you were there? Any scrap of paper? Anything?'

'No sir.'

'Good.'

Then turning to the Commander, he said, 'I have spoken to the UN Observer Group and informed them that the Pakis are jittery and have unnecessarily overreacted when one of our patrols lost their way and crossed the Cease Fire Line and came up to one of their posts. We have put the Pakistanis on the back foot by reporting to the UN Observer Group that indiscriminate firing by the Pakis caused unnecessary damage to our posts and it is they who have broken the ceasefire and put the peace talks at Tashkent at risk. The UN Observer Group as well as the Pakis are now more anxious than us to put a cap on this incident. The Corps and Command Headquarters are also keen to close the matter considering what is happening in Russia. The GOC has asked me to check all facts before proceeding further. Can I speak to the GOC?'

The Brigade Commander seemed to be happy at the way the issue was progressing and that his part in the matter would not be discovered. He called the signal exchange and asked them to get the GOC on the line. Addressing me, he said, 'Get out and stand outside. Tell the BM to also standby.'

I saluted and got out as quickly as I could. The BM was already standing outside. He put his finger on his lips, motioning me to keep quiet.

The Commander Artillery spoke with the GOC. The conversation was clearly audible from where we were standing. It was not our intention to eavesdrop but we were only following orders and frankly we were also keen to know what was being said.

The Commander Artillery briefly told the GOC about what had happened and that he had spoken with the Brigade Commander as well as with me. He said that he was satisfied that there was no evidence whatsoever left behind at the Pakistani post and that neither the Gorkhas nor anyone else had fired a single shot in retaliation. He also told the GOC that he had spoken with the UN Observer Group and they had in turn spoken with the Pakis and that all concerned wanted the matter to be amicably resolved.

The GOC said something that we could not hear but from the conversation it appeared that the GOC wanted to know as to what was to be done with me.

The Commander Artillery said, 'Sir you would be aware that the Gorkhas have done well during the war and even though this officer has created a situation that could well have been avoided, he has proved that we are in total control of the Cease Fire Line and if he is punished it would send a wrong message to the young officers of the division with regard to initiative and boldness and courage and that should not happen.'

The GOC said something else which we could not hear and the Commander Artillery responded, 'Yes, sir. First, we could send him on some leave so that he does not keep talking about what happened. Secondly, we can issue a Special Order of the Day stating that although courage and initiative are well appreciated, balance and maturity are also required when taking action on the Cease Fire Line and that it is important to keep one's seniors informed of action contemplated – something like that... and yes sir, I will keep BGS[13] Corps and Command informed.'

With that the telephone conversation ended. The BM grinned and gave me a 'thumbs up' and answered the Commander who had shouted out for him.

The BM returned and said that the Commander wanted me inside. I went in and saluted.

He said, 'We have been considering your stupid, irresponsible action from all angles and have decided to let you off this time. You will proceed on leave and stop babbling about what happened. It will give you the time and opportunity to think about what you have done and to realize that you need to think before you act. Before you leave, I want your plan and no funny stuff this time. Now beat it before I change my mind.'

With that, the matter of my nearly having started a war was concluded. I submitted my plan for the raid on *Badmash Post*. I think it was a good plan because it had important details as to the best approaches to raid or capture the post, the direction of attack and the placement of support weapons and reserves.

Ultimately, as far as the brigade was concerned, all turned out well. The Brigade Commander was promoted to Major General; I got my leave and the episode of my crossing the CFL and entering an enemy post was given a decent burial. However, at the national level things did not go well at all. Prime Minister Shastri passed away in Tashkent and we had to give Haji Pir back after capturing it with so much effort and sacrifice. This expectedly did not go down well with the army.

The Pakistani Army tried to say that they had won the war and some people on both sides tried to state that it was a draw. However, that is not true. The writings of Frederick Von Clausewitz, Mao Tse Tung and Chanakya are all in agreement that the destruction of the enemy's war machine and the will to fight is the best indicator of victory. We had in this war destroyed 97 Patton tanks at Asal Uttar and 64 enemy tanks at Sialkot. In effect we had destroyed the bulk of their armour, a sure indicator that the Pakistani war machine had been effectively neutralized. Pakistani ammunition had reached an all-time low and they would never have been able to carry on with the war. Once again, we gave in to the intervention of the UN and agreed to a ceasefire.

As far as my battalion was concerned, we had proved beyond doubt that we dominated the CFL and that we were in charge of the area in front of us. The men too had something to talk about during the dull period after the war.

A few months later an incident occurred in the battalion that gave us much to think about.

Tensions once again rose between Pakistan and India and both sides tried to dominate the no man's land in the area of the CFL. We had received information that Pakistan was contemplating a raid in our sector and that we needed to be alert.

In addition to patrolling the area up to the CFL and the ambushes that we laid, we were also carrying out 'link-patrols' between our posts on a nightly basis. The link-patrol would leave its post and link up with the next post ensuring that the area in between was clear and would return the next morning to its own post.

One particular night, the sky was overcast due to low lying clouds that blotted out all starlight and the night was very dark indeed. A link patrol from one of our posts approached an area where some of our men had laid an ambush. It was pitch dark and when the patrol came close to the ambush site, the ambush look-out challenged the approaching patrol asking it to identify itself. For some reason the patrol commander who had to respond, forgot the password. Three times the challenge was given and the patrol commander failed to respond. The lookout who was a Lance Naik fired five rounds. His fire was very accurate and all five rounds found their mark. The link-patrol commander was killed and four soldiers were wounded – so accurate was the fire on that pitch dark night.

The battalion was in a quandary. Was the look out justified in opening fire? If unjustified, should he be punished?

A Court of Inquiry was held and the Lance Naik was cleared of all blame. It was an example of our own troops being killed due to mistaken identity. In this case it was an issue of a Commander forgetting or not knowing the password on a dark night with zero visibility and the firer could therefore not be blamed.

Sometimes strange things happen in war and commanders have to look at incidents with balance and maturity, keeping in mind the facts and the consequences of their decisions on the morale of the men they command. Morale in fact is a very important factor in war and needs to be carefully nurtured.

The 1965 war was an eventful period in my life. I learnt a lot from the brave and loyal conduct of my men whose discipline, sense of duty, courage and loyalty were outstanding – that it is good to trust but also necessary to double check on information given to me by others. I was deeply grieved at the loss of the men from my company. I had over the years become very close to them and now they were no more. That's how life was in the army. It went on and we had to be ready for the next battle.

Notes

1. *Field Marshal Sam Manekshaw – the Man and his Times* by Brigadier Behram M. Panthaki and Zenobia Panthaki, Niyogi Books, New Delhi, 2014, p. 59.
2. Training of all elements of a unit collectively in all the operations

of war so that they are able to perform seamlessly in operations as integrated sub-units.

3. Divisional Reserve is a force which is not holding ground and therefore available to carry out contingency tasks for the division.

4. Napalm – an incendiary mixture of polystyrene, benzene and petrol, which when mixed forms a firm jelly used in flame throwers and incendiary bombs.

5. Ulloo in Hindi means owl.

6. An elongated lock of hair at the top of the head at the tonsure and one of the distinguishing marks of a person of the Hindu religion.

7. Although I had just seven years' service, I was promoted to major's rank as the rules permitted officers in operational areas with more than five years' service to be promoted to major's rank if a vacancy existed.

8. The 'Order' group of a Battalion Commander consisting of the company commanders and the platoon commanders of Support Company and the Battery Commander of the Artillery.

9. A holy man.

10. A rogue/rascal.

11. Irregular soldier.

12. A gardening tool.

13. Brigadier General Staff is a staff officer at a Corps/Command Headquarter dealing with operational matters.

St. Xavier's School Junior Hockey Team 1951 (*standing third from left*).

St. Xavier's College Hockey Team, 1953 (*sitting first from the right*).

With the Hero of the Soviet Union, Marshal Zhukov (*fourth from the left*), February 1957. Harpal Singh is on Zhukov's right. Generals Thapar and Habibulla are on either side of us.

Harpal and I accompanying Marshal Zhukov on a tour of the National Defence Academy (*second from the right*).

With Prime Minister Pandit Jawaharlal Nehru at the Cadets' Mess,
April 1957.

With my course mates 'G' Squadron, NDA, May 1957.
(*Sitting, left to right*): Lt Baijal I.N.; Flt Lt. D.S. Chhabra IAF; Squadron
Cadet Captain Balwant Singh, Cdr. P.S. Bhar, I.N.; Academy Cadet Captain
Ian Cardozo, Captain M.N. Rawat IA.
(*Second row*): Cadets Jasmail Singh Gill, N.C. Mahajan, Satpal Singh, N.R.
Khanna, Surinder Bawa.
(*Last row*): Cadets P.K. Mehta, S.K. Phani, D.K. Kapoor.

General K.S. Thimayya, DSO at our Passing Out Parade 12th Course, 7 June 1957. SBL Kapoor is on my left.

Under Officers of the 21st Course Indian Military Academy with the Commandant and Staff, May 1958.

Looking at the valley of the Andhi Khola, Nepal,
February 1959.

With L/Naik
Amarbahadur Gurung
– Simi Tanje on the
Nepal-Tibet border,
February 1959.

Battalion Group 1/5GR(FF) and others at Ziro in Subansiri district of NEFA, December 1959 *(first row, sitting, centre)*.

Outside my basha, Daporijo, Subansiri District NEFA, September 1960.

With an MMG detachment
4/5 GR (FF) Mendhar Valley,
January 1964.

Being awarded the Sena Medal by Army Chief J.N. Chaudhuri, OBE,
15 January 1964.

With Lt. Gen. Sam Manekshaw (*standing second from the right*), MC and other recipients of the Sena Medal, 15 January 1964.

With Lt. Raghu Bidappa 4/5 GR(FF). Mendhar Valley, Jammu & Kashmir, July 1964.

Photograph taken during
Indo–Pak War, 1965.

At Lisrian Post, Jammu &
Kashmir, November 1965.

My marriage with Priscilla, 26 April 1966. Emerging from Sacred Heart Church under an arch of Khukris held by Regimental Officers 5GR (FF).

Wedding Group, 26 April 1966.
Left to right: My father Vincent Cardozo, Priscilla's brother Norbert, Priscilla's mother Effie deGuerra, my brother Colin, Self, Priscilla, Priscilla's bridesmaid Avril deGuerra, Priscilla's father John deGuerra, my mother Diana Cardozo, Priscilla's brothers Leslie and Darryl.

On our honeymoon,
Mussoorie, April 1966.

On our honeymoon, Naini Tal Lake, May 1966.

Priscilla, on a visit to 1/5 GR (FF), Ferozepur, May 1966.

Lt Gen Jehangir Sataravala (Jangu) MBE, MC; GOC 1 Corps.

'My Family', Mathura 1970.

President V.V. Giri awarding Lieutenant Colonel A.B. Harolikar with the Maha Vir Chakra for his outstanding courage and leadership at the battles of Atgram, Gazipur, and Sylhet during the 1971 War.

Capt Kipgen and I with Capt Jayalakshmi MO Upper Officers' Ward MH Pune and a Red Cross official, March 1972.

With Priscilla and Capt Kipgen (Kippy) Upper Officers' Ward, MH Pune. Kippy and I had just been fitted with our artificial legs.

Left: With Priscilla, Sunith, Arun and Vikram, Mhow, after being discharged from the Artificial Limb Centre (ALC) September 1972.
Right: At the NDA. On an outpass from the Artificial Limb Centre Pune. (Hut of Remembrance in the background).

Photograph taken at a studio at Pune of four of us who became close friends at the Artificial Limb Centre. They are clockwise – Capt Kipgen (Kippy), Self, Capt Yeshwant Rawat and Major Abu Taher (Bangladesh Army).

Being awarded with the Ati Vishist Seva Medal by the President of India, February 1985.

Above: Briefing Javed Abidi and persons with disability on the meaning and significance of India Gate on World Disability Day.
Right: A keen marathon runner: with Priscilla at the Mumbai Marathon.

With Lal Krishna Advani and George Fernandes at the release of the Hindi edition of my book *Param Vir* in 2005.

With Priscilla and our sons 2/Lt Sunith, Arun and Vikram, Akhnur, Jammu & Kashmir, December 1989.

Group photograph 4/5 GR (FF) Sundarbani, Jammu & Kashmir circa 1990 (Major Dalbir Singh, who later on went to become the Army Chief, is seen standing second from the right).

The Cardozo family. Flagstaff House, Akhnur, Jammu & Kashmir, December 1989.

CHAPTER FIVE

'Jangu' and Memories of Mathura

*The essence of good leadership is influence
– not authority.*
ANONYMOUS

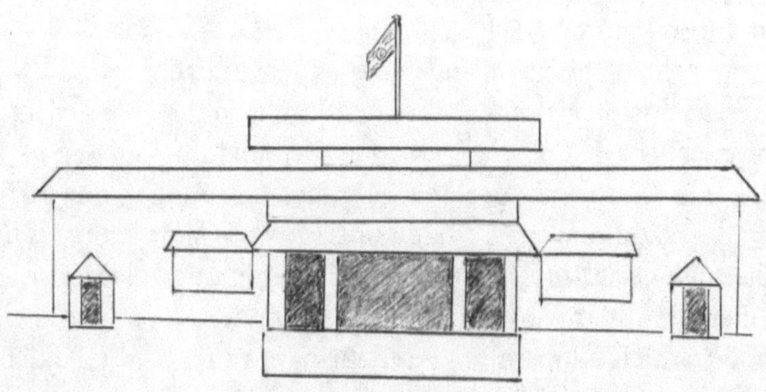

Flagstaff House Mathura

Flagstaff House – Mathura

Towards the end of 1965, when the war had come to a close, I had completed seven years of service in the army – all of it in the battalion. I was overdue for a posting on the staff. Lieutenant General Jahangir Sataravala, one of our senior generals from the regiment had taken over a corps and had asked for a regimental officer to be appointed as the Deputy Assistant Military Secretary at his headquarters. It was a staff appointment but it also had an overlap of regimental duties – the person selected would be carrying out the duties of a staff officer and he would also be heading the team that involved the aide-de-camp (ADC), the JCO ADC, and personnel of the regiment on his staff. The General had looked at my record of service at Army Headquarters and selected me for the job.

I did not want to leave Alpha Company and the battalion. My company was located as an independent picquet and within my given role and charter of duties, I could practically do what I liked as its company commander. Due to the heavy casualties that Alpha Company had suffered during the 1965 War, I had to reorganize, rebuild and train the company for its future tasks.

I valued the trust and independence given to me by the CO. In this regard, I was fortunate to have the able assistance of excellent JCOs with Subedar Gajbahadur Gurung as my 2ic and Naib Subedar Narbahadur Gurung as one of my platoon commanders. I had constructed a short range where the men could fire from standing, sitting and lying positions when on their way to the water point and a good view point which allowed an excellent panorama of the Pakistani positions in POK (Pakistani Occupied Kashmir), a Raike's Range,[1] a boxing ring, and volleyball and basketball courts. Subedar Gajbahadur Gurung had come in place of Subedar Bhimbahadur Rana who had been killed during the war.

Gajbahadur took over the administration of the company and that left me free to handle the training with Naib Subedar Narbahadur Gurung. In addition, I had a young officer from the battalion to be trained, a Forward Observation Officer from the Artillery, along with detachments from the mortar and MMG platoons and a detachment of mules. It was an excellent 'hands on' appointment and I revelled at the range of my command.

We trained hard, played hard and dominated the CFL very effectively. Command of my company truly gave me a lot of satisfaction. I was therefore most reluctant to hand over the command of Alpha Company to anyone else. However, I was told that orders were orders, that I had been specially selected by General Sataravala and I had to go. There was, however, an advantage of being posted to a peace station – I was married a year earlier, and Mathura was a family station.

I wrote to my parents to say that I was posted on the Staff to a high-level formation headquarters as its Deputy Assistant Military Secretary (DAMS). My mother, however, was not impressed. In her reply, she expressed concern at the appointment that I had been given and said, 'Son, what is this appointment that you have been given? What can be smaller than a deputy assistant and that too, a secretary?' She had a point. I did not have a suitable answer!

I left Alpha Company with a feeling of deep regret. There is probably no command in any army which gives an officer such closeness to his men as command of a rifle company. As a company commander, I knew each man of my company; and the loss of my best JCOs, NCOs and men during the 1965 war had grieved me deeply. Perhaps it was also the knowledge that I might never get command of a rifle company again that made the parting with Alpha Company all the more difficult.

The General Officer Commanding the corps, Lieutenant General Jehangir Sataravala MBE, MC was known throughout the army as 'Jangu Sataravala'. Jangu was over six feet tall, fair, fit and slim. He had three rows of medal ribbons, which for those days was a lot. He was commissioned into the 6/13th Frontier Force which is now in Pakistan and had won his Military Cross in 1944 during the Second World War at the Battle of Trigno in Italy. The Military Cross is a pretty ribbon – white with a broad purple stripe running down the centre and is equivalent to our Vir Chakra. He had also been awarded the MBE for excellent rescue work done during the Quetta earthquake. His hobbies were shikar and angling, which were typical of the senior officers of his time and his main game was golf.

By the time I joined the corps, it had moved out on a big exercise. A vehicle from the GOC's fleet had been placed for me at the railway station and I moved directly to the exercise location. Somewhere around 7 p.m. I caught up with the Corps Headquarters. It was the first time that I witnessed a large formation on the move. It was setting up camp for the night and I found everyone too busy to pay attention to me. I slept on the ground in a field that night and I remember that vividly because I had to share my bed with a field mouse who got between my sheets. In the morning I was called by the Brigadier General Staff, Brigadier P. Chowdry who was also from the regiment. Besides welcoming me, he congratulated me and told me that Priscilla had delivered a baby boy. I was granted a few days' leave to meet my wife and son, and I took the first train from the nearest station and met Priscilla while she was still at the Military Hospital at Mhow.

Sleepy and dishevelled, I went to the hospital straight from the railway station. Soon after our marriage and honeymoon I had to return to my battalion, which was in an operational area. I was seeing Priscilla after quite some time, I had missed her and had eyes only for her. She had to remind me about our son fast asleep in his baby cot right by her bedside. It was then that I moved towards our first born. Just as I was about to lift him and take him into my arms, the nursing sister asked me if I had had a bath. I probably looked like a mess because she sent me home and only after I had bathed, was I allowed to pick him up. He opened his eyes and looked at me with curiosity. He seemed so small. I could not imagine at that time, that he would one day follow me into 'First Five' in keeping with the tradition of the regiment.

We named our son Sunith, after Sunith Francis Rodrigues,[2] who was from my school. He was the son of Francis Rodrigues, a senior editor at the *Indian Express* and a very close friend of my father.

I met Jangu very briefly and did not have much to do during the exercise except to look after the Commander's Mess and the GOC's fleet of vehicles. My work would start in earnest when we returned to the permanent location of the Corps Headquarters – the personnel management of all officers of the corps.

My first major interaction with Jangu took place on our return to the Corps Headquarters. I was called into his office through his intercom with the ADC, who said, 'The Boss wants to see you.' I knocked on his door and went in.

He looked me up and down and said, 'Sit down.'

'I hope you know that I have specially selected you for this job after going through your dossier at MS Branch, Army Headquarters. I hope you will be happy working with me. I have high expectations from you.'

He then elaborated. 'Your job involves the handling of the Annual Confidential Reports (ACRs) of all the officers of the corps, including very senior officers of General's rank. These reports are confidential and their contents can make or mar the future of the officer involved. A quality which I hold to be very important in an officer is "trust". My trust in you is total and I expect you to honour that trust. You come directly under me in the matter of confidential reports and under nobody else. Confidentiality has to be maintained at all cost not only by you, but also by your staff. Since these reports are important in the career profiling of every officer, you will need to ensure that the formation commanders initiate the reports to their officers in time. As my representative in these matters, you have the privilege to initiate correspondence on such issues and to follow up, and you are free to come to me when you feel that the matter is beyond you. Make sure that you are polite and circumspect in your attitude, behaviour, and in your correspondence. Don't let this authority go to your head.'

He continued, 'The middle alphabet of your first name is "A". I therefore expect you to be alert and to anticipate issues and events and not be told what is to be done. There are two "O"s in your surname. "O" stands for opportunity and I expect you to use this opportunity of being posted to a Corps Headquarters to develop professionally. You can learn a lot in this formation and if you wish to sit in on any operational or logistical presentation or discussion, go to the BGS[3] or the Brig Adm[4] and ask for their permission. I have spoken with them. I expect you to also look at the needs of the personnel from the regiment and see that they are met.'

He then asked, 'Any questions?'

'No sir.'

'All right then. Welcome to the team. You can learn a lot, provided you keep your eyes and ears open and you take this opportunity to learn. I hope you have a satisfying and happy tenure with the corps and with me.'

I said, 'Thank you sir,' and left.

There were reports by the previous corps commander that had to be initiated and followed-up and so I had my hands full following-up on all the reports – past and present.

Within a few months of my taking over, Captain Ashok

Malhotra, the ADC was detailed to go on the Commando Course and instead of asking for a replacement, Jangu informed me that I would have to do the duties of the ADC as well. He said it would be a good learning experience.

It was not easy handling two jobs and I did not have a spare moment to myself. A week later, I was informed that the General was to attend a divisional exercise and I would have to go with him.

I liaised with the staff at the Corps Headquarters and learnt that the General and some senior staff officers and I would travel by air to the exercise location. The GSO 2 (Ops)[5] would be handling all aspects of the exercise, so I would only be concerned with the job of the ADC and anything concerning ACRs, which was my basic job as the DAMS.

During the 1965 War, the manager of the CSD canteen at Mendhar in Jammu & Kashmir was trying to get rid of his stores because the area was under heavy shelling by the Pakistanis. I bought an HMT watch from this canteen. It was a hand wound watch with a black dial with radium tinted hands and numerals and I liked it because I could read the time at night.

I got up early on the day of our departure for the exercise. We were scheduled to take off at 9 a.m. and would have to leave the Corps Headquarters at 8 a.m. I had lined up the vehicles at Flagstaff House at 7.30 a.m. and was waiting, when I received a message that the GSO 2 (Ops), who was to accompany us was unwell and that I should go to the Corps Headquarters and collect the briefcase that contained the exercise papers immediately. I looked at my watch. I had just thirty minutes to collect the exercise papers and be in time to take off. I got into a jonga and rushed off to the office, collected the briefcase and was back in double quick time. On reaching Flagstaff House, I looked at my watch and found there was still ten minutes to spare.

The Corps Commander came out after a few minutes and said, 'Is it time to take off?' I looked at my watch and said, 'No sir, we still have time.'

The Corps Commander went back inside. After about five minutes he again came out and said, 'Isn't it time to leave?' I looked at my watch. It was still showing ten minutes to eight. I realized that my watch was showing ten minutes to eight for the last ten minutes or so. My watch had stopped!

I quickly said, 'Yes sir, it's time to leave.' The GOC gave me a funny look but did not comment further. I got into the front seat next to the driver of the staff car and we took off. The watch on the dashboard showed 8.15 a.m. We were fifteen minutes behind time! It wasn't an auspicious start for my first tour with my corps commander!

We arrived at the airfield about ten minutes late. The Corps Commander was known to be on time wherever he went. This was out of sync with his reputation and I was the cause! I am sure that he knew that we were late but he did not say anything to me.

The air crew and the other staff officers were waiting. Jangu and the rest of the officers went into the crew room for a cup of tea while I had the luggage loaded. I had just finished having the luggage loaded when the pilots came aboard followed by Jangu and the rest. I followed and took a seat at the rear near the baggage which was held in place by a net. The aircraft was a propeller-driven *Otter*. It took twelve passengers.

After about 30 minutes of flight time, I wanted to use the washroom and to my dismay I learnt that the *Otter* did not have a 'loo'. I began to feel uncomfortable. It was a two-hour trip to the Divisional Headquarters. Luckily, I was at the back so no one could witness my discomfort which escalated to agony. I kept twisting, turning and squirming, but to no avail. I held on until I thought I would burst.

Meanwhile the whole of the township where we had to land had assembled at the airstrip to witness an aero-plane at close quarters. The airstrip was cordoned off by a string of barbed wire and huge crowds had gathered on both sides. The military police made sure that the crowds were kept some distance away and stayed behind the barbed wire. The crowd watched the *Otter* grow from a speck in the sky till it reached full size.

As soon as the airplane landed and the pilots opened the door and let down the steps, I shot out of the aircraft and went to the other side of the fuselage, unzipped and relieved myself. The crowd did not expect this additional bit of entertainment and they laughed and clapped their hands in glee. They must have concluded that after all, these '*burra Saabs*' who travelled in these sophisticated forms of transport, were just ordinary mortals like anybody else! The Corps Commander wanted to know what the shouting and laughter was all about. I kept a discreet silence but I think he knew.

Jangu was met by the GOC of the local formation who accompanied him to the inspection bungalow (IB) and they had a cup of tea together. I sat in the adjoining room with the ADC of the GOC of the local formation and learnt that there would be a briefing that day in the formation headquarter Ops Room till 1 p.m. followed by lunch, an hour's rest, then a round of golf and later a dinner reception at the Formation Headquarter Officers' Mess. Fortunately, Jangu's batman had accompanied us, otherwise as the officiating ADC, things would have become more complicated. As it was, the visit to the division had started on a shaky note, and I kept my fingers crossed that all would go well for the rest of the visit.

Normally, as a staff officer to the Corps Commander, I would have been accommodated at an officer's mess.

However, since I was also doing the job of the ADC, I was put up in the same inspection bungalow, two rooms away from Jangu's VIP suite.

The next morning, I was up early. Jangu's batman had told the mess detachment what the Corps Commander would like for breakfast. I placed my order, and we were both served breakfast together. We had barely sat down when Jangu said, 'Brief me.'

'Beg your pardon sir. Brief you about what?'

Jangu looked surprised. 'Why have we come here?'

'For the exercise, sir.'

'So?'

'Sir, the GSO 2 (Ops) was supposed to come, but he took ill and hasn't come.'

'So, who will brief me? You have come, haven't you?'

'Yes sir.'

'So, shouldn't you have studied the exercise papers, knowing that the GSO 2 (Ops) hasn't come?'

'Yes sir.'

'OK then. Go and read up on the exercise.'

I got up, picked up the exercise briefcase, went into the ante-room and opened the file. I had hardly read the introduction to the exercise, when I saw the General walking briskly out of the dining room and heading for the vehicles that had been lined up outside. I shoved the errant file into the briefcase, jammed my Gorkha hat on my head and started running towards the transport.

Jangu had already got into the driver's seat of the lead Jonga and the engine roared into life. Everyone was taken by surprise and the officers and drivers started running towards their vehicles including the CMP[6] Jonga that was to lead the way. I got into the passenger seat of Jangu's Jonga just as it was about to take off, and banged the door shut. The vehicle had already started to move.

Jangu shot out of the gate of the inspection bungalow, turned and belted down the road. I wondered where we were going. I thought to myself that he obviously knew the way otherwise he would not have left the CMP vehicle behind.

I was wrong! Apparently, he did not know the way! As far as I was concerned, this was the first time that I had ever come to this location. But it appeared that Jangu expected me to know the way!

The CMP jonga was desperately trying to catch up but Jangu was too fast.

I said, 'Sir, the CMP Jonga is trying to catch up to lead the way.'

'Let him. I am not stopping him!' he said.

After about ten minutes we approached a cross road.

'Right or Left?' he asked.

I had no idea whatsoever, but how long could I keep saying that I didn't know?

'Right sir.' I blurted out.

Jangu took the turn in style. I looked back at the remaining vehicles of the convoy which were far behind and desperately trying to catch up.

After some miles we came across another cross road.

'Right or Left?' he once again asked.

I had no idea but having said 'Right' the last time, I said, 'Left, sir.'

Jangu however, turned right instead of left and carried on down the road without letting go on the speed.

I had no idea where we were heading and I kept picturing the GOC of the division and all the officers of his formation waiting for us in the exercise area and here was I, without a clue, guiding the Corps Commander goodness knows where, and once again getting him to be late again by giving him wrong directions. Things were not going well for me, or for the Corps Commander for that matter.

I stuck my head out of the car to look at where the rest of the vehicles were.

Now sticking your head out of a speeding Jonga with a Gorkha hat perched on top of your head with only a chin strap to hold it in place, is not a very wise thing to do. And lo, my hat took off!

'Sir!' I said urgently.

'What is it?'

'My hat's taken off, sir.'

Jangu brought the Jonga to an abrupt halt.

I got out and ran towards my hat which had fallen quite far away.

The CMP officer, however, had seen what had happened and picked up my hat, brought it with him and screeched to a halt.

'Are we on the right road?' I asked.

'Yes,' he said. 'Don't you know the way?'

'No,' I said. 'For goodness' sake lead the way.'

By this time, the remaining vehicles had caught up with us. I took my hat from him and got back into the Jonga. The CMP officer took off in a burst of speed and thereafter led the way.

The Corps Commander asked me, 'Are we on the right road?'

'Yes sir.'

'Do you know the way?'

'No sir.'

'Hmm,' he said. 'I thought so!'

Jangu was cool and detached and acted as though nothing had happened.

We reached the exercise area well in time and I breathed a sigh of relief. I placed the exercise file and his reading glasses on the table in front of where he was supposed to sit.

Tea was organized before the exercise presentation

commenced and Jangu was moving around talking to the officers. I realized that as his staff officer and the officiating ADC, I needed to keep him within my eye vision and hearing distance in case he wanted me for anything. Once the exercise started, I sat at the rear from where I could keep an eye on him. I began to realize that the job of an ADC wasn't as easy as I had thought it would be.

Since the presentation was meant for all the officers of the division, it started from scratch and I found it interesting. It was a river-crossing exercise at a divisional level with the utilization of a heliborne force. Little did I know then, that one day I would be part of a heliborne force in actual war and that I could learn a lot from this exercise.

In retrospect, I understood the game that Jangu was playing. He wanted me to learn my job the hard way. No fooling around and no spoon feeding. He wanted me to learn that as an officer from his regiment I ought to be alert to every opportunity to learn the art and science of soldiering. When the GSO 2 (Ops) failed to appear for the exercise, he had hoped that I would use the opportunity to take his place and in that too, I had failed. I was content to just carry the exercise files, instead of using the opportunity to get acquainted with the exercise.

I remembered his initial interview when he had said that 'A' was the middle letter of my name and that in my dictionary 'A' ought to stand for anticipation. He had said a good soldier needs to anticipate events before they happen, and that there were two 'Os' in my surname which ought to tell me that I need to doubly understand the meaning of the word 'Opportunity'.

The understanding of those words now made sense to me and I realized that I had to work on these values and others that would make me a better soldier.

A month later, Jangu was to officiate as the Army

Commander and he decided to travel to the Command Headquarter in the Army Commander's reserved railway saloon. I was in a coupe that was part of the saloon meant for the ADC and a staff officer. With the dual responsibility, I had the coupe to myself. The saloon had its own bedroom, dining room and kitchen and a separate compartment for his security and staff.

By this time, I had begun to understand that I had to anticipate the Corps Commanders' requirements, and not wait to be told what he would require to know. It was a night journey and before turning in, I handed over to him a list of the officers that he would meet at the Command Headquarters with some information on their background and also the names and appointments of the officers who would meet him at the railway station. He nodded his head in approval and that was good enough for me.

On our return to the Corps Headquarters we started visiting the divisions and independent brigades and it was my job to not only brief him on the commanders and principal staff officers that he would meet but to also bring to his notice any officer, JCO, NCO or jawan who had done something worthy of note, so that he could meet them and speak with them. On the way back in the car he would make sure that I sat next to him and he would ask me, 'So, what are they saying?' He was asking about the morale of the officers and men in the units and formations. He expected me to be his 'eyes and ears' so that he had a finger on the pulse of his command. In addition to the formal feedback that he received from the Staff, he wanted to know from informal sources about what was going on in his corps. He believed that the true picture lay between the formal and informal knowledge that a commander at any level received. At my level, it was easier for me to get informal first-hand knowledge of the state of morale of his command. I was careful not to exaggerate or colour events but to be factual, direct and to not pass on gossip.

I had also learnt by this time that on our seemingly 'mad' drive to the exercise area during that divisional exercise, Jangu actually knew the way to the exercise location! As a young officer of the 6/13 Frontier Force before India had become independent, he had done a weapons course in the general area of this division during a time when it was home to the Small Arms Weapons Training School. I also discovered that it was he who had designed the exercise and he was just trying to bring home to me that I ought to have known the area we were going to operate in and studied the map or made a sketch or whatever; that I should never go 'blind' into an area where I would be required to operate. All these were valuable lessons that helped me eventually in operational situations in command of a battalion, brigade and division and as Chief of Staff of a corps.

However, being who and what I was, I continued to make mistakes as the situations changed progressively faster than I could learn, but learn I did. I remember my platoon commander at the IMA once telling us: 'the best soldier learns from the mistakes of others; the good soldier learns from his own mistakes and the bad soldier never learns.' I hoped that I would measure up to the Corps Commander's expectations of me at least as a 'good soldier'.

After our return from the first tour, we were driving to the office the next morning when he asked me whether the tour notes were ready. I had not yet prepared the notes, although I had made my rough notes on all matters concerning the corps and its formations at the various meetings, briefings and discussions.

'No sir,' I said. 'I will work on them this morning.'

'Ian you are not learning! Make sure I have them on my table first thing tomorrow morning, and in future make sure that I see the tour notes in draft form first thing in the morning the day after we return from tour. Ensure that there is a column for "Action to be taken" and make sure that there is a suitable time line. Have you got it?'

'Yes sir.'

'And by the way, organize a coordinating conference latest by tomorrow on what happened at the exercise for all branches of the Corps Headquarters. And since you were present on the exercise, you will brief the HQ on the exercise and how it was conducted.'

'Yes sir.'

To tell the truth, I felt that Jangu was being unnecessarily tough on me. I was only carrying the blessed exercise papers because the concerned officer fell sick and could not come. Now I had to prepare the tour notes, organize the coordinating conference and do the initial briefing on the exercise and on the rest of the tour with hardly any time for this multiplicity of tasks.

It was at this time that I learnt the meaning of responsibility and the art of delegating. Although I was the junior most officer at the Corps Headquarter other than the ADC, I sent for the errant GSO 2 (Ops) and told him what had happened at the exercise location and made him fair the draft notes that I had made on the exercise. Since the ADC was still on the Commando Course, I made him sit at the ADC's table so that he was on hand, if he wanted to consult me. I got chairs put in front of my desk and had the staff officers of all the branches edit the draft notes that I had made on other aspects of the tour concerning their respective branches. I called the GSO 2(SD)[7] and told him to organize the coordinating conference for the following day and to issue an inter-office note informing all concerned. I used the GOC's PA to fair the tour notes along with what I thought was the action to be taken.

I was now beginning to enjoy my new found authority. All concerned were doing what I told them to do and they were doing it well. By afternoon the tour notes were faired and put up to Jangu. Although they were supposed to be draft tour notes, I had faired the tour notes leaving space for his remarks in red ink.[87] There were none!

By the following morning the tour notes went out to all the formations and to all the branches of the Corps Headquarters. The Coordinating Conference went off well and I think everyone learned that Jangu worked his personal staff to the limit. The formations were surprised to get the tour notes so quickly and also understood that this was expected of them too.

I also began to understand Jangu better!

After two months and a number of these tours, Ashok Malhotra the ADC, returned from the commando course looking half his size, with a zero haircut. I was glad to have him back – it gave me more time to do my actual job of processing the ACRs of all the officers of the formation.

By this time, the ACRs had been pouring in and I was expected to bring to Jangu's knowledge the reports that were biased or irregular so that corrective action could be taken. Here, I had a problem with a report that was written by Jangu himself!

It so happened that a very senior officer came on posting during the big exercise that was held when I joined the corps. This officer was posted as General Officer Commanding (GOC) of one of the divisions. Naturally he did not know anything about the exercise. But he took charge and was soon in control of his division and ran a happy and efficient formation.

A senior officer at that level got only two reports before being considered for Lieutenant General's rank. In this, his first report, Jangu gave him a very good pen-picture but had remarked 'Not Yet' for promotion, perhaps because he had barely seen him for four months. There was a dichotomy here and I was in a dilemma as to whether I should bring it to his notice. I decided to speak to him about it. I called on the intercom and said I wanted to see him.

'What about?' He asked.

I told him it concerned the report of a senior officer.

'Who is it?' he asked and I told him the name of the officer.

He asked me to bring the report in.

'What about the report?' He asked after I had entered his office.

I decided not to beat about the bush. I said, 'Sir, you have given General XYZ an excellent pen-picture but given him a "Not Yet" for promotion. Maybe you would like to reconsider whether the officer is fit for promotion to Lieutenant General's rank and either change the pen-picture or your recommendation for promotion.'

I could sense annoyance and irritation flitting across his countenance at being told how to write a report on a very senior officer by a 'piddly' Major. However, he was magnanimous enough not to say anything to me except, 'OK give me the report. I will look at it again.'

Jangu looked at what I had said. I knew that he must have deliberated on the report long and hard and that he was honest in his reporting but he realized that what I said was also correct.

After a few days he rewrote the report. Now the pen-picture and the recommendations matched and that officer some years later became the Army Chief. Once again, I had acted on what I was taught at St. Xavier's School, that one needed to do what is right irrespective of the consequences and the army and the country got a good chief!

I learnt also, that as a staff officer, however junior, one can influence important decisions by commanders, which could have far-reaching consequences.

Jangu, like most people of the Parsi community, was a conscientious and honest person who practiced the right values. He was an excellent human being and had a loving family. His wife, Perin Sataravala was gracious – kind, considerate and caring. She was Jangu's strength. She kept a happy family and ran an efficient home. As the senior-most lady in the formation, she was a mother figure to all of us and we were glad that she was around. She was informal and practical and a breath of fresh air for all of us.

General and Mrs Sataravala used to entertain guests to dinner at Flagstaff House when senior officers visited the station and also for all those who had called on them. Priscilla and I would be invariably invited and we learnt how one had to entertain in the army, keeping the traditions and customs of the Service in mind.

Mathura as a military station had nothing much to offer those days in the way of entertainment. Being the birthplace of Krishna, it was a city of worship. There was a proliferation of temples and it was a city on the banks of the River Jamuna, one among many such across the length and breadth of India. Off duty, the only place we could go to was the Officers' Mess which doubled up as an Officers' Institute. It had tennis courts and a squash court and every week a film was projected on a make-shift screen. The station also had a nine-hole golf course.

Our married accommodation was a barrack-like structure – like a train in fact. It consisted of a series of rooms one after another. The first room was the dining room with a small kitchen attached as an outhouse. The dining room was followed by a sitting room, a large bedroom followed by two smaller rooms one of which we used as a bedroom for the children and the other as a study. Both bedrooms had attached bathrooms. The house had a lawn in front with a verandah that ran along the entire length of the house and a vegetable patch at the back.

As young families, we had to find means to entertain ourselves. Our immediate next-door neighbours were the Moorthys – Ahobala Krishna Moorthy and Sharada. Opposite and some distance away were Madhav from the Ordnance Corps and his wife, Sara Prasad. There were others but these were two families that we were most friendly with. Major Moorthy was from the Garhwal Rifles. Moorthy was a die-hard, thorough-bred Infantry Officer who took no nonsense from anyone but he knew his job well. The Prasads and the Moorthys were excellent families, ever ready to help anyone in need. We used to entertain at our respective homes and Madhav and Sara one evening held a fancy dress party. It was fun to try and put together home-made costumes and pretend to be characters that we were not. Priscilla went as a Japanese girl. She wore a kimono lent to her by Sara and had her hair put up with two knitting needles in place just like pictures we saw in Japanese prints and no one could recognize her – so well did she look the part! In fact, Priscilla has been mistaken for a Parsi, a Punjabi, a Muslim, a Nepali, a Gujarati, a Maharashtrian – anything other than a Goan from Para,[9] Goa.

Our next two children, Arun and Vikram, were called 'Mathura ke Krishnas' because both were born at Mathura. However, both births were not without some element of drama.

Sunith was a year and a half old and Priscilla was pregnant with our second child. She woke me up early one night to say that she had a pain in her stomach. I told her to go back to sleep and we could go to the doctor in the morning, if she was not alright by then. As soon as it was light, she woke me up again and said that she needed to go to the hospital. I saw she was in pain and I realized that she needed to be taken to the hospital immediately. I ran to Madhav Prasad's house as he was the only one amongst us who had a car. He was in the middle of a shave and had lathered his face with soap. As I told him that we had to get Priscilla to the hospital urgently he quickly wiped off the lather, changed into a pair of trousers, threw his shoes into the car, backed it out of his make-shift garage and took us post haste to the hospital.

We were just in time! Soon after we arrived at the hospital Arun was born. Madhav was sitting on the steps of the hospital putting on his shoes when a nursing sister came out and said that Priscilla had delivered a baby boy and that mother and child were both well. That was pretty close and as Madhav always says, he has a claim on Arun!

Before Priscilla was discharged from the hospital, her mother had arrived and thankfully took charge of looking after Priscilla and the baby.

All went well as long as her mother was there. After a month, my mother-in-law had to leave and Priscilla had to handle the two children on her own. Sunith was all right, but after a while Arun became quite cranky, was not sleeping properly and used to cry all the time.

Sharada Moorthy, next door, must have heard Arun crying. She came over and asked Priscilla what was wrong and why was he crying. Priscilla said that he was probably missing her mother. Sharda did not quite accept that and zeroed in on the actual problem. 'When did you last give him a bath?' She asked. Priscilla replied that she had only been sponging him because he was so small that she was scared to give him a bath. Sharada straight away took charge. She sat on a small stool in our bathroom and put Arun on her legs just like they do in our villages. She first massaged him with coconut oil, and then bathed him with warm water, all the while talking and singing to him and Arun just loved it. Soon afterwards, Arun went off into a deep contented sleep and there could not have been a happier baby thereafter – all thanks to Sharada.

It was during my tenure with the corps that I had to study to appear for my Staff College entrance examination. Priscilla made sure that after I came home from work, I was not disturbed. Guests were entertained by her and I was left to study. At night, after she had put the children to sleep, she would come to the study with a mug of tea for me and she would sleep there while I was studying, just to be close to me.

By the time our youngest son Vikram was born, the Moorthys and the Prasads had moved out on posting and I was away from Mathura appearing for the Defence Services Staff College entrance examination. One day, during the time that I was away, Priscilla realized that she needed to go to the hospital and that she needed assistance. She did not know who to ask for help, so she rang up Mrs Sataravala who was having lunch. Mrs Sataravala left her lunch and drove immediately to our house in her own car and had the staff car take Priscilla to the hospital along with our new neighbour's wife. She then relaxed on our bed reading because Arun and Sunith were sleeping. She waited till they woke up and then took them along with the orderly to Flagstaff House and looked after the two boys herself although the family had two civil domestic servants. During the next few days, every evening, she would send a note to Priscilla informing her about what the children were doing, what they had eaten etc. When I returned after the examination, Priscilla was still in the hospital. I went across to Flagstaff House to take Sunith and Arun home but she refused to hand over the children to me saying that I would not know how to look after them and waited till my mother-in-law arrived. She was that caring and considerate a person.

Part of our small family was Rifleman Tekbahadur Thapa of Alpha Company. He was in the final years of his service and had been my batman earlier when I was with the battalion. He volunteered to come with me on my posting to the Corps

Headquarters and I was glad to have him with me because we knew and understood each other.

Tekbahadur took it upon himself to take charge of us and our home as our protector, guardian and guide. Our three sons – Sunith, Arun and Vikram were separated by just about a year each and were a handful for Priscilla. Tekbahadur stepped in and took charge.

On one occasion, the corps had gone on a short exercise and during that time, when I was away, the Jamuna that passed close to the Corps Headquarters, broke its banks and flooded the cantonment. The water started rising in the middle of the night and by the early hours of the morning it had entered the garden. Priscilla and the boys were asleep.

Tekbahadur, however, let them sleep and blocked the entrance of all the doors with mud from the garden and kept monitoring the rise in the level of the water all night. It was only after dawn at 6 o'clock that he woke Priscilla up by tapping on the bedroom door, showed her what was happening and rang up the Military Transport (MT) and asked for a vehicle to take them to safety.

Priscilla meanwhile rang up Major Vishi Khanna, an armoured corps officer from the Central India Horse and his wife Cynthia and asked for advice about where she could go. They said that she and the children should straight away come to their home. Priscilla and Tekbahadur had the house packed up and had moved out within an hour. The luggage was moved out to my office and they moved in with the Khannas.

By this time, the exercise was called off. I returned to the cantonment to find that our house was under four feet of water. I had to swim to the house. I looked in through the windows. All I could see was the fridge on top of the dining table and the rest of the furniture floating inside.

Major and Mrs Khanna did not have a large house but

generous, as most Service families are, they made us feel welcome and shared their house with us.

After the flood waters had receded, I returned to the house to find the floors awash with mud and the walls damp and covered with mildew. I asked for leave and left Priscilla and the children with my parents in Bombay. After two months we returned to our house and made it a home once again. It took a lot of effort but we managed.

It was now mid-1970 and the Staff College results were declared. I was happy to find that I had passed. Those days, the results used to be published in the newspapers and my name appeared as number two on the 'Competitive Vacancy List' – I had secured the second rank amongst the first twenty in the order of merit.

Those days, the first three used to be sent to foreign staff colleges to UK or Canada or Australia. I had visions of being sent to one of these institutions but was told later that the names in the list were in alphabetical order and that in fact I was twelfth in the order of merit!

It was around this time that I became acquainted with Major Kanian who was an officer from the Electrical and Mechanical Engineering Battalion (EMB) at Mathura. Kanian had the unique ability to recall the past and foretell the future. If you asked him a question, he would note the time the question was asked, the date, time and place of the birth of the person who asked the question and he would give the answer the next day. His forecasts were unbelievably accurate and this brought him a lot of unwanted attention. Kanian had become a friend and used to tell me stories about the forecasts that he had made and his stories were quite astonishing.

A cousin of mine, John Charles – a state level hockey and football player, was on holiday at Shimla and decided to break journey at Mathura to spend a few days with us. We had been at school together and he lived next door to us at Colaba in Bombay. We were very close to each other and were talking about old times when the topic of destiny came up and I spoke about Major Kanian. John was very skeptical about an army officer being able to forecast the future and said as much. I asked him whether he had any question about the future. John said 'Yes' and so we requested Major Kanian to come over for a cup of tea.

John asked him, 'When will I get married and to whom?'

Kanian said, 'Is that all?'

'Yes,' said John.

Kanian asked him about his date, time and place of birth etc. He returned the next day and told him that he would get married to a teacher in April the following year.

John now revealed to Kanian that he was engaged to a girl who was a secretary to a senior person in a very prominent company in Bombay and that she had gone to the UK to be with her sister and to shop for her trousseau for the wedding and that they were to marry that year i.e. in September 1970.

Kanian smiled. He seemed to understand that John was trying to test him. He told John that if the information given by him was correct then there would be no change in what he had said.

After Kanian had left, John repeated his belief that Kanian was wrong and that we should not rely on his ability to forecast the future.

John left for Bombay and two months later he telephoned to say that the wedding had been called off because his fiancé had been offered a very good job in England and that she wanted him to give up his job in India and join her in the UK, which he was not prepared to do.

Subsequently he married a professor in April the next year just as Kanian had predicted. When I mentioned this to Kanian, he merely smiled.

Kanian's ability to forecast events also aroused my

curiosity about my own future. I popped the question to him one day and he took down all the necessary details. Strangely, he did not give me his response the next day or the day after. After a week I spoke with him on the telephone and asked him whether he was very busy.

I wanted to know the answer to my question. He seemed evasive but said that he would come over that evening and would give me an answer.

He came that evening looking very troubled. I asked him what was the matter and he said that the answer to my question was very strange.

'What is it?' I asked, concerned.

He said, 'Sir, the feedback that I am getting is that you will be involved in some very heavy fighting next year and will be severely injured but you will survive.'

I was taken aback and said, 'Fighting! What fighting Kanian? There is no war on nor is there a threat of any war in the near future, so what fighting are you talking about? Within a month's time, in January next year, I will be going to Wellington to do the Staff Course and the course lasts for a year! So, what is this all about?'

'That's what, sir. That is why I am confused and that is why I hesitated to come back with this response.'

We once again checked the data I had given him on which he had worked. It was correct. There was no change.

I then asked whether he believed in destiny. He reflected for a while and then said that destiny was inevitable. It was fixed. We could, however, choose the route to our destiny i.e., how we lived our life on the road to our destiny. It was our behaviour and attitude to life that were important. From his experience so far in answering questions about the future, he felt that it is better not to know the future but to live life the way it comes. Both of us were perplexed as we had no idea as to how his prediction would pan out. That was December 1970.

By January 1971, I had left Mathura for the Defence Services Staff College course at Wellington and I had tried to put Kanian's forecast about my future out of my mind. However, by the end of March we became aware of the problem brewing in East Pakistan. By the end of April 1971, the world became aware of the large-scale massacres by the Pakistani Army in East Pakistan and the exodus of ten million East Pakistanis as refugees to India. By October, I learnt that Pakistan was getting increasingly aggressive on our border with East Pakistan and that my battalion had moved to the border. War clouds now loomed on the horizon and Pakistan President General Yahya Khan was threatening a war with India.

Keeping all this in mind I decided to be practical and to get myself insured. I went to an insurance agent in Wellington and asked for an insurance policy on my life and on injury in war and warlike situations. The agent, I think his name was Mr Malik, told me that the Life Insurance Corporation (LIC) did not insure soldiers against loss of life or injury in war.[10] So, I had no policy. Kanian had correctly predicted the possibility of war and I wondered if what he had predicted about me would also happen. I told myself that maybe my answers to his questions were flawed and decided once again to push his prediction out of my head.

* * *

We, as a family, have fond memories of our stay at Mathura, of the Sataravala family and the friends that we made. The camaraderie and the realization that the army was one big family was very reassuring. Despite serving far apart on postings thereafter, we stayed in touch with the Sataravalas, Moorthys and Prasads and continue to do so even after retirement. Strangely, it was only on a recent visit and a relaxed chat that Moorthy and I realized we had walked the same jungle paths, crossed the same turbulent rivers and survived similar skirmishes in NEFA a few years apart! In fact, he was the same Lieutenant who had recovered the body of Major Ripu Daman Singh after the massacre of the Assam Rifles platoon by the tribals in 1954.

As an officer of the Indian Army, I learnt a lot professionally from General Sataravala whose tough attitude concealed a kind heart. He was the epitome of the ideal 'Officer and a Gentleman'. Priscilla and I benefited much from the kindness of Mrs Sataravala and we learnt from her how to manage an army home and the little social courtesies of life in the army.

Priscilla and I kept in close touch with the General, Mrs Sataravala, their elder daughter Sheku Fey and their elder son Cyrus. We used to visit them often after General Sataravala had retired. He was initially at Delhi and after a while they shifted to Pune. Priscilla and I used to make it a point to visit them whenever we went to Pune, and it was always a joy to meet up with this grand and gracious couple.

The world does not make persons like them anymore! They have since passed away. Mrs Sataravala passed away in 2019 after her 90th birthday. Priscilla and I were privileged to visit her earlier that year. We are in touch with the children and share a special bond with them.

Notes

1. A sand model of a piece of terrain corresponding to the grid lines of a map on which the fall of artillery shells/mortar bombs can be indicated by vapour/smoke. It is a training aid to train personnel to direct artillery/mortar fire.
2. Sunith Francis Rodrigues, who many years later was appointed as the Army Chief.

3. Brigadier General Staff is a senior staff officer at a Corps/Command HQ, responsible for all matters concerning operations, training and staff duties.

4. Brigadier in charge of administration is also a senior staff officer at a Corps/Command HQ. He is responsible for all administrative matters.

5. GSO 2 (Ops) – General Staff Officer Grade 2, dealing with operational matters.

6. Corps of Military Police who in addition to their policing duties also handle traffic and normally lead a convoy of a VIP.

7. GSO2 (SD) General Staff Officer Grade 2 (Staff Duties)

8. Military Convention lays down that in written correspondence, the senior-most officer, normally a commander, writes in red ink, the senior-most staff officer uses green ink and the remainder use blue or black ink.

9. A village in Goa. Our former defence minister, Late Manohar Parikar was from this village and his surname derived from the name of this village.

10. Since the Life Insurance Corporation did not insure soldiers against death or injury during war, the Indian Army took a decision to institute what was called the Army Group Insurance Policy that insured soldiers against death and injury in war and warlike situations. However, that happened many years after the 1971 War.

The Indo–Pak War of 1971

Battles are won or lost in the mind,
before they are won or lost on the ground.

The Indo–Pak War of 1971 was yet another war forced upon India by our neighbour, led by her arrogant and devious leaders. This time, Pakistan had aligned itself with the United States of America and the Peoples' Republic of China.

I was still at the Defence Services Staff College, Wellington when my unit, the 4th Battalion of the 5th Gorkha Rifles (FF) moved to the international border (IB) in East Pakistan. Border incidents in the Eastern Sector had multiplied – the Pakistanis were crossing over in pursuit of the Mukti Bahini[1] who were carrying out raids on Pakistani units and installations in an effort to free their homeland from the vicious grip of West Pakistan. Multiple casualties had been inflicted on our Border Security Force (BSF) personnel by the Pakistanis due to indiscriminate firing and it was decided that army units needed to be moved to defend the IB from the depredations of the Pakistani Army. To understand the root causes of the war, one needs to delve briefly into the past.

Ever since the creation of Pakistan, West Pakistan had relentlessly usurped the authority and resources of East Pakistan. The first president of Pakistan, Mohammed Ali Jinnah's avid promotion of Urdu as the national language and the military takeovers of Pakistan festered a simmering discontent among the Bengali population in East Pakistan. Resistance strengthened under the leadership of Sheikh Mujibur Rehman who was jailed repeatedly by the military while he was campaigning for autonomy. In the general elections held in West and East Pakistan in December 1970, the Awami League led by Sheikh Mujibur Rehman won a landslide victory and emerged as the majority party in the National Assembly. This meant that the president, prime minister and most of the ministers of Pakistan would be Bengalis from the Awami League. This, the Western wing was not prepared to accept.

Dismayed by this unexpected result, Zulfikar Ali Bhutto,

and Yahya Khan, the president of Pakistan, colluded to prevent domination of Pakistan by a Bengali majority at all cost. Their first step was to postpone the Assembly session. This infuriated the Bengalis and the brewing unrest from decades of oppression broke loose.

All government and quasi-government offices, central and provincial were closed, as students and agitated crowds took to the streets. Curfew was imposed in Dhaka but by 3 March 1971, Mujib's writ ran wide in East Pakistan. Lieutenant General Sahibzada Yakub Khan, the Lieutenant Governor of East Pakistan was recalled to Pakistan since he refused to collude with the nefarious subterfuge of the West Pakistan government. He was replaced by Lieutenant General Tikka Khan, who was soon to become notorious as the 'Butcher of Bangladesh'.

Tikka Khan let loose a reign of terror that has no parallel in modern history. In what was to become infamously known as 'Operation Searchlight', the armed forces of Pakistan used machine guns, tanks and artillery against unarmed civilians and Bengali para-military forces. The targets were intellectuals – the catalysts of the uprising. Teachers and students at universities were lined up and shot and buried in mass graves. Women and girls were raped in front of their men and then slaughtered in the most bestial genocide of modern times. Over a million citizens of East Pakistan were butchered by a renegade army led by debauched generals and perverted officers of the Pakistan Army.

Operation Searchlight triggered off a mass exodus of terrified civilians to India. Their number eventually totaled to over ten million. Their shelter, food, hygiene, medical and sanitation needs became the responsibility of the Government of India. The burden of refugee relief was estimated to be at over $700 million. India protested to the United Nations (UN) and the leaders of the Western world. The world, led by the

US, however, turned a blind eye to these horrific developments in South Asia. The UN, proved to be a toothless enforcer of global rectitude and did nothing more than mouth pious platitudes. Worse still, it equated Pakistan the aggressor, with India the protector of human rights.

Prior to these developments, US President Richard Nixon and his Secretary of State Henry Kissinger had been keen to establish relations with the People's Republic of China, led by Chairman Mao Tse Tung. This much sought-after meeting was arranged through the good offices of General Yahya Khan. Thereafter, Pakistan became the favoured protégé of the US and could do no wrong.

The least that the US government could have done was to condemn the horrific genocide being perpetrated by the West Pakistan Government against her own people. Instead, she chose to ignore this horrible blood bath of Bengali Hindus and Muslims and declared that this butchery was an internal problem in Pakistan and that the refugee problem should be resolved bilaterally between Pakistan and India. Strangely, the rest of the world also killed its conscience and followed the malignant lead of the US President.

India now stood alone against a malevolent triumvirate of Pakistan, China and the US. In order to offset this imbalance, Prime Minister Indira Gandhi entered into a Treaty of Friendship with the Soviet Union.

An agitated Indian public now began to clamour for military action against Pakistan but Mrs. Gandhi decided to explore all available options to prevent a war. She visited all the major capitals of the world and the UN headquarter, to request world leaders to convince Pakistan to stop the genocide and allow the refugees to return to their homeland. The world, however, had lost its moral moorings. Other than a bit of cursory lip service, no one even chose to condemn the genocide unleashed in East Pakistan. Gary J. Bass, an officer posted at the US Consulate at Dhaka was witness to what was going on and protested against his country's policy and misconduct. He was withdrawn, sent home and replaced by someone who would toe the official line. He went on to write the book *The Blood Telegram* that has damned the American president and his secretary of state in particular and the United States' government in general.

When the situation reached an intolerable state in April 1971, Mrs. Gandhi called the Army Chief and broached the issue of military action. The Army Chief informed the Prime Minister that the time was not ripe. There were valid reasons against immediate military action – political, military, climate and weather, all of which demanded a self-imposed delay.

A review was carried out that took into consideration the state of arms and ammunition, equipment, training, commerce and industry, road communication, climate, weather, morale, world opinion and enemy options. All these factors pointed to a particular time-table for war that would be suitable to India. Indian political leaders heeded the advice given by the military. The armed forces used the intervening period to gear up for the expected Pakistani offensive.

By the middle of November 1971, it became clear that Pakistan was preparing for war. The Indian Army recalled all service personnel from leave and terminated all ongoing courses. At the Defence Services Staff College, we were close to the end of our course, when we were told that our training would terminate a month earlier. We would be required to join our units after leaving our families home.

As expected, Pakistan launched her offensive against India on 3 December 1971, but this time India was prepared. By 4 December, the Indian Army, Navy and Air Force had launched their counter offensives.

On the evening of 3 December, the Pakistan Air Force attacked Indian airfields at Srinagar, Avantipur, Pathankot,

Uttarlai, Jodhpur, Ambala and Agra. Some of my Staff College coursemates and I were on the Frontier Mail heading for Delhi at that time. We were scheduled to fly by the Assam Courier[2] the next morning which would take us to Guwahati from where we would have to find our way to our units.

We arrived at Delhi Railway Station in the dark. There was a complete 'blackout' due to the Pakistani air raids and it was only then that we learnt that the Pakistan Air Force had attacked our airfields that evening at 5.45 p.m. This was a declaration of war and meant that the shadow boxing of the past few months was over. India was now at war with Pakistan.

While we were still at the Staff College, Satish Sondhi who was also with me at the NDA, invited me to spend the night at his home after I reached Delhi by train, so that we could catch the Assam Courier together at Palam the next morning. I reached Satish's home around 10 p.m. His family was glued to the radio, listening to news about the war.

At around 11 p.m. we learnt that Prime Minister Indira Gandhi would be addressing the nation and at midnight we heard her stirring address. She explained to the citizens of India that she had done all within her powers to avoid a war but if Pakistan was bent on war, we would give her a fitting response; that we now had no option but to defend ourselves and that we would do so with all our might. The next morning, we caught a taxi to the Palam airport, put our names on the Flight Manifest[3] and waited to embark onto an AN-12 which had lined up a short distance away.

After about an hour of waiting, we were called for what we thought was a briefing. Instead, we were assembled and told that the courier had been cancelled because a slow-moving transport aircraft filled with officers and men would be an attractive target for Pakistani jet fighters. We would have to find our way to the units on our own.

Satish and I and a few other like-minded officers decided not to waste any time and caught a cab for the New Delhi Railway Station. The cab driver, a Sikh, was more than happy to take us to the station and refused to be paid. In Punjabi, he said words to the effect, '*Saab ji, give them a fitting reply. May God be with you.*'

We rushed off. We were told that the Assam Mail was ready to depart and we better hurry up if we wanted to catch it. The train had started moving by the time we got to it. Luckily, the over bridge brought us to the centre of the train. We clambered on board the moving train and pulled the chain because some of us with heavier baggage had not yet caught up.

A harassed conductor lumbered up to find out who had pulled the chain and why. We explained. We also informed him that we had no tickets and that we needed his help to see that we got to our units on time. He said, 'This is the first time I am welcoming ticketless travellers. No problem, sir. You all are on your way to defend our country. Be the guests of the Indian Railways.'

That made us feel good. First, the taxi driver and now the ticket examiner! He even managed to make sure we had a four-berther to ourselves all the way to the Northeast.

The train literally crawled, or maybe we felt that way because we wanted to get to our units post haste, given the urgency of the hour. There were no mobiles those days but one amongst us had a transistor radio and All India Radio was giving the nation updates about what was happening on the Eastern and Western fronts.

While on the train, we learnt that the Pakistani submarine *PNS Gazi* had been sunk off the port of Vishakhapatnam; that the Indian Navy was attacking Karachi; that the Indian Army was attacking Pakistani defences on the Eastern and Western fronts; that the Pakistani Air Force had not been able to do any damage to Indian airfields on 3 December; and that the Indian Air Force was battling for the conquest of the skies over East Pakistan.

On the morning of 6 December, we reached Dharmanagar Railway Station in North Tripura and I was happily surprised to see a JCO from my battalion on the railway platform. He was equally surprised to see me. He said that the battalion was expecting me to get off the Assam Courier at Bagdogra and that they had no news about me after they heard that the courier had been cancelled.

The JCO brought me up to date on what had happened in the fighting so far. He said that the battalion had launched two attacks at places called Atgram and Gazipur and had earned a great name in its conduct in both these battles. It had, however, paid a price for its victories. Three officers were killed and four wounded. He suggested that I immediately get off the train since the quickest way to reach the battalion was by road and he had a jeep. I wanted to start immediately. He suggested that we wait for an hour instead. A hospital train full of wounded officers and men was passing through about then and four wounded officers from our battalion were on that train. It would be good if we could meet them, he said. They could also tell me more about the battles fought at Atgram and Gazipur.

I said goodbye to my friends on the train. We had travelled together for two days and nights. The time spent together had strengthened our bonds that had been forged at the Staff College. We wondered about the outcome of the war and whether we would meet again.

The hospital train took more than an hour to arrive. Until it did, the JCO and I walked up and down the railway platform talking about events of the recent past. I had been away from the battalion for more than five years and there was a lot to catch up on.

The hospital train finally arrived at around 11 a.m. This was the first time that I had seen a hospital train. It was full of battle casualties. There were officers and jawans who had lost limbs; some had received head injuries, some had eye injuries, others were wounded in the abdomen. I had never seen so many bandaged heroes! The train had an operation theatre, dressing rooms, kitchens and wards for different types of casualties. It was staffed by surgeons, medical specialists, nurses and nursing orderlies of various specialties. It also had an officer commanding the train. The four officers from our battalion had managed to stay together in the same compartment – they were all very young and in the prime of their lives. Captain Yeshwant Rawat had joined the battalion in 1963 and was commanding a rifle company at the battle of Gazipur. He had been injured by a grenade on his right leg which eventually had to be amputated. There were three more – Captain Virendra Rawat and Lieutenants Young Bharat and Rajesh Sherawat, the intelligence officer. They each had flesh wounds and would recover, but Yeshwant would have to go to the Artificial Limb Centre at Pune to get an artificial leg.

The train did not stay long and I didn't learn the stories of the battles of Atgram and Gazipur. I had just enough time to meet them before it was time for the train to leave. I could, however, gather that the officer casualties had been high. The battalion entered the war with eighteen officers. Now, with three killed and four wounded, it was already short of officers and the war had just about begun. Of the three who had been killed, one of them was the 2ic. He had been leading a two-company attack at Gazipur and it appeared that I would be replacing him.

It seemed that the jinx of the '2ic' had once again raised its ugly head. The battalion had lost three of its 2ics within the first six months of its raising. The next two 2ics had survived because they were able to pray at a temple and offer their respects at a *pir's* grave in Jammu & Kashmir. But here in the battle zone there was no temple or a *pir's* grave to offer prayers and so one more 2ic had been lost! I learnt from the JCO that the battalion was now waiting for its next task and that the CO, Lieutenant Colonel A.B. Harolikar was waiting for my arrival to take over as the next 2ic.

I realized that I would be the seventh 2ic in eight years from the day we were re-raised in January 1963 and I wondered what the future had in store for me. Kanian's prediction came to mind. He had said that the destiny of each of us was fixed and all that we could do was to live our lives as best as we could, on the path to our destiny.

We drove non-stop with the driver and me taking turns at the wheel. We passed military units and formations along the way – long columns of men and vehicles bound for their respective objectives on the different and disparate thrust lines of battalions and brigades. Our battalion had reached a place called Killaura.

We reached Killaura around 3 a.m., the morning of 8 December. The jeep bumped across barren fields and stopped some distance away from a fleet of four helicopters on the ground. The moon was in its third quarter and sinking slowly into the horizon. By its pale light I could see groups of soldiers lying asleep on the ground. Soldiers learn to sleep wherever and whenever they can because we never know when there will be another opportunity for rest. NCOs were checking on their sections, ensuring the presence of all members of their brood. The helicopters were etched against the setting moon like some dark denizens of a different age.

While I was taking in the scene, I saw what appeared to be a small group of officers standing some distance away. I walked up to them to investigate.

One of them came forward and asked in a kindly but authoritative voice: 'Who is it?'

'Major Ian Cardozo, sir,' I said. '2ic designate Four Five Gorkhas.'

'Welcome to the division, Ian. I am General Krishna Rao, GOC of the division.'

'Good morning sir.'

The other two officers were the Brigade Commander, Brigadier Bunty Quinn and Lieutenant Colonel 'Billoo' Suri, the Commander Engineers of the division.

Brigadier Quinn took me aside and briefed me. The battalion had been tasked to capture a landing ground at Sylhet, a road junction and the broadcasting station in the Indian Army's first heliborne operation. Part of the battalion, about 300 soldiers, had been heli-lifted the previous day and the remaining were in the process of being moved.

Sylhet is a city about 250 kms northeast of Dhaka, rich with tea plantations, forests and rivers. Militarily it was part of the chain of strong fortresses that General Niazi, the Commander of all armed forces in East Pakistan had organized, as part of his strategy to defeat Indian forces attacking his defences. The 'Fortress Concept' envisaged strong defensive positions based on river obstacles, which in this case was the Surma River.

Brigadier Quinn said that the division had been informed by the corps that there was minimal opposition at Sylhet because information had been received that the brigade defending Sylhet had moved to Dhaka. It was on the basis of this report that the battalion was being heli-lifted to Sylhet. As it turned out, there was more opposition than we had anticipated at Sylhet and the battalion was fighting to take control of the ground that we had captured.

This looked like another operation where infantry battalions are sent into battle with minimal information of the enemy they would face. Good leadership skills, hard training, sound battle drills and the will to win are all that they have to ensure success. This has happened time and again and it is to their credit that they came out on top each time.

The troops that I could see before me were the last that would be heli-lifted and afterwards the choppers would leave for other tasks. After the briefing, I asked to be excused so that I could meet my JCOs and NCOs and men.

Was I glad to meet them! It had been five years since I had left the battalion and the JCOs were NCOs when I had left. Much had happened during the intervening years but just then, time fell away and we went back to the days when I had left them when I was in command of Alpha Company before, during and after the 1965 war. The JCOs and NCOs were talking to me in hushed voices. There was no reason to speak in whispers because the enemy was very far away, but the occasion seemed to demand it.

While we were catching up, we could hear the hum of the helicopters of the previous wave that were now returning from Sylhet. As they came closer, the noise of their engines increased and shattered the peace of the early morning. The JCOs and NCOs were busy urging those who were asleep to be ready to embark. I realized how lucky I was to be in time to catch the last wave.

The MI-4 choppers – there were four of them, appeared overhead and descended like giant birds of prey. The sound from their engines prevented any worthwhile conversation, until finally the roar reduced to a whine and clatter when the engines were shut off and the rotor blades finally stopped rotating. The pilots clambered down and asked for help to off-load the casualties that they had brought back. For the injured, the war was over but different battles to recuperate and rehabilitate were just beginning. The number of wounded that were off-loaded indicated that a fierce battle was going on for the capture of the landing ground.

The returning pilots briefed the crew who would go in next about enemy positions and the type of fire that they could expect. They examined the choppers and the many bullet holes caused by the enemy's small arms fire. Luckily, no fuel tanks or fuel lines were hit and the pilots were unharmed. The helicopter pilots were young and brave and ever ready to take risks. Their mission was full of danger considering the amount of ground fire that was aimed at the choppers. The fact that the helicopters were thin-skinned and meant only for administrative tasks made the risks even greater.

Soon the engines of the last wave of helicopters started humming as they readied for take-off. I got on board one of the choppers. Each chopper could take a section of ten fully armed men. I had not been issued with a weapon until then and wondered what sort of a reception we would get from the enemy when we landed.

The choppers rose one after another, hovered for a while above the launch pad like giant birds of prey and then took off for Sylhet. I had overheard the returning pilots saying that the landing area was protected and clearly marked by 'goose necks'[4] to indicate the boundary within which they would have to land.

As the choppers descended towards the landing area, we could hear the cracks of bullets as they pierced the thin metal skin of the helicopters. We desperately hoped that we would be spared the indignity of being shot in our bottoms! We could now hear the sound of small arms, mortar, artillery and MMG fire – the enemy were doing their best to destroy the choppers as they landed.

As soon as I jumped off, I was met with the grinning faces of three of my Alpha Company boys who had been with me during the 1965 war. Oblivious of the enemy fire that was raining down on us, they hoisted me on their shoulders and danced around with cries of '*Cartoos Saab – Ho ki hoina!*'[5] I finally persuaded them to put me down so that I could meet the CO, Lieutenant Colonel Arun Harolikar.

Lieutenant Colonel Harolikar was sitting on the ground hooked onto his wireless set, speaking to the company commanders and controlling the battle. He was speaking in Nepali so that even if the Pakis intercepted our conversations, they would not be able to decipher their content. When there was a break in his communication with the company commanders, he stuck out his hand and said, 'Welcome to the battalion, Ian. I have been waiting for you for a long time.'

'Happy to be back, sir.'

The CO apprised me that the Corps Commander, Lieutenant General Sagat Singh had been insistent that 202 Pakistani Infantry Brigade that had been defending Sylhet had moved out, probably to defend Dhaka. He had specially selected our battalion to occupy Sylhet before it could be occupied by other Pakistani troops and had organized the heli-lift to have the move executed speedily. These orders were conveyed to the CO through the GOC of 8 Mountain Division. Lieutenant Colonel Harolikar mentioned that he disagreed with the Corps Commander's assessment. The situation would be dangerous if the brigade had not moved out, but he was overruled and told to follow orders and occupy Sylhet without delay. The Battalion had moved as ordered, in the Indian Army's first-ever heliborne operation. The Rifle Companies and the Battalion Headquarters had landed the previous day, 7 December, and the remainder landed on 8 December, bringing the strength of the battalion to 384 soldiers of all ranks. The battalions had been reduced to this number because of earlier casualties suffered at the battles of Atgram and Gazipur and because of the fact that some of our leave parties had not yet caught up with the battalion.

The fact that the landing was heavily opposed indicated that Lieutenant Colonel Harolikar was right – the brigade had probably not moved out. Several enemy counter-attacks had been beaten back but it was causing a strain on the battalion's limited resources of ammunition. Some of the casualties had been evacuated in the returning helicopters that morning but more casualties had built up. The CO had been told that the helicopters were moving elsewhere for other tasks. So, we were now on our own until the promised link-up took place.

The corps had communicated that the battalion would be linked up within 48 hours and based on that premise, the battalion had moved only with ammunition that we could carry on our person (pouch ammunition) and rations and water for two days.

Doubtful of the corps' assessment of the enemy strength at Sylhet, and the expected link-up within 48 hours, the CO had decided to leave personal equipment and dry rations behind, and to carry extra ammunition and grenades instead. Fortunately, we had a troop of mountain artillery and an Air Control Team (ACT) with us.

This was the situation on the evening of 8 December. Luckily for us, the ground was soft and digging posed no problem. Half the men continued to prepare the defences and the remainder manned defensive positions.

The Regimental Medical Officer (RMO) reported that the regimental aid post (RAP) bunker had been dug and that he already had three severe casualties. He informed us that the overhead protection would be ready only by the next day. No trench had been dug for me, so the CO invited me to share his L-shaped trench. We could just about fit in. The wireless set was kept at the end of the trench with the antennae poking out to ensure proper reception. It was a tight fit but we managed like this throughout the Battle at Sylhet which would last for eight more days.

The soil beneath the top layer was soft and moist and in my mind's eye, I can still smell the soft soil of what is now Bangladesh.

That night, half-hearted attacks by the enemy were beaten back. Later, we learnt that Pakistan's 31 Punjab and 30 Frontier Force, earlier battered by the battalion at Atgram and Gazipur, were part of the forces defending Sylhet. They had probably passed on the message to their units that the soldiers that had landed at Sylhet were from a Gorkha Battalion that used khukris with abandon and were not to be trifled with.

During a lull in the battle, the senior-most subedar came up and said that he wished to speak with the CO. Speaking in Nepali, he narrated the story of the jinx of the 2ic of the battalion. His narration went back to the Burma campaign during the Second World War where two 2ics were killed and two COs who had been promoted from 2ic had also been killed. He then went on to more recent times when four 2ics had become casualties one after another.

Lieutenant Colonel Harolikar, who all his life had served with the 3rd Battalion, listened to the JCO patiently and after he finished, asked the JCO what he expected him to do.

The JCO replied, 'Saab, we are happy that Major Saab is back but please don't call him 2ic.'

'Then what shall we call him, Saab?'

'Saab, the Pakistanis call their officers by code names like "Bada Imam, Chota Imam, Kazi, Vazir". Call him by some such name.'

'So, what do you recommend?'

'Saab, we could call him Vazir – that is the closest term to the appointment of 2ic.'

Lieutenant Colonel Harolikar turned to me and asked, 'Is that OK, Ian? Can we call you "Vazir"?'

'Yes sir. You can call me anything you like.'

'All right, Saab. We can use "Vazir" for second-in-command from now onwards. Please tell the Adjutant to pass this order down to all the companies and to the Rear and to speak to me if anyone has any queries.'

Subedar Saab was happy. He saluted and left. So, on 8 December 1971, it was decided on the battlefield of Sylhet that the term used for second-in-command of the 4th Battalion the 5th Gorkha Rifles would be 'Vazir'.

The next morning, the ACT managed to whistle up close air support and an enemy force that was massing up for an attack was broken up by our fighter jets operating from Kumbhigram airfield. The appearance of our fighter jets was a great morale raiser for our troops and we could only watch in awe as our MiG 21s repeatedly attacked the enemy. We could not see what they were shooting at but they kept Flight Lieutenant Sharma of the ACT informed of the targets they were attacking. They reported that they had broken up forces gathering together for an attack. From the information being relayed to the ACT, it was clear that we were facing a very large enemy force and that 202 Pakistani Infantry Brigade had evidently not moved out of Sylhet.

What we didn't know then was that on 7 December at the same time that the battalion was landing at Sylhet, 313 Pakistan Infantry Brigade had also arrived there to reinforce 202 Brigade and the Sylhet Garrison. These two brigades and the Sylhet Garrison commanded by a Brigadier made the force opposing us close to the strength of a division.[6]

During the day, the enemy was kept at bay by our air force fighter aircraft but at night we were on our own. In those days the Indian Air Force did not have night fighting capabilities.

On 9 December, to our delight, we heard the BBC reporting that a Gorkha Brigade had landed at Sylhet! Could we use this piece of disinformation to deceive the Pakistanis that we were a brigade of Gorkhas when we were in fact only half a battalion?

During those days, there were three broadcasting stations reporting on the war – Pakistan Radio, All India Radio and the BBC. Nobody, including the Pakistanis, believed in the reliability of the Pakistan Radio Channel. All India Radio did broadcast credible news but they were invariably late with their broadcasts because they were getting their inputs from Army Headquarters which had to be accurate and truthful. The Indian Army had, however, given permission to foreign war correspondents to accompany our troops into battle as they advanced into East Pakistan on four different thrust lines. We had nothing to hide and were happy if reliable reports could reach the world that our operations conformed to what was ethical in war. These correspondents were able to provide minute-to-minute reports on what was happening on the ground. They lived with our troops, marched with them, ate what they ate, and slept alongside. Now, it appeared that the BBC war correspondent had mixed up 'battalion' and 'brigade' and forwarded his report that a brigade of Gorkhas had landed at Sylhet, while meaning a battalion. We decided to take advantage of this fortuitous mistake.

Lieutenant Colonel Harolikar and I decided to redeploy the companies to simulate that we were a force larger than we actually were. There were disadvantages to this as well. Trying to project that we were a brigade would mean bigger gaps between the rifle companies, which in turn would adversely affect the arcs of fire, the interlocking of our automatic weapons and our ability to effectively cover the gaps between our companies. We were already short of troops and this would make a bad situation worse. It would mean that the enemy, if they were worth their salt, could by active patrolling, find out our true position and use the opportunity to destroy the companies one by one. It was obviously a grave risk, but one worth taking and Lieutenant Colonel Harolikar, the brave and resolute officer that he was, took it.

Alpha and Delta Companies were told to advance forward silently at night and to spread out laterally so that the Pakis would not realize that this was a re-deployment of troops. The companies redeployed on the night of 9/10 December and by morning they had occupied their new positions.

Pakistani artillery however redoubled their shelling of our defences. We requested our air force to locate the enemy guns and destroy them. Our fighter aircraft were overhead within minutes and took on the enemy guns. Their firing stopped immediately. The enemy guns kept changing their positions to avoid detection by our air force and resorted to firing at us at night and in the early hours of the morning.

On the night of 12 December, I received a message from the RMO that one of the wounded was repeatedly requesting my presence. The enemy artillery was doing its best to pulverize our defences but their infantry attacks had reduced. We, on the other hand, gave orders to our troops to shoot only to kill. We were running low on ammunition.

When I reached the bunker of the regimental aid post, it was around three in the morning. I was led inside only to find Naib Subedar Bhim Singh Khatri in a bad way. He had joined 'First Five' along with me many years ago and then transferred along with me to 'Four Five'. A splinter from a Pakistani artillery shell had ripped open his abdomen and his guts had spilled out. All that the RMO could do was to put the contents back inside and bandage him up with a field dressing. He was in urgent need of proper medical attention.

Bhim Singh's eyes lit up when he saw me but he was in great pain. He said he had been asking for me because he wanted me to get him evacuated in a helicopter to an Indian military hospital. I said I would try. But perhaps he guessed that it might not be possible. He said, 'Come back soon Saab. If I die, I don't want to go away alone. Please be with me.'

I hurried to the signal link with the Brigade Headquarters. There was in fact a dire need to get the wounded and the dead away from the battlefield. It was bad for the morale of those who were still fighting to have to see so many of their own dead and wounded. The smell of death pervaded the area and the wounded were in urgent need of medical attention. Most were in the open, some distance from the regimental aid post since the bunker was too small to accommodate all. They were quietly bearing their pain without complaint. A nursing assistant was looking after their needs and the RMO kept shuttling between the bunker and the wounded. Some were asking for water but the only water available was the dirty water from nearby ponds which we were all forced to drink.

I managed to get through to the Brigade Headquarters and to convey to them that helicopters were urgently needed for evacuation of casualties. I could not say too much – we knew that the Pakis were listening in. After I confirmed that my request was understood, I briefed the CO and made my way back to the regimental aid post. I was approaching the regimental aid post around 5 a.m. when I heard the Pakistani artillery opening up with their early morning salvos.

When an enemy artillery round passes over an individual, one can hear the whistle of the passage of the round through the air. It's a sign that one is safe. The danger is when you hear the sound of the guns but not the passage of the round because it means that the round is going to fall directly on you or very close by.

This is exactly what happened that morning! Two enemy artillery rounds landed close to me without warning – one landed directly on the regimental aid post. The artillery rounds threw up great mounds of earth and the medical aid post was completely destroyed. The wounded who were in the RAP were blown to bits. They, and broken parts of medical instruments went wheeling above our heads before they rained back on the ground. Nothing was left of the medical aid post except a dark gaping hole. There was no trace of the wounded.

That evening, around 8 p.m., two of our choppers landed to take away the remaining wounded. I wanted them to take away the dead too, but at the time the air force did not carry dead bodies. However, after some altercation they agreed and took off safely with the dead and wounded, despite the best efforts of the Pakistanis to destroy the choppers. I breathed a sigh of relief. Not being able to do anything for our many dead and wounded was very disturbing.

Later that night, we learnt that an enemy patrol had come close to our defences and was forced to withdraw after a sharp engagement with one of our patrols. What was of concern however, was whether the Pakistanis had now learnt that we were not in fact a brigade and were spread very thin on the ground.

The CO and I considered what the enemy might do now and brainstormed about what we would have done had we been in their place. There was no doubt, they would attack in force the following day or night. In counter, we needed to face them with a consolidated front to give them a good fight and prevent their attempts to remove us. So, at around 2 a.m., orders were passed to 'Alpha' and 'Delta' companies to withdraw to their original positions, keeping an intact front throughout the withdrawal.

The next day, 13 December, was spent in improving the defences and dispatching strong patrols to dominate the ground in front of us. The enemy was strangely quiet. I had learnt that silence was always dangerous – it meant that the enemy was up to something. We concluded that they were planning a big attack and we alerted the air force in case they planned a day attack. Meanwhile, through coded messages, we had informed the brigade that we were short of ammunition and we were informed that a Caribou transport plane would drop what we needed at dusk that evening. We lit the 'goose necks' to help pilots identify the area in the fading light. The drop commenced at around 6 p.m. and the enemy did their best to destroy our slow, lumbering transport plane circling around the battle zone and to destroy our loads on the ground. The pilots did an excellent job with the ammunition, coming down with parachutes on the designated areas while the enemy rained down ammunition on our small dropping zone (DZ).

Armed with khukris, I led a party to quickly cut away the loads from the parachutes despite enemy artillery concentration on the dropping zone and rounds falling all around us. The CO was annoyed when he learnt that we were dodging enemy artillery shells with the team. He said that he had been waiting for my arrival for so long and that I would have to take over command of the battalion if anything were to happen to him. He remarked that I should not be taking unnecessary risks on small tasks. I accepted his admonishment with good grace. He was right.

We learnt later that the Caribou had been damaged from ground fire but managed to reach the base safely.

That night, on 14 December we waited for the expected attack but it never came. Our patrols dominated the ground in front of us. It appeared that the Pakis had lost the will to fight. That evening we heard that our Army Chief, Sam Manekshaw had issued an ultimatum to the Pakistani Army in East Pakistan to surrender or accept the consequences.

Calls for a ceasefire are typically fraught with danger – both sides try to improve their defensive positions in order to have an advantage when the bargaining of captured territory gets underway and the side which has captured more territory is at an advantage. Here that was not the case.

On 15 December, we heard that General Manekshaw had repeated his ultimatum both to the Army Chief of Pakistan and GOC-in-C, East Pakistan to surrender. General Niazi, however, continued to negotiate for a ceasefire, but the Indian

Army Chief would have none of it. He reiterated that Niazi must surrender or he would resume the war.

On 15 December at around 5.45 p.m., the company commander of 'Charlie' company informed the CO that a group of Pakistanis was approaching his company defended locality, waving white flags. Lieutenant Colonel Harolikar ordered the company commander to fire a warning burst to tell them not to come closer. The group stopped and two Pakistani officers came forward with a note stating that the Pakistani forces at Sylhet wished to surrender.

The situation was tricky. It was quite possible that this was a ruse to trick us into complacency and then mount an attack on us with large forces that were available to them. Even if they chose to surrender, it was quite possible that once they discovered how few we were in number, they could change their minds and attack. We were extremely low on ammunition and fighting for another few days without reinforcements would mean that our disadvantage would keep increasing.

Lieutenant Colonel Harolikar sent a message back through the Pakistani officers that we had till then, not received any orders to accept their surrender. The Pakistani officers then asked whether they could speak with the Brigade Commander.

So, now we knew that our bluff of being a brigade had worked! The Pakistani officers were told that these were the orders of the Brigade Commander, and that they should wait till we had confirmed that we could accept their surrender.

The Pakistani officers went back and we checked up with our own brigade at the headquarters. We were told that offers for surrender by Pakistani forces were being received all over the war zone.

We informed our Brigade Commander that the Pakistanis were under the impression that we were a brigade of Gorkhas and that they wanted to surrender to the Brigade Commander and he better come to take the surrender.

Brigadier Bunty Quinn, the Brigade Commander came from his headquarters in a chopper and landed within the battalion defended area. The CO briefed him. The Brigade Commander congratulated the CO and said that the battalion had done a great job in tying down more than two Pakistani brigades and the Sylhet Garrison and prevented them from contributing to the war.

An armed escort was provided for the Brigade Commander, with the men's khukris very much on display.

The leader of the Pakistani delegation, Brigadier Iftikhar Rana, Commander 202 Pakistani Infantry Brigade and two other brigadiers came to meet our Brigade Commander.

They greeted Brigadier Bunty Quinn but could not restrain their curiosity and asked, 'Who has come in this chopper?'

Bunty Quinn replied, 'I have. Why do you ask?'

'But you are the Brigade Commander. Were you not here?' they asked perplexed.

'No.'

'Then who is here?' they asked.

'The 4th Battalion, the 5th Gorkha Rifles.'

'Only a battalion?' they asked in disbelief.

'No,' said Bunty. 'Only half a battalion!'

There was a murmuring amongst the crowd of Pakistani officers who could not believe what they had heard.

It was then our turn to be shocked when we learnt that we had been fighting a force whose strength was close to that of an infantry division. The surrendering force included 202 Pakistan Infantry Brigade, 313 Pakistani Infantry Brigade and the Sylhet Garrison. Three brigadiers, two colonels, 173 officers, 290 JCOs and nearly 8,000 troops surrendered to a mere handful of Gorkhas. Our strength had now dwindled to 352 due to the casualties we had suffered. Undisputedly, we were successful in our mission but the price we paid was heavy. In the fighting at Atgram, Gazipur and Sylhet, four officers were killed and seven wounded, three JCOs killed and two wounded, twenty-four other ranks killed and 115 wounded.

That day, the 15 of December, the Pakistani force at Sylhet surrendered to Lieutenant Colonel A.B. Harolikar and Brigadier Bunty Quinn.

As the 'Vazir' of the battalion, I realized that we were now responsible for thousands of prisoners who had surrendered to us. So, on 17 December, after taking the CO's permission, I walked across to the Pakistani Camp to ensure that all was well. All I had for protection was my armed runner.

When I reached the Camp area, I found that the Pakis were quite capable of looking after themselves and nothing was required to be done. On my way back, I saw a Pakistani truck loaded with blankets.

December was cold and all that we had to keep ourselves warm were our rain capes. I called the Pakistani JCO and asked him whether the blankets in the truck were meant for his men or if they were part of the Quartermaster's Store.

He replied in Hindustani and said,

'Jenab, all our men have their blankets. These blankets are for the Store. Do your men not have blankets?'

I said, 'No Saab. We came here to fight, not to sleep.'

After he had digested that reply from me, I said, 'I would like you to give me those blankets for my men. Please speak to your officer. I will give you a receipt for them and after distributing them to my men, if you still have any left, I would like to also give blankets to my officers.'

The Pakistani JCO was astonished. He said, 'Jenab, are you saying that even your officers do not have blankets?'

I looked at him in the eye and said, 'Saab, if our men do not have blankets, how can our officers have blankets?'

The Pakistani JCO came to attention and said with deep emotion, 'Jenab, if we had officers like those in the Indian Army in our Army, we would not have seen this shameful day.'

What the Pakistani JCO said was true. The Pakistani officer class is different. They are all powerful and the relationship between the officer and the men is feudal – they are not as close to their men as we are. In our case, in keeping with the Chetwode motto – the country comes first, the men under our command come next and our own needs come last.

Now that the war had ended, the commanding officer felt it was no longer necessary to call me 'Vazir'.

So, he said to me, 'I have a problem with the word "Vazir" and keep calling you "Kazi"! Now that the war is over, is it OK if we revert to calling you 2ic?'

I said that it was OK and word was passed around that we would no longer use the word 'Vazir' and I would go back to being referred to as '2ic'.

On the morning of 17 December, a new station suddenly appeared on the radio-net and the conversation was in Gorkhali! We broke into the conversation and were happy to learn that it was 5/5 GR of our regiment. We discarded our code signs and resorted to excited calls of 'Four Five' to 'Five Five' and 'where are you?'

We were happy to learn that they were part of 101 Communication Zone and were approaching Sylhet from the North. That evening, the officers of the two battalions met and briefed each other on all that had transpired so far.

There was a new development the next day, on 18 December, we got a call from a BSF Platoon Commander who seemed to be in panic. He protested that armed Pakistanis were moving around his area and he felt very threatened. I told him that the Pakistanis who had surrendered to us were now our prisoners and would carry out our orders. If he so desired, I would order them to keep away from his area.

This did not seem to reassure him and he continued to be agitated.

I spoke to Lieutenant Colonel Harolikar and asked for permission to go across to the BSF Platoon Commander before he did something drastic. The CO appeared hesitant. Perhaps he had some intuition. I don't know and I never asked him. He said, 'Ian, the war is over. What is the point of getting involved in someone else's problems? We don't know where this BSF platoon has come from and they don't even come under our jurisdiction.'

'Sir, what if he opens fire and causes an international incident now that the war is over?' I tried to reason.

Very reluctantly, he gave me permission to go. He was right. I should never have gone.

Taking my runner along I went across to where I thought the BSF Platoon was located. Standard procedures worldwide require the forward and rear edge of a minefield to be marked and wired off. No such marking or wiring had been done.

After I had gone some distance, I stepped on a Pakistani P2 mine which blew up and I came crashing down. My leg was in a mess. A Bangladeshi man in a lungi who with some others witnessed the incident, had the guts to enter the minefield and, with my runner's help, lifted me up and took me to a nearby jeep.

Looking back, things are a blur. Whose jeep was it? What was it doing there? I only remember that my leg was bleeding profusely and the floor of the jeep was awash with my blood. I don't know how we reached the Battalion Headquarter but we did, and the CO came to meet me. I remember apologizing to him for what had happened and asked him if it was possible to get me to an Indian military hospital as quickly as possible. I was drifting in and out of consciousness, perhaps due to excessive loss of blood.

I was carried into a hut and the CO sent for the RMO

and then went to the radio set to request for a helicopter for my evacuation.

My leg, or what was left of it, was bleeding profusely, with the blood gushing out in spurts. The main artery must have been severed. The RMO came rushing up and tied a tourniquet around my thigh and the blood slowed down to a trickle, but by this time I had lost a lot of blood. I asked him for some morphine to kill the pain and he reminded me that all medications had been destroyed in the Pakistani shelling that had demolished the regimental aid post. I requested him to find something to cut off my leg and he went off to do so. He had been gone for a while, and clearly both of us had failed to realize that only khukris were available.

I knew that there was no point in trying to save what was left of the leg. It was in a bad shape. The foot, within the blasted boot, was hanging from shreds of flesh and cartilage, with bits of bone and flesh loosely connected to my leg. In addition, there were fragments of shrapnel and mud all over the wounded area. Balbahadur, my batman, was looking visibly upset and shaken.

'Balbahadur,' I asked in Nepali, 'where is your khukri?'

Balbahadur brought it to me.

I handed it back to him and asked him to cut off my leg. He responded that he couldn't bring himself to do that, and that I should wait for the doctor saab.

Knowing that my leg was beyond saving, I took the khukri from him and severed what was left of it. The severed part of the leg fell to the ground.

'Balbahadur, please go and bury it,' and Balbahadur did as he was told.

When the RMO returned with a knife, he looked with dismay at what I had done.

'What have you done, sir? You have completely messed it up.'

'Never mind, Doc,' I said. 'Please bandage it up.' I told Balbahadur to give him my first field dressing.[7] He took it and used another one as well to bandage what was left of my leg, which now looked a little more presentable.

■ ■ ■

The jinx of the 'second-in-command' of 'Four Five' had come back!

By this time the CO had returned. Somberly, he said, 'Ian, I have tried very hard to get a chopper for you but none is available due to commitments following the surrender. The Pakistani Garrison Commander has however heard about what has happened and has offered medical assistance. They have a hospital here.'

I didn't like the idea of being treated by Pakistani doctors, so great was my distrust of Pakistanis and I said as much.

I did not realize then that I was being unreasonable. Lieutenant Colonel Harolikar, however, was being very tolerant and patient. He tried to explain, 'Ian, if you don't get treated immediately, gangrene will set in. You are making things very difficult for yourself and for me.'

'Sorry sir,' I said. 'I will do what you say but I have two requests.'

'I do not want them to infuse me with Pakistani blood.'

'All right then. I will talk to the RMO and see what we can do. What is your other request?'

'Sir wherever they operate on me, I request you to be there. I don't want them to cut off my good leg.'

'OK, Ian,' he said and told the adjutant to inform the Pakistan Garrison Commander to immediately send an ambulance.

I remember being put onto a bed in the hospital. From the medical documents that accompanied me to Indian military hospitals thereafter, I learnt that a Pakistani doctor, Major Mohamad Bashir, operated on me. He did a good job but I have never been able to thank him. Maybe, if he reads this account, he will know that I am grateful. And as it so happens, my right leg is intact! I don't think it required Lieutenant Colonel Harolikar's presence at the operation theatre and I did not dare ask if he was there.

I remembered Kanian's prediction that I would be wounded but not killed – better that this happened at the end of the war rather than at the beginning!

I now know that doctors are doctors the world over and that they generally stick to the ethics as demanded by their Hippocratic Oath.

I was told later that the land route to Sylhet was opened after the surrender. When the road was cleared, our Quartermaster and our rear administrative echelon were able to connect with us. The men were able to eat hot food after more than two weeks. Gone were the days of drinking dirty muddy water from ponds and scrambling for grain from deserted huts for food. The ADS (Advance Dressing Station) had sent a medical detachment and our battle casualties were able to receive reasonable medical attention.

Meanwhile, Group Captain Douglas King Lee of the Indian Air Force, who I had served with in Mathura, had heard that I was wounded and needed to be evacuated by helicopter. During the war he was posted as part of Air Defence at Shillong, under Headquarter Eastern Air Command. He arranged to have a chopper pick me up and take me to an Indian Army Military Hospital. A lot of things happened in the chain of evacuation but that's another story.

The surrender of General Niazi to our Eastern Army Commander, Lieutenant General J.S. Aurora is now history and the photograph of the defeated Pakistani General signing the surrender document was everywhere. Every newspaper carried the headlines of the largest ever surrender of military troops after the Second World War. Major General JFR Jacob did a great job in ensuring that it was a surrender and not a ceasefire which Niazi was trying to insist upon.

The surrender of 93,000 Pakistani soldiers was followed up by the Shimla Declaration. Unfortunately, senior members of the Indian Armed Forces were debarred from being part of the negotiating team, contrary to the practice worldwide. Bureaucrats were once more at the helm of affairs to ensure that the Armed Forces did not get their rightful place at the negotiating table. The outcome is for all to see. What we gained on the ground was lost at the negotiating table. We were back to square one!

The 4th Battalion the 5th Gorkha Rifles (FF) had executed an impossible mission vindicating the faith and trust of the Corps Commander, Lieutenant General Sagat Singh. It had held two Pakistani infantry brigades and troops of the Sylhet Garrison for nine days and nights with very little food and water and a diminished amount of ammunition, thereby preventing these Pakistani forces from interfering with the 4 Corps offensive across the Meghna. Major General Jacob has acknowledged this in his book *Surrender at Dacca*.

All this was made possible by the 'never say die' attitude, outstanding courage and exceptional leadership of the Battalion Commander, Lieutenant Colonel Arun Harolikar, and the officers and men he had led into battle.

However, those nine days at Sylhet extracted a heavy price in fourteen men killed that included one officer, two JCOs and eleven other ranks, and thirty-nine wounded that included officers, JCOs and men. During the heli-landing at Sylhet, the adjutant, Captain Karan Puri was mortally wounded. He passed away subsequently at Guwahati military hospital.

It is a matter of regret that the exemplary courage and leadership of Major Shyam Kelkar who was the 2ic at the

Battle of Gazipur and was killed leading a 2 company attack, company commanders Yeshwant Rawat, Mane Malik, Dinesh Rana and Virender Rawat and the Battery Commander K.D. Segan has not been recognized. If the Corps Commander repeatedly put his faith and trust in 4/5 Gorkha Rifles (FF) to deliver outstanding results at the difficult battles of Gazipur and Sylhet after displaying their mettle at Atgram, then should he not have insisted on the battalion to be better recognized? Unfortunately, this did not happen.

In this memorable battle we all need to also recognize and appreciate the extraordinary courage of the brave, young helicopter pilots who landed the battalion against very heavy ground fire. More so, because the helicopters were unarmed and had no armour protection.

It is said that 'fortune favours the brave.' This is what happened at Sylhet, when an understrength battalion turned the tables on a far superior enemy force. Undoubtedly, God was also with us during this historic battle.

Postscript

1. As far as the blankets are concerned, we eventually did not get any blankets from the Pakistani garrison. The only blanket that we got was the one that I was wrapped in at the Sylhet Garrison Military Hospital. It was a well-worn civilian blanket which had the name of the soldier to whom it perhaps belonged. The name of the soldier, 'Mureed' was etched onto a piece of cloth and stitched onto the blanket. On checking, I learnt that the name means 'disciple'.

2. I did not 'hack off' my leg or amputate it, as some people have stated. My foot was hanging by strands of flesh. It was clear that it could not be saved. A quick cut was all that was required to separate the foot from what was left of the leg, and that was

what I did. The above action would have been taken by anyone else in a similar situation. There was nothing 'heroic' about it as some persons have made it out to be. This incident has been magnified and exaggerated by others.

Notes

1. A force raised from Bengali personnel of the Pakistan Army who had escaped from Pakistan and had regrouped to fight for the liberation of their homeland.
2. An aircraft that carried officers and men from Delhi to the Northeast, thus saving many days of journey by train.
3. Flight Manifest is a list of passengers/baggage that would be loaded on a military aircraft.
4. Kettle-like contraptions with elongated spouts which were filled with kerosene oil. When lit they gave out a bright flame that indicated the location suitable for landing at night.
5. Actually, a joyous cry – literally meaning 'Cardozo Saab – to be or not to be'.
6. A battalion consists of about a thousand men, a brigade normally consists of three battalions and a division normally has about three brigades along with supporting arms and administrative units.
7. A first field dressing is a medicated bandage that is issued to all ranks. As the name suggests, it is to be applied to a wound as a first aid application as a prelude to proper medical treatment.

CHAPTER SEVEN

Aftermath of the War

*A nation reveals itself not only in the men it
produces, but also by the men it honours – the men
it remembers.*
President John F. Kennedy

During the fighting at Sylhet, we did not have the time to think of anything except our only objective – hanging on to the ground that we had captured against overwhelming odds. It was only after I was removed from the scene of battle that I began to think about the future and wondered what it would hold for battle casualties like me.

The Indian Air Force helicopter that evacuated me from Sylhet landed me and my batman Balbahadur at an old, abandoned airfield in the state of Tripura that borders Bangladesh. This airfield was last used during the Second World War. It was around 3 p.m. and there was not a soul around. Darkness falls quickly in winter particularly in the

Northeast and the helicopter kept its engines running while I was offloaded. It took off soon after I had been jettisoned because it did not have night flying capability and had to reach its base while there was still some visibility left.

Far away, I could see a villager cycling on a track that ran alongside the airfield. I told Balbahadur to run after him and request him to go to the nearest military unit and ask them to send a vehicle to pick me up and take me to the Advance Dressing Station (ADS)[1] which I had been told was located somewhere near this airfield. It was wishful thinking! The villager, on seeing a soldier running after him, got alarmed and began pedalling away furiously. However, in his haste he fell down. Balbahadur caught up with him and told him he meant no harm and tried to explain our predicament. But the villager, scared as he was, refused to go to any military unit, especially in the evening. Balbahadur somehow convinced him to loan him his bicycle, pointed in my direction and told him to keep me company, till he could get some help.

It had become dark by then, and the villager approached me in the darkness shouting something that was unintelligible. I shouted back but I was on a stretcher on the ground wrapped up tightly in a blanket and he could not see me until he came closer. I told him to sit next to me. I tried to converse with him but he was not very communicative and after a while, we lapsed into silence.

After about an hour the night began to get cold and windy. Jackals were calling to each other in the quiet of the night and I wondered what they were saying, whether there was some language in their calls. The villager began to shiver and lamented about how he had landed in this situation. He was away from his home minus his cycle and told to guard some *fauji* on a stretcher who was wrapped up in a blanket, while he was freezing in the cold. There was nothing I could do, except listen to his lamentations.

Around 10 p.m., I heard the barking of dogs and the sound of a vehicle some distance away. The twin beam of the vehicle's headlights pierced the late-night mist as the vehicle climbed the embankment on which the airfield had been made and then having reached the tarmac, turned towards us. I asked my reluctant companion to stand up. As he was dressed in white, the vehicle which happened to be a Dodge one ton, caught him in its headlights and came to where we were.

Balbahadur was in the vehicle with the villager's cycle.

The villager was relieved that his ordeal had come to an end and that he would get his cycle back. I would have liked to have given him some money for the inconvenience that we had put him through, but neither Balbahadur nor I had any, as soldiers don't go into battle with money in their pockets. So, all I could do was to say, 'Thank you.' We offered to drop him to his home but he would have none of it. He was more than happy to get his cycle back and to be allowed to proceed to his home and his family.

The ADS was a tented facility meant to receive battle casualties but it was not on the line of evacuation of any battlefield. It had no battle casualties and I was probably going to be the first and last that it would receive during the entire war. I wondered what it was doing here, all by itself, far away from the scene of battle. It must have been part of some plan, that was later abandoned and that in the confusion of war, it remained out on a limb – forgotten. An ADS was authorized a medical officer but considering the lack of utility of this particular unit, he must have been sent elsewhere where he was more needed.

The JCO in charge of the ADS had been called to Dharmanagar, about 40 kms away, where a 20-bedded hospital had been set up for the war wounded and so there was nobody to give me the medication that I was supposed to receive. My medical file from the Pakistani military hospital at Sylhet had accompanied me but what we needed was someone with a medical qualification and the requisite authority to continue with the medication that I was being given.

That night I slept on my stretcher on the ground with Balbahadur sleeping next to me. The next day I asked Balbahadur and the nursing orderlies to carry me to the shade of a tree and there I spent the next day far away from my battalion and my family – in the middle of nowhere.

It was now that I began to go over the last couple of weeks. I thought of Priscilla and the children and wondered whether they knew that I had been wounded. There was no way I could communicate with her. I longed to hear her voice and to tell her what had happened and that I would soon be well.

I also began to think about whether I would be retained by the army. Would I ever be able to return to my battalion and the Gorkha 'johnnies'[2] who had become such an important part of my life? What would happen to my family? If the army did not keep me, what would I do to support my family? My eldest son was four years old and the youngest was just one. I had left St. Xavier's College without getting a degree, to join the NDA and at that time, passing out from the NDA was the equivalent of an Inter-Science/Arts qualification, which was neither here nor there.

The JCO in charge of the ADS returned around 4 p.m. from Dharmanagar. Looking at my condition and my medical papers, he gave me the requisite medication and suggested that I be evacuated to the Military Hospital (MH) at Dharmanagar as soon as possible.

Early next morning I was placed on the stretcher that had accompanied me from Sylhet and loaded onto a one-ton vehicle en route to the MH at Dharmanagar. I remember that it was a winding road because the stretcher which lay on the floor of the truck kept sliding from side to side, despite Balbahadur's best efforts to keep me steady. The leg began hurting very badly and sliding around the floor of the truck did not make things any easier.

The MH at Dharmanagar was a temporary make-shift facility that consisted of a series of *bashas*[3] and tents. What was left of my leg is called a stump and the bottom of the stump was kept open for the mud and splinters to drain out but it was bandaged tight and had been like that ever since I had left Sylhet. I was overdue for a fresh dressing and the nursing orderly here, who was an NCO, was pouring hot water with acriflavine to pull the bandage off which was stuck to my skin.

The stump began to hurt badly because along with the bandage, the NCO was pulling off what was left of my skin and so I asked him whether I could be given a pain killer. The NCO replied, '*Saab, hukum nahin hai*' (Sir, we don't have orders). So, I asked him to call a JCO. The JCO gave me the same reply. So, I asked him to call the officer who had given the *hukum* that a pain killer could not be given. It took a while for the doctor to arrive. When he finally came, he looked grim and irritated. He was a major. Although we both were of the same rank, I was much senior to him. Regimental Medical Officers (RMOs) of units are looked upon as friends, philosophers and guides and are usually called 'Doc'. I said, 'Doc this change of dressing is hurting badly. Could I be given a pain killer?' His answer shocked me. He said, 'I am not "Doc" to you or anyone else. I am Major Sharma[4] and you don't need a pain killer! Bear with the pain. You are suffering for your sins!'

I was shaken by his answer. 'Anything else?' he said. I was too stunned to give him any reply, so he turned and walked away, satisfied I suppose that he had put me in my place. The JCO and NCO were standing by. Judging by their expressions, it seemed clear to them that I had been ticked off by the medical officer and being refused a pain killer.

I told the NCO to carry on with his job and I gritted my teeth and bore the pain as he tore off the blood-soaked bandages along with my skin.

That afternoon, Colonel Jog, the Commanding Officer who had re-raised 'Four Five' many years earlier, came to visit me. He considered all the officers and men of 'Four Five' including myself, as his children. I was hurting badly – as much from what the medical officer had said, as from my wound and I was glad to see him but did not tell him what had happened that morning. We talked instead about old times, the battalion and what had happened at Sylhet. He stayed with me for a couple of hours and left in the evening as he had to travel far.

After he left, I ruminated on what had happened that morning and I remembered the saying that 'power corrupts and absolute power corrupts absolutely'. I was aware that all medical officers of the Indian Army are wonderful persons who closely identify themselves with the troops they serve, but I concluded that this medical officer was an exception who felt that he was 'playing God' because he thought that he had total control and power over me.

However, his words that I was suffering for my sins, did have an effect on me. I knew that none of us are perfect but I began to wonder whether I was really suffering for my sins and what about all the other battle casualties and all those who had died in the war? Were we all suffering for our sins?

A couple of days later, I was told that I would be transferred to the MH at Silchar and I was glad to leave. We had to go by train and there was no military coach. My stretcher was laid on the floor of a very crowded railway platform next to baskets of fish packed with ice. Water from the melting ice was dripping down in small rivulets. The nursing orderlies were doing their best to keep me away from sniffing dogs who wanted to know what was going on, and from curious onlookers who gathered around to look at me. They meant no harm. They wanted to express their sympathy but did not know how!

We had to travel in a third-class compartment because there appeared to be no provision for officer patients along with the nursing orderlies to travel first class. The nursing orderlies were a cheerful lot and that helped. Getting a stretcher through the doorway and aisle of the compartment was difficult but they managed. There was no food or water but the nursing orderlies fed me cheerfully with food bought at the railway station with money from their own pockets and they looked after me very well. I shall always be grateful for the generosity of the Indian soldier who gives of himself in so many different ways without counting costs.

We reached the Silchar MH on Christmas Eve and for the first time after nearly a month, I was able to sleep on clean white sheets. We had reached the hospital around 11 p.m. Dinner had finished but they gave me a nice omelette with buttered toast and a mug of hot tea. I shall always remember that meal as one of the finest I have ever had!

Early next morning, I woke up to find a nursing sister standing at my bedside and staring at me. I said, 'Happy Christmas, Sister.' She burst into tears and ran away. I had no idea as to what I had done to make her cry!

Her outburst made me think of different times. Of Christmas Eves spent helping my mother and my brother Colin making special sweets, sending cards, waiting for Santa Claus and the gifts we hoped he would bring, of going to church for midnight mass, of hymns and songs so reminiscent of the spirit of Christmas, brotherhood and love. Later on, it was Christmases spent with Priscilla and the boys in our own little family, in the battalion, and in the formations I later served in; when Priscilla used to make umpteen plum cakes to share with the many friends and colleagues who used to come calling on Christmas Day. It used to be so festive – but those were different times! The war had changed my world and turned it upside down.

Later in the day, a group of nuns came along to pray over the patients. They were a cheerful lot. They prayed over me and they informed the parish priest who in turn informed Major Eustace Fernandes,[5] an old friend, that I was there. The parish priest came over and prayed with me and later that evening, Eustace Fernandes came over with a bottle of whisky and we drank together and sang old songs. Liquor is not permitted in military hospitals, or in any hospital, but the doctors and nurses pretended that they were not aware of what we were up to.

After a few days, we were evacuated to Guwahati MH. I don't remember how we travelled. It must have been a comfortable journey, or I would have remembered.

When I reached the ward at Guwahati MH, the sister in charge of the ward informed me that there was a movie being screened for the patients in an open-air theatre and she asked me if I would like to go. I sensed that she wanted to go, so I said 'yes'. She wrapped me up in a blanket, put a towel around my head, transferred me onto a trolley and wheeled me to the movie theatre. This was the only time I saw a movie lying down. I don't recall the story because I fell asleep soon and didn't wake up until I was wheeled back to my bed.

I remember asking if there was anyone else from my battalion in the hospital. I was told that Captain Karan Puri, our adjutant, was in the ICU. He had been grievously wounded in the abdomen during the heliborne landing at Sylhet. I asked permission to meet him but was not allowed for fear of infecting other patients. The next time I asked about him I was told that he had passed away.

That night, I walked down memory lane and recalled the days spent in happier times with Karan Puri. Four officers had died and seven of us had been wounded. This was quite a large number of officer casualties, for a war of just thirteen days. Karan had spent a weekend with us when we were posted at Mathura. His face kept spinning in front of me till I dropped off into a fitful sleep.

On 31 December 1971, some other patients and I were taken to the airfield at Guwahati. We were being air lifted to Pune. There was an AN 12[6] on the tarmac. The interior of the fuselage had shelves along its length to accommodate stretchers, one above the other, to take the maximum number of patients. There was a long line of military ambulances bringing in patients who were to be evacuated.

Those who came in early, and I was one of them, were loaded first and by the time the last patients had been loaded, we had been baking in the plane's hot, oven-like interior. The soldier above me was in great pain and was crying out loud. I felt sorry for him but he was making life very uncomfortable for all of us.

There must have been over fifty of us in that aircraft – mostly amputees and all on stretchers. Pune was the key location for amputees because of the Artificial Limb Centre, but some of the patients had multiple injuries like the one on the shelf above me. The journey was long; the aircraft rattled and vibrated as if it was going to disintegrate and we were all shaken up – the heat was intense and we were perspiring and the stench of blood and sweat of so many unwashed bodies was overpowering.

We landed at the Lohegaon airfield at Pune early on the morning of New Year's Day 1972, and our stretchers were taken out of the aircraft and laid on the tarmac. A cool, fresh breeze was blowing and I felt like I was in heaven as compared to Dante's[7] inferno in the aircraft.

Apparently, there were not enough beds at Pune MH, so some of us were sent to Kirkee MH. All along the way, our ambulance was stopped by revellers celebrating the arrival of 1972 and they kept banging on the body of the ambulance with cheery shouts of 'Happy New Year'.

I wondered what the new year had in store for us.

At Kirkee MH, I was put into a ward with the other battle casualties and we quickly made friends. There was a constant stream of visitors from Pune and Kirkee. Nobody knew us, but they came to tell us that they appreciated what we had done in defence of the country. It was good of them. Later, word had got around that I was there, and some friends from Pune came to see me including a nun who I had known as a girl, who would later go on to become the principal of Jesus and Mary Convent at New Delhi. She cheered me up immensely.

On one side of my bed was Major Mahalingam[8] from the Madras Regiment. He had a shoulder injury and one of his ears had been injured. On the other side was Captain Kipgen of the Assam Regiment. 'Kippy' had been an instructor at the NDA. He too had lost a leg on a minefield.

Admiral 'Ronnie' Pereira, the deputy commandant of the NDA came over to see Kippy. He was cheery and jovial and made it a point to speak to every officer in the ward to make us all feel good.

During the day, the officer patients in our ward exercised control over their pain but at night whilst they were asleep, pain used to take over and one could hear them groan and mumble in their sleep. Maybe I did the same. At one end of the ward sat the night duty sister at a table with a shaded lamp writing her reports. She would get up every now and then to attend to our needs.

Priscilla continued to be with her parents at Mhow along with the children. I did not know whether she had been informed by Army Headquarters that I had been wounded. From Guwahati MH I had written her a letter to say that I had been wounded. Explaining what had happened, I had written, 'I was alive and kicking – except that I was kicking with only one leg'. She told me later that she didn't find that remark funny!

After a couple of days my parents came from Bombay to see me. They were worried but tried not to show it. My father asked if I was in pain. I confirmed that I was, but told him that the duty sister had said that absence of pain was not a good thing. That seemed to reassure him. My mother, typical of all mothers, wanted to know when I had last had a bath! I probably did not smell very good when she kissed me. My mother, intuitive that she was, had got it right! It had been over a month that I had last had a bath! She was aghast and she shared her discomfort with the nursing sister on duty.

The nursing sister reported my mother's concern to the matron who directed that those who could walk should be taken to the bathroom and to be assisted if they needed help to bathe, and those of us who could not walk should be given a sponge bath in our beds.

Screens were set up around my bed and a mackintosh placed below me and a nursing sister commenced 'Operation Clean up'. My clothes were removed and I was asked to cover frontal nudity with a hand towel and the nursing sister commenced washing me with water from an aluminum basin. I was sponged from head to toe with soft hand towels, warm water and soap and after so long, the accumulated grime and dust of the battlefield was finally scrubbed away. The sister was gentle and I shall always remember that gentleness. She washed my hair, my ears, face, arms and the leg that had remained. Along with the grime of battle she scrubbed away my memories of the violence of war. It was a rather sensuous feeling to be washed by a woman who was neither my mother nor my wife; but she was a nursing sister, so I put my head back and gave in to her ministrations. While washing my leg she pulled out a few splinters of shrapnel that were lying just below the surface of my skin of the leg that had remained. After the application of soap and water and another round of scrubbing, she dried me with a towel and sprinkled me with eu de cologne. After she finished, I fell into a deep and contented sleep, smelling good and feeling clean.

My parents were with me for a few days and it was good to have them over. They asked me if there was anything that I needed. I told them that I needed some underwear, a couple of shorts and shirts and some money which they readily gave me. My mother was praying for me that I would get well soon. I assured her that in fact I would be up and about once I got my wooden leg. I now felt slightly more comfortable with some money in my pocket and some clothes other than the standard night clothes that were issued to all of us.

The surgeons – Majors Majid and Chahal were operating night and day without respite because there was a huge line-up of battle casualties that needed immediate attention. From the day I was admitted to Kirkee MH, I was due to be administered my antibiotic medicines to prevent infection but the ward medical officer, a lady doctor – a lieutenant of the Army Medical Corps, kept telling me that only the surgeon could give directions for what medication I could take.

I told her that I had passed through many military hospitals on my journey to Kirkee MH and had been given antibiotics all through and therefore at the very least, I should be given what I was already being administered earlier; the prescription for which was available on my file. But she insisted with stubborn irresolution that I should wait for the surgeon. While I waited, ten days passed without medication. By this time, the complexion of the pain in my stump had changed and a sharp throbbing pain had taken over. Even I, with no knowledge of medicine, was aware that infection had set in – but the doctor remained indecisive. By now I was getting apprehensive, annoyed at this lack of attention and decided to take the matter to higher authorities. I asked to see the commandant but that too was refused.

Late next morning, I noticed that the telephone in the ward MO's office was unattended; I rang up the taxi stand and called for a taxi. Within a few minutes the taxi arrived. I had been given a pair of old-fashioned under arm wooden crutches. I grabbed hold of them and went towards the taxi.

As I was getting into the taxi, I heard someone shout, 'Stop him!' It was the commandant on his rounds! With him were the chief matron, the ward medical officer, the ward sister, and the ward master. I tried to get into the cab and the Sikh taxi driver seemed to be greatly enjoying the unfolding drama. He started the engine and would have taken off, if it was not for the ward master who had caught hold of the door, opened it, and tried to physically remove me. I warned him not to touch me by which time, the commandant arrived hot and breathless.

This was the first time that I saw him!

'Where do you think you are going?' he demanded.

'To Command Headquarters,' I replied.

'Why?'

'To meet the Army Commander.'

'Why?'

'Because I've been here ten days and no one has attended to me yet.'

The commandant was furious.

He said to the ward master, 'Take him to the ward.' The ward master took a step forward.

I told the ward master not to touch me. The ward master stepped back. I took out my wallet to pay the taxi driver but he refused to accept any money.

By this time, some of the battle casualties had come out and were witness to the scene. They were ordered to go back to their beds and I proceeded on crutches to my bed with as much dignity as I could muster.

By this time my lunch had come on a tray but I was in no mood to eat.

The colonel and his posse of hospital functionaries went back to wherever they had come from.

The ward nursing sister came to me after a while, with concern written all over her face. 'What happened, sir? Why are you so angry? Why did you talk like that to the commandant? He is a good man.'

'Sister,' I said, 'I do not know or care about how good or bad he is. You have been a witness to the number of times I have been practically begging for my medication. Yet no one has had the time to see me – neither the surgeon nor the commandant and I have been here for more than ten days! The pain in my stump has changed and I think that serious infection has set it. Who will be responsible if gangrene sets in?'

The ward sister kept quiet and after a while said, 'Have your lunch, sir.'

'No. I am in no mood to eat.'

After a while, there were sounds of boots in the corridor outside the ward. The ward master entered with another nursing orderly and told me that I was being shifted to MH Pune. I was told to collect my things and proceed to the ambulance outside.

I had no time to say goodbye to my friends in the ward. Everybody looked upset and serious. I too felt sorry. I had never spoken like this to a senior officer in my short life in the army but I had been pushed to my limits. It appeared that the medical staff at Kirkee MH viewed me as a troublemaker and decided to get rid of me. The thought made me unhappy.

The admission procedure at MH Pune took a while and I was given precedence over some other battle casualties on wheelchairs who were waiting to be admitted.

I was first taken in a wheelchair to the Lower Officer's Ward because my details had to be recorded in the office. While there, I saw a number of young officer amputees – some on wheelchairs, some on crutches. The ones on wheelchairs were racing around playing with a ball and those who were on crutches moved easily as though they had known how to use crutches all their young lives. There was much laughter and shouting and the doctors and nurses did not seem to mind. The atmosphere was positive; no one seemed to have a care in the world.

Since I was a Major, I was admitted to the Upper Officer's Ward. Captain Jaya Lakshmi, the Ward MO of the Upper Officer's Ward welcomed me with a warm smile, told me to go along to Room No. 4 of the new wing of the Upper Officer's Ward and said that she would join me there soon.

This new wing had been built after the Sino–Indian War of 1962 when the medical authorities realized that if another war took place, a big influx of battle casualties would require more room. They were right. Captain (Dr) Jaya Lakshmi later told me that besides the other war wounded, there were nearly fifty officers in the Upper and Lower Officers' Wards who were all amputees.

On my way to Room No. 4, I was stopped by someone who didn't appear to be a battle casualty and looked much older than any of us.

'Hello,' he said. 'What's your name?'

I told him who I was. I didn't know who he was, but he spoke with an air of authority. He had what looked like medical papers in his hand.

'Have you been admitted?'

'Yes,' I said.

'Which room?'

'Room Number 4,' I said.

'Well, wish you the best of luck. The previous three occupants of that room have all died, and the last occupant passed away this morning.' He said this with a laugh and waved me off.

I wondered who he was. He seemed to be an unpleasant sort, so I put him out of my mind.

The room allotted to me was nice. It had an attached bathroom, a built-in wall cupboard, a writing desk and chair and two easy chairs – quite a luxury compared to the dormitory ward at Kirkee. Majors, it appeared were considered to be reasonably senior and this new-found status for me was most welcome. Just then, a nursing orderly came to the room with drinking water in a flask, two glasses and a hand towel. He asked me if everything was all right.

I asked him whether the previous occupant of the room was discharged that morning. Pointing upwards, he said, '*Yes sir, final discharge!*'

'Was he a battle casualty?' I asked.

'No sir,' he said. 'He was the father of an army officer and he died a very painful death.'

'What did he look like?' I asked.

The nursing orderly gave me a description of the person, and his description matched the man I had met that morning, on my way to Room No. 4! I am not a superstitious person but this didn't seem to be a good omen.

I lay on the bed and went over what had happened at Kirkee MH and then after all the excitement, the pain hit me again – a deep, intense, throbbing pain. I thought of how my mother had told me to take my medicines and antibiotics regularly. I had not told her that no doctor had seen me until then, and that there were no antibiotics to take.

A while later, the commandant of the Artificial Limb

Artificial Limb Centre

Centre – Colonel 'Tommy' Das came to see me. He was accompanied by the deputy commandant of the hospital. They looked very stern and I realized that the commandant of the Kirkee MH must have spoken to them about me.

Colonel Das said, 'What was the matter at the Kirkee MH that made the Commandant send you here?'

I was glad that I was asked for my version. I explained to Colonel Das what had happened. Though he didn't say anything, he seemed to understand my predicament because he requested the Deputy Commandant to have the Operation Theatre (OT) ready for an immediate examination. Within twenty minutes I was wheeled into the OT. I was given a pain killer; my dressing was removed and a culture taken from my stump. A fresh dressing was applied and I was wheeled back to my room. The next day an X-ray of my stump was taken.

The following day, Colonel Das came to my room in the evening and confirmed my worst fears. According to my reports, infection had set in and the bone in my stump had been severely infected. Another amputation would be necessary and the operation could not be done until the infection had abated.

I had learnt by this time, that the length of my stump was important if I wished to lead as normal a life as possible. I had no idea how much of the bone had been infected and how much more of my leg would have to be cut off. I had no way of knowing how this would affect my ability to walk and run and swim. I was angry and frustrated that the doctor at Kirkee MH failed to do her duty with regard to a simple thing like giving me antibiotics that I was already taking, but there was nothing I could do about it.

The infection was so serious that I was subjected to a course of intravenous injections that lasted for ten days. I could be operated upon only after the infection had subsided. Priscilla wanted to come to Pune to be with me but I told her not to come then, because things were so uncertain. I was left with my own thoughts and fears – how much more of my leg would be cut off and how would it affect my ability to perform as an infantry officer. I knew that much would depend on this operation. Unfortunately, there was no one I could share my thoughts with at the time. A week later, I decided to call Priscilla to Pune because by then, a coursemate's sister,[9] a doctor herself, offered to put her up at their home. Their house was within walking distance from the hospital.

That morning Rev. Father Valerian DeSouza[10] came along with some young boys and girls from St. Patrick's Colony. He had brought his guitar with him and all the patients gathered around. They sang songs for us and asked if they could help in any way.

One week later, I was declared fit for the operation. I was taken to an air-conditioned waiting room. The room was a bare, cold place and I was left alone with my thoughts as I waited for the operation to start.

Finally, I was wheeled into the OT by two nursing orderlies and put onto an operation table, next to which was a trolley on which I saw an array of saws, hammers, chisels, knives and needles. The OT looked like a carpentry shop and I wondered what they were going to do to me! The surgeon saw me looking at these implements and signalled to a nursing assistant to have them covered.

There were two surgeons, masked and gowned – one of whom I learned later on was Colonel 'Tommy' Das. The other surgeon told me that he was going to give me an anesthetic called sodium pentothal which I remembered was also a truth serum. He told me to count to ten but I remember reaching only up to five and I don't remember anything after that.

I woke up in my room sometime later and Priscilla was there. I wondered if it was actually her or whether I was hallucinating as a consequence of the anesthesia that had been given to me! I slipped back into unconsciousness.

When I woke up again, Priscilla was actually there. I told her to look at my leg or what was left of it, and she said, 'Shush, I don't have to look at it now. We have the rest of our lives to look at your leg. What is important is that you are alive!' That settled all my apprehensions of how she felt about my losing a leg and an intense sense of peace descended upon me and I dropped off into a deep, drug-induced sleep.

Colonel Tommy Das the surgeon and Commandant ALC had apparently told Priscilla that after the amputation I should walk on my crutches. The blood needed to flow to the end of my stump to help with the healing process. I was happy to have her there, pushing hard to make me walk up and down the room on my crutches.

At that time in 1972, the Amritraj brothers – Vijay and Anand, were making their debut on the world tennis circuit and were playing in Pune at the Asian Lawn Tennis Championships and the battle casualties were given passes.

Priscilla accompanied me, carrying pillows for me to rest my stump.

The hospital at this time was short staffed for nurses and Priscilla had been helping them with their tasks. She was everywhere. All the battle-casualties knew her even though they didn't know me. Up to then, I had been restricted to my bed and when I started to move around, I was known as 'Mrs Cardozo's husband!'

In a month it was time for Priscilla to go back to her parents' home – the boys were missing her. By now I had become very close with three other amputees – Major Abu Tahir[11] of the Bangladesh Army, Major Kipgen[12] of the Assam Regiment and Major JV Raju[13] of the Artillery.

None of us had any idea what the army would do with us. The percentage of disability according to a standard international formula depended on the length of our stumps. All of us had a disability of 60 per cent or more and we were told that we could be invalided out of the army if we chose to leave; and if we did, then we would be eligible for a number of Central Government and State Government concessions. The government was making it attractive for us to leave the army while it was giving us a choice – to leave or to stay! But it was a 'take it or leave it option!' Did we even know then what we really wanted? The route to leave meant that we would have to choose to be invalided out!

Being invalided out seemed like a dismal option considering that I knew, in my heart, that even with an artificial leg I could be nearly as good as I was before I got injured. I had read *Reach for the Sky*, the story of Douglas Bader, an RAF pilot. He had lost both legs and continued to fly Spitfires during the Second World War. He had become an air ace by shooting down 21 German fighter-aircraft. If he could do it, why couldn't I face my challenges in the same way?

I did not want to leave the army. This was a way of life for me and I knew no other. Although money is important, I had not joined the army for money and no concessions in the world could compare with life with my battalion.

A fundamental issue was whether battle casualties would be eligible for command of troops and promotion in the command stream. Nobody had answers to this most important of questions. It was this concern that loomed over me. To be a 'babu' in uniform, for the rest of my professional life was not an attractive proposition at all. We would, however, have to prove to ourselves and to the world at large that we were as good as the non-disabled officers of the armed forces. But we did not know the first thing about how we could do that! We would have to find out for ourselves how good we were. But would we be given a chance? Would I really be able to prove that I was as good as anyone else or was I chasing an impossible dream?

It felt as if we, who had fought for the flag and been part of that great victory of 1971, were now being left behind. India and the army were moving forward without us. Had the Indian Army forgotten us? Did we not 'belong' anymore? We, who did not count the cost! Was I being punished for being wounded in battle? Were we, the battle casualties, winners or losers? It was as if something died inside of me. My small world had been turned upside down. Would I never go back to my battalion again? What choice did I have, what path could I take, and what fate was waiting for men like us?

During the day, in the company of my new-found friends, we did all that we could to distract ourselves and we lived as if there was no tomorrow. The night was different. Alone in my bed, all these worrying thoughts came rushing back to torment me. I would lie awake for hours, playing out different versions of the same scenario, my thoughts churning this way and that, until I would finally succumb to a fitful sleep.

Paradoxically, in the beginning, when I was told that the door to command troops had been shut in my face, a sense of relief swept over me. I would no longer be a part of the 'rat race'! That was over and done with! I could now just relax, get invalided out and let life take me to my destiny and accept the perks that were being offered. It was certainly a comfortable option. But my thoughts would instinctively return to my troops, my battalion and the Gorkha Johnnies who had become part of my life. If I was being true to myself, there was no other life than to be with my troops to face the challenges that came my way and to find the answers to overcome them.

I revisited conversations with Kanian about predictions for the future and their relationship with destiny. I remembered asking him if our destinies were inevitable and added that I was of the opinion that, *'Destiny is a matter of choice and not a matter of chance.'* After having thought about it for a while, he said that my statement was not entirely true; destiny had an element of choice as well as an element of chance. Each one's destiny was fixed; this could not be changed because a prediction, if it is true, is what would eventually happen to a person, fashioned by individual choices and actions. I remember him saying that there was a relationship between values, habits, behaviour and actions that could result in good or bad outcomes; the fate of an individual began from home. Good values fostered by the family encouraged good habits which in turn resulted in good actions which resulted in good outcomes. However, there were factors over which the individual had no control, which introduced the element of chance that had an influence on the destiny of an individual and even the collective destiny of a nation.

Keeping in mind what Kanian had said, I decided to make my destiny a matter of choice and accept whatever the element of chance would throw my way. In the matter of choice, the first thing that I needed to do was prove that battle casualties were as good if not better than non-disabled soldiers. I had no difference of opinion with those who chose to be invalided out. That was the route to their destiny, but that was not what I wanted.

The chance to face the challenges that disability offered was the way out for me. I had to find my own path to my own destiny and break the boundaries that limited the dark and blinkered vision that others had fashioned for battle casualties. It became an opportunity for me to reset our narrative.

At the hospital we could not get measured for our artificial legs until our stumps healed. It took approximately four months for that to happen. During this time, we were all over Pune on our crutches and our bandaged stumps – at the bar of the Southern Command Officer's Mess, at the races, at the movies, at Poona Coffee House on East Street and at the restaurants on Main Street (now called MG Road). The citizens of Pune had become used to us and accepted us as their own.

All the activities that we were indulging in required money and regrettably we lived beyond our means by drawing cash from a money lender and spending it recklessly. His shop was on an offshoot of Main Street and he allowed us to use post-dated cheques and charged us exorbitant rates of interest. Looking back, I think we lived as if there was no tomorrow because we did not know what 'tomorrow' held for us.

Around this time, Headquarter Southern Command decided to organize a reception for the battle casualties lodged at the Pune and Kirkee military hospitals. The Army Commander was the host and so I decided to speak to him. The Army Commander was from the Gorkhas and Colonel McKean, a senior staff officer from Headquarter Southern Command was from Darjeeling. Both spoke Nepali. So, I went and spoke to Colonel McKean in Nepali and asked him whether I could meet the Army Commander. 'Sure,' he said and asked me why I wanted to meet him. I told him that we battle casualties were in the dark about our future and that we wanted to know whether we could go back to our battalions. Speaking in Nepali, he introduced me to the Army Commander. I was on my crutches.

The Army Commander was speaking to some senior officers. He excused himself and turned around to meet me and after being introduced, he said:

'So, are you from the RIMC?'[14]

'No sir.' I said slightly taken aback.

'Then are you from the 11th Gorkhas?'

'No sir.' I said, even more mystified.

Colonel McKean explained the reason why I wanted to speak with him.

The Army Commander turned to me and said, 'That is for the doctors to decide.'

I answered, 'Sir, how can the doctors decide what I can or cannot do? It is for the chief and the army commanders to decide how battle casualties can best be employed.'

The Army Commander was more than annoyed. He said, 'It is not for you to decide what the chief and the army commanders should do. As far as I am concerned, army doctors will decide what your medical category will be and that will decide how you can best be employed. Is that all?'

The Army Commander's attitude was discouraging. It appeared that the mindset of the military hierarchy was biased against battle casualties, and that would exclude us from the command of troops.

I was disappointed. The chief and the army commanders were our last resort and it appeared that the Southern Army Commander, at least, was not inclined to support our claim that we should be permitted to join our units and that at the very least, we should be given an opportunity to prove our credentials one way or another.

By then, it was almost four months and our stumps had healed. Now began the serious business of being measured for our artificial legs, trying out our prosthesis till we got a perfect fit. This involved a lot of hard work that started at 8.30 in the morning and lasted until 4.30 p.m. with only a break for lunch in between. Much depended on the shape and health of our stumps – the healthier the stump, quicker we could begin to walk.

The aim was that we should be able to walk normally; that our gait should be so seamless that no one should be able to guess that we had an artificial leg. For below knee amputees like myself, it was easier to walk naturally. However, for above knee amputees like Abu Tahir and Yeshwant Rawat, an officer from my battalion, it was more difficult to conceal a pronounced limp.

Major Abu Tahir was promoted to the rank of Lieutenant Colonel by Bangladesh while he was still with us at the Artificial Limb Centre. A month later he was promoted to Colonel's rank. Suddenly, he had became senior to us, rank wise.

I was posted to Military Secretary's (MS) Branch, Army Headquarters, New Delhi. During my interview with the MS I was told that Gen Manekshaw had specifically asked that I be posted to MS Branch to be part of a committee to evolve a policy for battle casualties.

Maybe General Manekshaw saw from my record that I was from his regiment and that was probably why he directed that I be part of this committee.

It was around this time that we first heard the term 'post traumatic disorder' – that some battle casualties could not accept the horrors of war to which they had been subject or the events which led to their disability and this adversely affected their emotional make-up. None of us at the Artificial Limb Centre appeared to be affected in this way. There were so many of us who were amputees and we became a strong support to each other. However, a Major from the artillery, who had lost both his legs above the knee took it badly. He had been fitted with two wooden block-like legs that reduced his height considerably which made him look like a dwarf. It was difficult for him to walk and he had to waddle around – that too with a stick. We heard later that he shot himself. Was this a part of post-traumatic disorder? We did not know, but it felt terrible to learn that a disabled soldier had ended his life.

The Major was senior to most of us and while there were lots of us single-leg amputees who had each other for company and were able to move around Pune on our crutches, he was alone and lonely in his room. We sometimes went to his room to keep him company but he probably sensed that this was more an act of charity rather than our desire for his company. We discovered that he was not married but there was a girl somewhere in his life that he had been fond of, but things had come to an end before he lost his legs, and now there was no question of being able to pick up the threads of a lost relationship. When we talked about the war, he often said that he wished that he had been killed rather than forced to live his present existence.

Later on, when I heard that he had killed himself, I felt a sense of remorse, perhaps even guilt. Would this have happened if I and others like me, had spent more time with him and given him the companionship that he must have longed for? Was this what post-traumatic disorder was all about? It's something most of us knew very little about – mental health issues that affect soldiers due to the violence of war had not been examined in depth until that time i.e., what needed to be done to alleviate the pain that some soldiers suffer; with no one to understand what they are going through. Many soldiers had died in the war but there was nothing more tragic than for a soldier to take his own life because there was no one to empathize with his plight.

'Sam Bahadur' cared for his officers and soldiers. He reminded MS Branch and AG's Branch[16] that personnel of the Indian Army needed to know that if they were wounded their interests would be taken care of. He had remarked that if such conditions were not created, who would stick their necks out in a future war? Having himself been badly wounded in the Second World War at the Battle of the Sittang River in Burma in 1942,[17] he understood what it was like to be wounded. This is something the present and future military and political hierarchy need to think about!

Kautilya[18] has written extensively on kingship, governance, leadership and war as an instrument of state policy, the meaning of morale and its effect on the will of the soldier to fight well, but the politician, and the bureaucrat of today appear to have forgotten him and his teachings. It is also about time that Kautilya's *Arthashastra* becomes part of the syllabi of schools and universities but it is unlikely to ever happen because it will expose the inadequacies of the people in power.

Colonel Abu Tahir, Major S. Kipgen (Kippy), Major J.V. Raju, Major Yeshwant Rawat and I chased our own dreams and chose our paths to our respective destinies. Abu Tahir, Yeshwant Rawat and I chose to soldier on and take our chances with what our respective armies offered us, while Kippy and Raju decided to leave the service by getting invalided out. Raju, Kippy and I had the same percentage of disability i.e., 60 per cent; whereas Abu Tahir and Yeshwant Rawat's percentage of disability was more since they were above knee (AK) amputees.

What happened to me is encapsulated in this book, but

what happened to the rest of the foursome, are stories by themselves which will have to be told separately. Kippy's story has been told by his wife Maman Kipgen in *A Life in Service – the Biography of Major S Kipgen, SM*. The story of the four of us is told in a short story 'And then there was one' that forms part of my book of short stories on the 1971 War.

Although I did not fully comprehend how tough it would be to prove myself fit for command of troops, I realized that I needed to fight not only for my own perceived destiny but also for the collective destiny of all battle casualties who wanted to prove themselves. Upbringing at home and at school, training at the defence academies, regimental camaraderie in all the wars I had fought alongside my troops, gave me the impetus, motivation and stubborn confidence to not give up on my dream without a fight. Even though I did not know at that stage how long and how difficult that journey was going to be, I was determined to battle it out.

Notes

1. This is the second rung in the chain of evacuation of battle casualties. Medical assistance is available here at a slightly higher level than what is available at the Regimental Aid Post.
2. A Gorkha soldier is called a 'Johnny', just as a Tamilian soldier is called a 'Thambi', a Maratha soldier is called a 'Ganpat' and a Garhwali soldier is called a 'Bula'.
3. A bamboo hut with a thatched roof.
4. Name changed.
5. Eustace Fernandes did well in the service and was promoted to Lieutenant Generals' rank. Unfortunately, he was tragically killed in an explosion soon after he was promoted. His wife Melanie has settled down at Pune. They have two daughters – one has married an army officer and the other has married General Sunith Rodrigues' son.

6. A transport aircraft.

7. The Italian poet Dante Alighieri wrote the *Divine Comedy* which gives a graphic description of Hell which has come to be known as *Dante's inferno*.

8. Major Mahalingam, later on, was promoted to Brigadier's rank and has become a defence correspondent and defence analyst and is nowadays often seen on TV.

9. Surgeon Commander Barbara Ghosh and her husband Surgeon Commander Debu Ghosh opened up their home to Priscilla and gave her love and affection and looked after her for a whole month. Barbara was the sister of my coursemate Vincent Lobo.

10. Rev. Fr. Valerian DeSouza had a brother in the army – Colonel Bunny DeSouza of the Engineers. Rev. Fr. Valerian, popularly known as 'Father Valy' was a favourite with the youth of Pune. He was later appointed as the Bishop of Pune and was known as 'The Singing Bishop'. Three girls from the group of young friends became nuns – two of whom joined Mother Teresa's order.

11. Major Abu Tahir had escaped from West Pakistan and joined the Mukti Bahini in order to fight for the freedom of his country. He lost a leg while leading an attack against a Pakistani unit.

12. Major Kipgen of the Assam Regiment lost his leg while trying to rescue a soldier of his company who had been blown up in a minefield in J&K.

13. Major JV Raju of the Regiment of Artillery was a Forward Observation Officer providing artillery support to the infantry when he lost a leg while assaulting an enemy objective.

14. Rashtriya Indian Military College.

15. Although I had been awarded the Sena Medal for an act of gallantry in 1959 on the Sino–Indian border, it had not been possible for me to attend the investiture parade until 1964 due to my being in NEFA followed by the Sino–Indian War of 1962 and the re-raising of 4/5 Gorkha Rifles (FF).

16. Adjutant General's Branch. This branch amongst its many other roles also looks at the welfare of soldiers.

17. On 22 February 1942, Captain Sam Manekshaw, in command of 'A' Company 4/16 Frontier Force Rifles launched a counter-attack on a strong Japanese position at Pagoda Hill in Burma during the battle of Sittang River. In true tradition of the Indian Army, Sam led his company from the front. Pagoda Hill was recaptured but Sam was hit by an LMG burst that lodged 9 bullets in his abdomen that perforated his lungs, liver and intestines. Sam was given up for dead but his batman, Sepoy Sher Singh carried him on his back to the Medical Aid Post which was clogged with casualties. Sepoy Sher Singh forced the doctor to operate on Sam, thereby saving his life.

18. Kautilya – an ancient sage who was the advisor on kingship to the kings of the Mauryan dynasty. His writings on governance and on war are exemplary in its clarity of vision and understanding which helped in making the Mauryan dynasty one of the greatest empires in ancient times.

CHAPTER EIGHT

Priscilla

*Behind every successful man is
a very surprised woman.*
Anonymous

I first set eyes on Priscilla at the annual 'mela' or fair organized by the Mhow Cantonment Board. It must have been June 1962. My friend, Sylvester, and I were both doing different courses at the School of Signals[1] and we decided to take a break from our studies and go to the fair.

Priscilla was chatting with a group of her friends. She was slim and pretty and I was instantly attracted to her gorgeous smile. I couldn't take my eyes off her. Sylvester, a Captain from the Corps of Signals, asked me who I was looking at.

I said, 'That girl with the beautiful smile.'

'Come on Ian, all Mhow girls have beautiful smiles. Which one do you mean?'

'The one in the blue and white salwar kameez.'

'Hmm…,' he said. 'Would you like to meet her?'

'Of course, yes,' I said. 'Do you know her?'

He didn't say anything and moved towards the girls with me trailing behind. Sylvester broke into their conversation to introduce me to Priscilla. He obviously knew her. Priscilla was too gracious to show that she didn't quite appreciate his intrusion – to meet a perfect stranger! She smiled at me politely and said, 'Hello' and went back to talking to her friends. Without saying so in so many words, she implied 'thanks for the introduction and now can I please get back to my friends?'

I felt embarrassed at this forced introduction. After some small talk with Sylvester, she and her friends moved to another part of the fair. I kept looking for her and her friends noticed this and appeared to be teasing her.

I was disappointed not only because the introduction was a fiasco and I could not take it further, but also because the Regimental Signals Officers' Course which I was attending, was coming to an end and I wondered if I would ever see her again. She was too pretty and appealing to be forgotten.

Afterwards, I left for my battalion posted at Daporijo in the Subansiri district of NEFA. But I could not get her out of my mind and thought of her in those lonely days and nights, spent in a desolate corner of the world. I doubted if I would ever see her again.

As luck would have it, two years later, I was back in Mhow. This time I was there for the Junior Commanders' Course. I wondered whether Priscilla was still around. All that I remembered was her first name and her smile. I had no idea where she lived; and if she had gone away, where she could have gone to.

Mhow, in those days, was a small military cantonment in the state of Madhya Pradesh that housed two military schools of instruction – the Infantry School and the School of Signals.

The cantonment had a small market town that met its needs. I have always felt that John Masters based his book *Bhawani Junction* on his life and time at Mhow Cantonment and the railway colony that was close by. Indore was the nearest city about twenty miles away. One could reach Mhow either by the BB and CI railway or the GIP[2] railway via two big railway junctions at Ratlam and Khandwa.

Some say that Mhow was actually an acronym that stood for the Military Headquarters of War (M.H.O.W.) which I don't believe to be true. Mhow in my opinion is a derivative of the name of a tiny village, which later blossomed into a town and cantonment and grew into its present size due to the military schools of instruction. Take away these schools and all that would be left would be a small town and its railway colony.

A few weeks into the course, I went for a swim at the Defence Officers' Institute known to all of us as 'The Club' along with a coursemate – Captain Inder Mohan Chowdhury from the engineers.

I plunged into the pool and did a few lengths switching from free style to breast to back and stopped for a break to chat with Inder, when I noticed a group of girls at the shallow end of the pool. One of them looked vaguely familiar. With a gasp I recognized that beautiful smile. It was Priscilla! The swimming cap made her look different! After a while, the girls decided to get out of the pool. I had eyes only for Priscilla. Her beauty took my breath away.

If she noticed me, she gave no indication. In any case, I wondered whether she remembered that we had been introduced to each other. But that was over two years ago. Most likely she had forgotten me!

All this while, Inder was watching me with an amused smile. 'What's the matter Ian? What's got into you? Are you OK?'

I told him about Priscilla and he said, 'Why did you not go and speak with her? You were introduced, weren't you?'

'Yes, but that was two years ago. What if she did not recognize me and cut me dead?'

After the girls left the pool, I asked the swimming pool attendant about the girls and if they came to the pool at the same time every day. 'No fixed time Saab,' he said with a smile. 'Today they came at 4 p.m. but on Saturday and Sunday they come early in the morning as soon as the pool opens, at 7 o'clock in the morning.'

I came to the pool the next day at 4 p.m. and the next day at the same time, and the day after that, but Priscilla and her friends did not come. I was at the pool at weekends early in the morning, but had no luck. I kept going to the pool around the time that the attendant had said, whenever the routine of the course allowed me to, but it didn't work out. I was disappointed.

Then, after a month, another officer, also from the Signals, who I had known at the IMA, came to the pool with his sister and that was the day that Priscilla and her friends were back in the pool. The officer's sister saw me doing the back stroke and wanted to learn. The officer knew Priscilla and the other girls, so I was introduced to all of them and once more to Priscilla. All wanted to learn new swimming techniques and now that the ice had broken, we began to get on very well with each other.

I divided the group into two teams and we swam against each other and time passed happily but too quickly, because all of us had other things to do. But we planned to meet at the pool on dates and at times convenient to all of us.

During the intervening days I could think of nothing else but Priscilla – her smile, her laugh, the way she spoke, her keenness to learn to swim better. I introduced the group to water games and how to swim under water. Looking back, I think those were the happiest days of my life. Unfortunately, all good things come to an end – Priscilla had to go back to college and there was no time for swimming, or to linger at the club and just talk and watch the way she spoke with that gorgeous smile flitting across her face and to snatch a few moments alone.

I wrote to my parents of Priscilla and learnt to my delight that they knew Priscilla's uncle who was a doctor. The de Guerras and a branch of the Cardozos were both old families from Mhow. My father told me to visit Dr Jerome de Guerra to renew old ties. I visited Dr de Guerra and we were sitting in his garden having tea, when to my surprise, I saw Priscilla walk by. Until then, I did not have the courage to ask where she lived. Now I learnt that she belonged to the same de Guerra clan and that she lived in the house next door. I was thrilled!

A branch of the Cardozo family had left Candolim, our village in Goa and settled down in Mhow about two hundred years ago. Priscilla's ancestors had also migrated from Goa and settled down in Mhow. Her family comes from Para, a village not too far from Candolim. Her grandfather set up a photographic studio in Mhow which was run later on by Priscilla's father and uncle. Their work was in great demand by the army and the local citizens of Mhow. Another of her father's brothers was the doctor I went to meet.

Strange that our two families – the de Guerras and part of the Cardozos – had their roots in Mhow and destiny turned full circle to bring me back to the place of my ancestors and to the family of the girl I was in love with.

After a while, I spent every moment that I could spare from the course with Priscilla and was delighted that she enjoyed being in my company.

Inder and I shared the same room and by this time he was a bit concerned that I was not paying enough attention to the course. Looking back, I know he was right, but I could not help behaving the way I did. Whereas I was all right in the class room and the TEWTS (Tactical Exercises without Troops) and sand model exercises, I did not do well in the written tests because I wasn't studying.

It used to be very hot in our rooms; so, Inder and I used to sleep at night on the terrace of our block. I remember those moonlit nights when I would think of her, and the moon became the symbol of my relationship with Priscilla. That year, a song, *Magic Moon* was a hit and it became our favourite song.

I passed the course with an average grading but my relationship with Priscilla had become very close. She was studying for her B.A. degree and my attentions to her must have affected her studies too. Despite these distractions she managed to do well.

Much of my courting was done on a friend's motorbike. On the last day of her exams, I picked her up from the examination centre. It must have been the month of June because it rained on the way back and we both were drenched. After we got to Priscilla's home, her mother asked me to stay for dinner but I was soaked and I had an exam the next day, so I asked to be excused. However, the invitation to dinner by her mother seemed to imply that I was an acceptable suitor for her daughter.

My course was coming to an end and although Priscilla and I had by this time decided to spend our lives together, I needed to formally ask her parents to consent to the match. So, one Sunday while I was at her home, I went up to her father and asked for his permission to marry his daughter. He looked at me kindly and said, 'Yes Ian. Permission granted. I hope you will keep her happy.'

'I will,' I said.

I have tried to keep my promise. I only know that we

have had great times together and that we have also had tough patches, particularly during our periods of separation through the wars and when I got wounded.

We were engaged on 10 April 1965 at Mhow and my parents, and my brother Colin came for the engagement. My father was happy to be back at Mhow and relive the days of his childhood because it was here that he used to come for some of his holidays when he was young.

Soon after our engagement, Priscilla headed for Bombay to do her B.Ed. at St. Xavier's Institute of Education. She stayed with her cousin for the duration of her course and I was happy that her degree would also make her a Xavierite.

I was lucky to get two months leave during May and June which I spent at Bombay while Priscilla attended her course. I had a scooter which Priscilla christened 'Dominique' and many happy hours were spent riding up and down Colaba Causeway and Marine Drive and towards Land's End.

Wanting to impress her, I went one morning to Bistro, a night club which was off Flora Fountain and reserved a table for two for dinner. It was the month of June and I wanted my leave to end on a nice note. I asked the management to have flowers and candles on the table and a card to say that the table was reserved. I asked the manager to request the band to play our favourite tunes and he noted them down. The manager was happy to participate in my scheme and I thought that with his cooperation, all would go well. He said, 'I would like to see this girl who you are trying so hard to impress!'

I said, 'You will, this evening.'

We had planned to see *My Fair Lady* which was playing at the Eros theatre at Church Gate. When we emerged from the theatre after the movie, I found to my dismay that it was raining heavily. We had gone to the movie on Dominique which was parked forlornly in the rain. I suggested that we take a cab for the dinner that I had so meticulously planned, but Priscilla said, 'Let's wait till the rain stops.' It did after a while, and we got onto Dominique and headed for Bistro only to be drenched on our way by another downpour. Priscilla wanted to go home but I persuaded her to have dinner, mindful of all the arrangements that I had made.

Bistro was a great little night club with a nice band and a crooner and a dance floor. The crooner was Brenda Lily, a gorgeous girl with a beautiful voice. Unfortunately, because of the rain there was nobody there but us. Even the crooner did not come because of the rain – but the card was there saying that the table was 'reserved' in a restaurant that was totally empty, and the flowers were there too with the candles which were lit after we arrived. It was disappointing but we made the best of it and the manager despite the loss of his clientele did his cheerful best to make us feel good and he gave me a 'thumbs up' for my girl. I persuaded Priscilla to dance on the small wooden dance floor and we danced to *Fascination,* another of our favourite songs, but we were too wet to be comfortable and after a couple of numbers we had dinner, thanked the manager and called it a night. When we left Bistro, it was still raining!

My leave ended soon after and I went back to my battalion. Two months later we were at war with Pakistan. My battalion was heavily involved in fighting the hordes of infiltrators that had come across as part of Pakistan's Operation Gibraltar. Priscilla's letters to me were full of encouragement to do my best during the war, and that helped.

A year after our engagement and six months after the Indo–Pak War of 1965, we were married on 26 April 1966. We emerged from the church under an archway of khukris held by officers from the regiment and we cut the wedding cake with a khukri. The wedding march was played on the church organ by Mrs Noella De Souza, wife of Major General

Eustace De Souza. Ashok Mehta who was six months senior to me raised the toast at my wedding. He had come all the way from the battalion which was in J&K. I have happy memories of our wedding surrounded by my family, friends, and officers from the regiment.

A year after the war, I was posted to Mathura as a staff officer to Lieutenant General Sataravala, a senior officer from my regiment who was the Corps Commander of the formation to which I was posted. It was during this posting that our three children were born. Except for one year at Ambala and a few months at Palampur this was my first peace posting in nine years but this posting lasted for three and a half years.

After the war, I was evacuated through a number of hospitals and Priscilla was kept informed by official telegrams from Army Headquarters that I was wounded. She said that each telegram informed her that I was wounded in action and was evacuated from one hospital to another. She, however, had no idea how badly wounded I was, or the nature of the injury, or at which hospital I was being treated, until I wrote to her from Guwahati military hospital. It was more than six weeks after the war started that she finally received my letter which had been heavily censored. I know she must have gone through a difficult time wondering what was happening during the war and to know later on that I was wounded and in hospital. But she has never shared the pain she went through with me. She could share this with the reader but she is not writing this book, so neither the reader nor I will ever know!

I would however like to say here that this was a different side of my wife that I saw during my long hospitalization. Her strength, her cheer, her ability to put aside her own fears and to be there for me, was simply amazing. She was also present for everyone else who were in the same ward. During this time, I was known as 'Mrs Cardozo's husband' because she was better known to them than I was!

While I was in hospital, our fifth wedding anniversary was celebrated with the nuns at St. Felix's convent on the banks of the Mula-Mutha River. It was good of the nuns to do this for us. It was also time for Priscilla to get back to the kids as they were missing her. I was thirty-four when I got wounded and the boys were just four, three and one year old.

Priscilla handled the aspect of my being wounded with circumspection and care. Vikram, our youngest son was not aware of the implications of my losing a leg and said he wanted a leg just like his daddy. However, Sunith the eldest was worried that his friends would make fun of his father because he had only one leg. She explained to him that he should be proud of his daddy because he had lost his leg fighting for India – but I don't know how much sense that made to a five-year-old. Arun, the middle one, just accepted it as a fact of life. Actually, this probably explains their attitudes and how each of them looked at life later on.

My battles off the battlefield continued and none of them would have been worthwhile without her by my side.

As a young girl, Priscilla was very actively engaged in sports and games. She played basketball for her school and college and always led her school team for the inter-school drill and marching competition and they always won. Also, a good swimmer and basketball player, she is primarily responsible for my sons turning out to be champion swimmers. She would drive them to the St. Columbus School swimming pool early in the morning before classes started and would follow up once again after school closed. My sons are what they are today mainly because of her. She is an avid follower of the World Cup in football and Brazil is her favourite team. She would stay up well past midnight to watch the matches and would wake me up to watch the action-replay when a goal was scored. Her love for sports continues to the present day.

I was lucky to have seen her that day long ago in 1962 when my friend Sylvester introduced me to her and to have had the good fortune that she agreed to be my life partner. I could not have made a better choice.

Notes

1. The School of Signals is now called 'The Military College of Telecom Engineering' (MCTE).
2. BB&CI – Bombay Baroda & Central India railway and GIP – Great India Peninsular railway.

C H A P T E R N I N E

Disabled? My Foot!

*Don't let anyone tell you what you can do or cannot
do. It's often a reflection of their own fears and
mental blocks. It's your journey not theirs.
Go for it! Dream big!*
ANONYMOUS

General Sam Manekshaw was not only a man of vision, he was also practical and humane and is acknowledged to be one of the best chiefs of the Indian Army. Of course, he led India to a great victory during the Indo–Pak War of 1971, but besides, he genuinely cared for his officers and soldiers. He is one chief who is not only honoured by the rank and file but is also remembered and loved by every officer and soldier of the Indian Army.

He knew what it was to be wounded in battle and that something needed to be done for the war wounded so that every officer and soldier would know that he would be cared for if he ever became disabled.

After the 1971 war, General Manekshaw had directed the Military Secretary to evolve a policy to take care of the careers of the war-disabled officers. He had said, 'Who will stick out his neck in the next war if we don't care for the war disabled?' It was with this in mind that he ordered the setting up of a committee to evolve a policy for the war disabled, so that every soldier would have faith and trust in the system. He understood the meaning of morale and what it takes to make men fight.

It was around this time that I received a letter from CDA (O)[1] saying that I would be on half-pay! The letter said that since I had been in a military hospital for more than six months, I needed to repay the government the expenditure on my hospitalization. We would continue to be on half pay until the expenditure due to the government for our hospitalization had been fully recovered. Other battle casualties who had been in hospital with me had also received similar letters. I was amazed at this attitude of the CDA (O) – it made light of the sacrifice that we had made fighting for our country. I had been amputated twice and it takes more than four months for the skin to grow and cover an amputated stump and more time after that to be fitted with an artificial leg and to learn how to walk again. And here I was, being made to feel that it was my fault that I had got wounded; that I should not have spent so much time in hospital recovering from my wounds.

Unfortunately, nothing was done to resolve this issue. On checking with battle casualties of the 1965 War, including Lieutenant Vijay Oberoi, I learnt that they too had been put on half-pay after being discharged from military hospitals. Many years later, around the year 2000, officer amputees of the 1999 Kargil War, stated that they too had been put on half-pay.

By this time, Priscilla and the children had joined me at Delhi. We were glad to be together again. The boys were too young to understand the implications of my losing a leg. Sunith was six years old, Arun was five and Vikram was two. I shared the letter with Priscilla. She was indignant and couldn't believe that this was the way soldiers who had been wounded in war could be treated.

At that time the waiting list for married accommodation for officers at Delhi was one and a half years. This meant that an officer posted to the capital would get married accommodation only for a few months before he was posted out. However, temporary married accommodation was available at Kotah House in the heart of New Delhi. This consisted of one-room out-houses on the periphery of the main building. The room had an attached toilet. It was a 'Take it or Leave it' choice. We were happy to accept the offer. After all, we were together as a family, and that was what mattered. The war and long months of hospitalization made us realize the importance of family life. Having to live together in a one-room apartment also brought us closer to the kids. Our sons too remember those days fondly. For them it was part of life as army brats. It also taught us to make the best of what life offered, instead of cribbing and complaining.

There now began a long spate of correspondence with the CDA (O), to get my pay restored. Why did this happen? Why was the CDA (O) so insensitive to our needs? If it had happened once, it could be pardoned as ignorance, but for it to have happened repeatedly, three times after three successive wars, was inexcusable. It was only in 2016 that the Seventh Pay Commission directed that this abominable order be rescinded. It took 41 years to see that justice was done on this issue towards those who were disabled in battle! This extended time lapse to sort out such a despicable injustice speaks for itself.

The composition of the committee to decide on the future of battle casualties was left to the chairman of the committee who happened to be the Deputy Military Secretary (B). Being a gunner, the brigadier would take care of the needs of officers from the Artillery. All the other arms and services were headed by colonels who were handling the HRD aspects of their respective arm/service/corps. Strangely, the largest corps i.e., the Infantry who had the maximum number of battle casualties was represented by me, a major, the junior-most member of the committee; junior to all the others by at least two ranks.

To my discomfort, the attitude of most of the members of the committee, right from the beginning, was prejudiced against battle casualties. Their general thinking was that retention of battle casualties would be a burden on the army which would be better off if the battle casualties were invalided out! MS Branch, the principal actor in this situation, felt that retention of battle casualties would cause major problems because they would need to be posted to peace stations and thereby deny the able-bodied access to such postings. There is no denying that these were real issues but however real the problem, solutions needed to be found.

The committee, in general, was against the option of placing officers like us in command because they felt that we would not sufficiently match up to the demands of peace and war.

These issues were not new; they had been debated after the earlier wars. The existing policy permitted the promotion of war disabled personnel only on the staff and that too, only up to brigadier's rank. In all the years since the Second World War, only two officers had been promoted to this rank – Brigadier Rathi Sawhney from the Gorkhas and Brigadier Jenkins from the Madras Regiment. General Manekshaw was not happy with the existing policy and wanted it to be overhauled so that battle casualties could be given more opportunities to contribute usefully to the Indian Army.

The debate and discussions continued for many months. Finally, the committee came to the conclusion that the *status quo* be maintained. During one heated discussion, I said that it was strange that a committee that would decide the fate of battle casualties had only one battle casualty on board. The composition of this committee was therefore skewed. I went on to add that the issue of command of troops and promotion of the war disabled had not been adequately examined and discussed. I requested that the comments of my dissent be recorded. The record of the discussions and the recommendations of the committee should be available in some file in MS Branch, Army Headquarters.

The conclusions and recommendations of the committee were finalized after Sam Manekshaw had retired, and the findings that the status quo be maintained found favour with the new regime. To say the least, this was deplorable. I did not know what I could do to set things right. As a member of the committee, I felt I had failed the battle casualties by my inability to convince other members that at the very least, the war disabled needed to be given an opportunity to prove themselves.

I am not sure whether the conclusions of this committee caused the setting up of another committee consisting largely of officers of the Army Medical Corps, which placed officers in various low medical categories. Perhaps this committee had been set up separately. These medical categories laid down the dos and don'ts for persons in these low medical categories, which would have a bearing on their postings on command, staff, instructional and other appointments. In other words, it would be doctors who would decide the future of battle casualties!

In accordance with the new rules, I was placed in a category labeled as S1H1A2P1E1, which if I remember correctly, stated that I could not be posted to an appointment that involved running, jumping, climbing and swimming, which in effect, ruled out command of troops. I came to the conclusion that if the formal route to a positive outcome on the future of the war disabled had failed, it was time to find other ways to prove that the war disabled were no less than the non-disabled and I realized that it would be up to me to prove the point. I had no idea how I could do this.

By this time, more than two years had passed. All my batchmates who had been approved for promotion to lieutenant colonel's rank were now about to finish their command tenures, but I continued to remain a major and was not even considered for promotion because the policies, rules and procedures that would govern battle casualties had not been approved. Although I had passed out high in my course, I was being superseded for promotion for no fault of mine. In fact, it appeared that I was being punished for being wounded in war!

It was around this time that I began getting sharp pains near the ankle of my amputated leg. However, when I reached down to touch the errant ankle, I found that it did not exist! It was then that I became aware of 'phantom pains' – pains that occurred in those parts of my leg that did not exist. I was told that the nervous system that is 'wired' to the brain was not used to the fact that this part of my body did not exist. The pain in fact was somewhere in my stump but my brain seemed to be under the impression that it had occurred in parts of my body that were no longer there. Even now, at night in my dreams, I keep walking and running around with both my legs. In the last fifty years since the war, I recall only one dream where I was functioning with one leg. My brain apparently has still not accepted that one of my legs is missing.

About that time, a circular was issued that Physical Proficiency Tests (PPT) would be held in a week's time and that all officers from Army Headquarters would be required to take the test which would be held at the National Stadium. The circular did not ban low medical category officers from taking the test. It was probably understood that we were not required to do it. I decided to take the test anyway, to see for myself how well I measured up to these tests.

On the appointed day, I joined all the officers from Army Headquarters who had assembled at the National Stadium. We had 'fallen in' (assembled) before a Colonel who was conducting the tests. We were all dressed in PT kit, which meant white shirts, shorts, socks and PT shoes. In view of the fact that I had an artificial leg, I wore white trousers instead of shorts and boots instead of PT shoes. This caught the attention of the Colonel.

'You there!' he said. 'Why are you wearing trousers and boots?'

'I have a wooden leg, sir,' I said.

'That means you are in low medical category. You are not eligible for the test.'

I said, 'Sir, the circular does not ban me from taking the test and I don't have a health problem.'

He said, 'Last year a low medical category officer took it and died of a heart attack. I don't want your death on my hands.'

'Don't worry sir. I won't die.'

There was a titter from amongst the assembled officers who apparently found my reply funny. I, however, was very serious.

'Don't argue or I will take disciplinary action against you.'

I said, 'Sir, you are welcome to take action against me if I commit an offence but until then please allow me to participate.'

The Colonel probably saw the logic of what I was saying. He relented, albeit very reluctantly, and allowed me to participate.

Fortunately, I was able to pass all the tests and in the two-mile run, I left several non-disabled officers behind me. The Colonel seemed pleased at my performance. He mentioned something in his report about a disabled officer who took the tests despite the fact that he had a wooden leg and had done well.

Sometime after this incident, I was approved for promotion to Lieutenant Colonel's rank, by a board that took into consideration the new rules concerning medical categories. According to this policy, I was approved for promotion on the staff and was posted to Military Operations Directorate as GSO1 MO3. The Director Military Operations (DMO) was Major General Arun Vaidya, MVC and bar. I was interviewed by him. He asked me why I had not commanded a battalion and whether I still wanted to do so. I explained the events that had transpired so far, and he asked MS Branch for a copy of my performance on the PPT tests. He told me that notwithstanding the existing rules and the policy for the war disabled, I should write an application to MS Branch for command of an infantry battalion. He asked me to draft the letter and send it to him for his approval.

The MO Directorate reported directly to the Vice Chief of Army Staff (VCOAS), who at the time was Lieutenant General A.M. Vohra. When the VCOAS went on a tour of an operational area, an officer from the Directorate had to accompany him as his staff officer. As GSO1 MO 3, I was dealing with three commands, so I would accompany the VCOAS on tours to these commands whenever they concerned operational matters. My application for command of a unit was approved by the DMO and was sent to the VCOAS for his consideration along with the report of the PPT tests.

The VCOAS was scheduled to tour Jammu & Kashmir and he directed that I be detailed to accompany him as his staff officer. I recalled what Lieutenant General Jangu Sataravala had taught me – 'anticipation', 'opportunity' and staff work, and I did my homework for the upcoming tour.

The tour went well. The visits to the forward posts were done by helicopter and there was no place for me in a helicopter, which could only carry the two chopper pilots, the VCOAS and the GOC. So, I moved along with the convoy of vehicles on the road.

On the last day of the tour, I reached the bottom of a hill on top of which was a post that the VCOAS had to visit. I reached down below at 3 o'clock in the morning and was told who the post commander was. He happened to be an officer from my battalion who had been posted to another regiment and I decided that it would be a good idea to meet him. The height of the post was about 2,000 feet and I started climbing up to the post. I reached the top after a couple of hours and had breakfast with the post commander. After some time, the VCOAS landed at the helipad. He was surprised to see me and probably thought that I had wangled a lift in a helicopter to get me there. He looked at me and asked, 'How did you get here?'

'I climbed, sir,' I said.

'You can climb?' he asked, not being able to conceal his astonishment.

'Yes sir. There are many things that I can do which my seniors don't understand or won't accept.'

'What do you mean?'

I said, 'Sir, the committee that has adjudicated on the future of battle casualties has not given the war disabled any opportunity to prove what we are capable of and has sealed our fate without giving us a chance to prove ourselves.'

The entire episode set him thinking. After he left in the chopper for the next post, I descended to where the vehicles were and drove to the airfield at Jammu where an aircraft was waiting to take us back to Delhi. While waiting for the

VCOAS at the airfield at Jammu, I worked on the tour notes and the next morning I had them faired and typed out and the draft tour notes were put up to him in the afternoon.

The VCOAS was impressed that the tour notes were prepared so quickly, and he said as much. I silently thanked General 'Jangu' Sataravala!

Soon afterwards, the VCOAS apparently spoke of me to the Army Chief, General T.N. Raina, MVC. He raised the issue about the existing policy, barring battle casualties from the opportunity to command units. He told him about the result of the PPT tests and my ability to walk, run and climb.

General Raina himself was a battle casualty of the Second World War and had lost an eye during the war. This had happened before Army Headquarters had evolved its policies to restrict battle casualties from doing what they were capable of. If MS Branch had had their way, at that point of time, perhaps General Raina would never have reached high rank – in fact the highest in the army.

During this time General Raina was due to visit Ladakh, and he said, 'Send Cardozo with me to Ladakh.' It was a heaven-sent opportunity and before we left, he summoned me to his office. I was in awe of being called by the Chief to his office. He briefed me about his schedule and what he wished to see on his visit. I liaised with the formation he was to visit and told them what General Raina expected. The formation was grateful to know what the Chief wanted and the Chief was happy to see them well prepared. The tour went off well and the Chief saw me walking in hilly terrain. Everyone benefited from the visit, including the MO Directorate. Once again as taught by General 'Jangu' Sataravala, I had the draft notes of the tour on his table the morning after we returned. I am certain he was impressed – the tour notes were issued the next day without any change.

General Raina then sent for the VCOAS and they

discussed my case. He sent for my file from MS Branch and made the following noting on my application for command of a battalion. He wrote: '*Yes, give him a battalion and also all war disabled officers who are not taking shelter of their wounds.*'

This single sentence from the Army Chief opened the way for battle casualties for the command of units. It was a very progressive step by an Army Chief, who used his powers emphatically, without having to run to the bureaucracy – military or civil, to get their concurrence.

Although I was the first battle casualty to be approved for command of a battalion, I was not the first battle casualty to be promoted based on the Army Chief's ruling. There was no vacancy either in 'First Five' or 'Four Five' at that time for command of the battalion, and the privilege of being the first battle casualty to be promoted in command of an infantry battalion was given to Lieutenant Colonel Vijay Oberoi, who in later years rose to the rank of a Lieutenant General and retired as the Vice Chief of the Indian Army.

This was the first step to open promotion of battle casualties to command appointments but it referred only to the command of units and in the euphoria of being given the opportunity to command a battalion, I did not realize that the chief's decision did not refer to higher ranks. The solution to this problem would be left to another time, another place and another chief.

Note

1. Controller of Defence Accounts (Officers). It is a civilian organization that handles the pay and accounts of all officers of the Indian Army. Our monthly salary slips are sent to us by this office, located in Pune.

CHAPTER TEN

Command of 'First Five'

God gives answers in three ways. He says 'Yes' and gives you what you want; or He says 'No' and gives you something better; or He says 'Wait' and gives you the Best!

By the time I was approved to command a battalion, seven years had passed since the war, and all my coursemates had not only completed command of their units but also their first tenure on the staff. I realized that I would be the oldest infantry battalion commander of the Indian Army – many years older than everyone else! I had, however, tried to keep myself physically fit by walking and running every morning and swimming at the DSOI[1] swimming pool in New Delhi.

I ran so much, that one day the metal bolt that connected the rubber foot of my artificial leg to the wooden shaft sheared off due to metal fatigue. I fell down and wondered what happened, till I saw my boot lying some distance away.

I got up and hopped on one leg and picked up my boot with the errant artificial foot, and waited for someone to give me a lift home.

After a while an army officer came along in his car. I flagged him down and asked if he could drop me home. I told him that it was close by at Sardar Patel Marg. I was standing on one leg.

'What's the matter?' he asked.

'My foot has fallen off,' I said.

'Whaaat!?!' he exclaimed in surprise.

'My foot has fallen off,' I repeated holding my boot up for him to see.

He could not comprehend the situation but he let me into the car. I explained to him that I was an amputee and that the foot of my artificial leg had broken off.

He brought me home and I told him that I would need to lean on his shoulder to negotiate the steps of our ground-floor flat which he gladly permitted. Fortunately, the Artificial Limb Centre gives all amputees a reserve leg just to meet such types of contingencies, so I did not have a problem once I got home.

During the summer holidays, the swimming pool at the DSOI used to be full of children and their parents. A chair used to be placed for me by the life guards, close to the entry point of the pool so that I could take off my leg before I dived into the pool. During the process of taking off my leg, all the noise and chatter around the pool would stop and I knew that all eyes were staring at me – this strange man with a removable wooden leg!

It still continues to be slightly embarrassing. However, I have to decide whether I want to swim or be bothered what people think about amputees like me. Now, as also in those days, I would ignore their curiosity and would dive into the pool and swim all the strokes that I knew, including the butterfly stroke to show that I was not something of an anachronism. Disabled persons are like that! We have to continuously prove that we are as good as the best among equals, if not better! I used to do about ten lengths and then take a break. That was the time that parents would come to me and ask, 'Would you please teach my child to swim?'

It gave me great satisfaction to teach many young boys and girls to swim and many years later these boys and girls, now parents themselves, bring their children to me and say, 'Do you remember me, sir? You taught me to swim so many years ago?'

I had requested that I be given command of 'Four Five', the battalion with which I had fought the 1965 and the 1971 wars and where I had lost my leg. But there was no vacancy there and so, I was posted to 'First Five', which had fallen vacant in January 1978, and that was equally good.

'First Five' was my first love because it was the battalion into which I was commissioned and where I had learnt all that I needed to know about the regiment and the rudiments of soldiering. I was returning to them after sixteen long years and no one there knew me except Major Emanuel Dewan, the 2ic who was officiating as the CO, and Subedar Major Deobahadur Pun, who had joined the battalion along with me in 1958. To reiterate, 'First Five' was a celebrated battalion of our regiment, with four Victoria Crosses and many battle honours and gallantry awards. At that time, the battalion was taking part in a Command exercise in the Rajasthan desert.

I had been informed that the CO, Lieutenant Colonel Vinod Badhwar had been promoted and had to take over a brigade. There was a delay in my replacement at Military Operations Directorate and I couldn't leave until I had handed over properly. Handing and taking over of appointments is considered an important duty in the army, where the new incumbent is briefed very thoroughly on his duties and this normally takes four days. However, my delay would break the chain of assumption of office of a whole lot of other officers, so Lieutenant Colonel Badhwar moved to take over his appointment and consequently was not able to hand over to me.

On 16 January 1978, I was met at the railway station by Subedar Major Deobahadur Pun and I reached the battalion late in the evening.

When I reached the battalion, the officers were in the mess which was a dugout in the sand. I had taken two bottles of Scotch whiskey to celebrate my return to the battalion but the reception was cold. The officers probably thought that they had been saddled with a commanding officer with a wooden leg who would be a burden rather than an asset to the battalion. The conversation was strained. When we broke off from the mess, I asked what the programme was for the next day.

Major Dewan said, 'Sir, tomorrow we are going on a 40-kilometre route march. We march off at 5 a.m. There will be a jeep for you.'

Frankly, I was taken aback. I had been doing 6-7 kilometres every morning at Delhi, but 40 kilometres on sand with a wooden leg, was a tall order. Nevertheless, I said nothing and went to my tent. Belbahadur Pun, my batman, faithful and loyal like all Gorkhas, was waiting to receive instructions from me for the next day. I apologized for keeping him waiting and asked him to prepare my web equipment[2] which I had brought along. He told me it wouldn't dry by the morning but I told him to do it up regardless, and asked him to wake me up at 4 in the morning.

I had not trained for a 40-kilometre march in the desert but I had been projecting all along that battle casualties were as good as able-bodied officers and now I had to prove the point. I could not do that by sitting in a jeep while the rest of the battalion marched on foot. This was my first test on arrival in the battalion and the test had come sooner than expected. If I sat in that jeep, it would negate all that I had been proclaiming all these years. It would also confirm what I thought were doubts in the minds of the officers, that I was not physically fit to command the battalion.

I told myself that I needed to face up to the challenge. If I could not do the march, then I would have to acknowledge that the doubts of the officers were right and I had no right to command 'First Five'. It was an unpleasant thought but it was a fact that I had to face.

At 5 a.m. the next morning, I took the report from Major Dewan that the battalion was ready to march off. He reported the number of officers, JCOs and other ranks that were on parade. It was a cold January morning in the desert, dark with only the stars in the sky.

After giving me the report, Major Emmanuel Dewan said, 'Sir, a jeep is waiting for you.'

I replied, 'That's all-right Emmanuel, I will march.'

He said, 'Sir, will you please come in the jeep?'

Everyone was listening, as voices carry far in the silence of the desert.

I decided that it was time to assert myself, so I said, 'Emmanuel, who is commanding the battalion, you or me?'

'You, sir,' he said.

'Right then, break off the jeep. I don't want it following me around. Give me an NCO from the Intelligence Section,[3] a map and a compass and give orders for the march to commence.'

Emmanuel passed the necessary orders and the battalion marched off with me marching at the head of the column. After a while I started trailing behind.

We had started at a few minutes past 5 a.m. After an hour, the battalion had gone ahead of me and in accordance with the laid down drill, had stopped for a brief break for the men to adjust their equipment. While they were taking this break, I crossed them.

Years later, I heard that when I crossed the battalion during that break, the men began asking, '*Buro lai ke bhayo?*' which means, 'What's happened to the old man?'[4] And they were told, 'He's got only one leg but he's marching'.

That was all right with me.

I was averaging about 4 kilometres an hour and that was not too bad. The good part was that although it was tiring and the day was hot, I was managing quite well but I also knew that if I stopped and took a break, I might have a problem with my stump.

The fear that I might not be able to complete the march gradually ebbed away and I began to feel a surge of confidence that if 40 miles in the desert was not a problem, then nothing could stop me. I began to understand the meaning of the word 'empowerment'!

After ten hours of marching non-stop, I could see the grove of trees on the edge of the desert where the battalion transport had arrived to pick us up. When I reached the grove, the adjutant gave me the report that the officers and men had just finished their meal and the battalion was ready to be marched off. I was glad that I had not kept the men waiting for their meal. I was also glad that I was able to prove to myself and the battalion that I was prepared to face all challenges to do all and everything that a commanding officer was required to do.

The exercise carried on and the battalion did exceedingly well. It had retained its flair for doing well at any task that was assigned to it. The 5th Gorkhas wear the chinstrap of their Gorkha hats under their lip rather than under the chin to signify their 'we do more and talk less'.

After about one more week in the desert, we returned to Thiruvananthapuram in Kerala, which was where the battalion was located. The brigade to which we belonged came directly under a Command Headquarter and there was no division or corps in between. We were left to ourselves with minimum interference. Professional and sport competitions were within the brigade and the best teams were sent to represent the Command at army competitions. The battalion therefore competed with itself and surprisingly we raised the level of our own professional competence and so it came to be that some of the Command teams were composed mainly of personnel from 'First Five'.

I held my first conference with the officers and told them what I expected from them and the areas where I expected the battalion to excel – professional competence, firing, physical fitness, boxing, football and cross country running.

We infused young blood into the teams and gave the old gladiators a rest. The football, boxing and cross-country teams were excused from PT and they trained instead to improve their competence in their respective fields.

I was lucky to have Major Dewan as my 2ic. He had been an instructor at Infantry School and had some very bright ideas about training. Thanks to him, well before the rest of the army switched to integrated weapon training, 'First Five' was well on its way to adapting this form of training as a matter of routine and soon became very good at it. Major Dewan took charge of the training of the football team, the unit cadres and the training of the specialist platoons. That gave me enough time to handle everything else.

The Brigade Commander, Brigadier NSI Narahari was the epitome of what a good commander should be. A paratrooper from the Bombay Engineers, he wore the maroon beret, a hallmark of the paratroopers, at a rakish angle that suited him well. He was physically tough, professionally competent, well read, and a friend of the battalion in every sense of the term. He spoke with an easy drawl and had an excellent sense of humour. He laid down his key result areas and left it to the commanding officers to come up to the high standards he demanded. He integrated himself with the unit in training, games and in our leisure activities. Firm when required, but humane and considerate when it mattered, he was more of a friend than a commander. During games, he was with us playing tennis, squash and basketball. At our barakhanas[5] he drank, sang and danced with the men and they loved it. The men would do anything he asked, but he had no demands. The battalion would have loved to go with him into battle.

He made no special concessions for me. And that is exactly what I or any other battle casualty would have wanted.

Many years later, General Narahari was commanding a corps in the Northeast, and the Chinese made the mistake of intruding into an area of his responsibility at a place called Sumdarongchu. Never at a loss to take decisions, he had the Chinese troops surrounded by the 3rd Battalion of the 5th Gorkha Rifles, and forced them to withdraw. The Chinese, who were used to delayed responses from India, were taken by surprise. General Narahari, however, was not one to look over his shoulder for decisions from higher headquarters. When asked why he acted on his own, he stated that this was his area to protect and he did not need permission from anyone else to do his duty.

He won the hearts and minds of every officer and soldier of the corps that he commanded. I think he would have made a great army chief, but regrettably age came in his way.

Unfortunately, my tenure under his command turned out to be just about a year because the battalion was posted out to Northern Command.

Prior to our departure from Thiruvananthapuram, the officers and families of the battalion went for our last picnic to Kovalam Beach. We invited the officers of the Brigade Headquarters and their families to join us. It was the month of June, just before the monsoon struck Kerala. The children were playing where the waves hit the shore. The lifeguards told us to keep an eye on the children as they themselves were moving elsewhere on duty.

After a while, we suddenly heard a shout for help and we saw one of our children – a twelve-year-old boy – being dragged into the sea by the backwash of a massive wave. Fortunately, he knew how to float, but the tide was moving out and he was being rapidly carried out to sea by the undertow. It appeared that no one had the ability to venture into the sea to bring him back. I knew that I was a reasonably good swimmer but I could not swim with my wooden leg. So, I took my leg off and I took the help of two young officers to launch myself into the sea. By this time Ravi, for that was the boy's name, had gone quite some distance. I swam rapidly to him aided by the speed of the outgoing tide. Ravi was floating on his back and naturally quite afraid. I swam up to him and told him not to try and catch hold of me because if he did, both of us would go down. I reassured him and told him not to panic and that as long as I was with him, he was safe.

'Yes, uncle', is what he managed to say. There was an outcrop of rocks that extended into the sea and if we reached there, he would be safe. Although the waves in the open sea were not as rough as on the shore, Ravi was finding it difficult to keep his face above the roll of the waves. I was worried that if a wave rolled over his face, he would choke and cling onto me and take us both down, so I used both my hands to support him to keep his face above the waves. That gave me the thrust of only one leg to push him towards the rocks. If we missed those rocks, we would have been taken out into the open sea. And then the only way we could be saved was for a boat to come out to rescue us. There were no boats on the shore. I said a silent prayer to help us reach those precious rocks. I don't know how, but after about ten long minutes, with God's grace, we were able to reach the last few rocks of the rocky outcrop and Ravi managed to clamber on top of them. But I could not follow him there because of my leg. Meanwhile, his father, who was away during this whole drama, arrived with the lifeguards, running across the rocky promontory and took him to safety. His mother and the rest of the officers and their families were watching from the shore with bated breath.

Now I had to swim back to shore against the strong current of a tide that was running out to sea and I was tired. A large crowd had gathered on the shore. It took me a long time to swim against the tide and to reach reasonably close to the shore. I had to be helped to get out of the water and many amongst the crowd were astonished to see that I had only one leg. Amongst the crowd was also a group of journalists and they all wanted a story. I told them that there was no story to tell. Maybe I was wrong. A story about the rescue of a boy by an army officer would have done the army some good and also strengthened the cause of disabled persons within the army and in the world at large.

A major tragedy was avoided and the incident put paid to whatever misgivings that some of the officers may still have had, about a one-legged commanding officer. This incident proved, beyond a shred of doubt, that I was better than them, at least in this respect. Am I being arrogant or conceited? I don't know. It is just that disabled people like me have to continually re-invent ourselves and prove that we are not that helpless and incapable. So, when we do something that others can't do, it makes us feel vindicated and empowered.

A week later, a military special[6] was designated to take the battalion from Thiruvananthapuram to Pathankot in Punjab and we would be on our way to move from the southernmost railhead of the country to its northernmost terminus, on our way to our destination in Jammu & Kashmir.

We decided to make it a memorable experience. The children were in the middle of their summer holidays, so I wrote to the new Formation Commander and asked for permission to bring the families along with me. I received a reply that the rules did not permit families to join their husbands until the unit had completed six months in location and the officers and men had become well-versed with their operational tasks.

This was understood and accepted by all of us, and some of our officers asked for permission to drop off their families at home. As school was still six weeks away, I suggested that they spend more time with the battalion and their families and travel on the military special. I could take the battalion to its new location with the Adjutant, the Quartermaster and the bachelors, and they could peel off, along with their families from the military special, at a station closest to their homes and join the battalion thereafter. They readily agreed.

Travel by a military special is a unique experience. The train is composed of coaches for unit personnel, and railway wagons for equipment and stores. In addition to the railway engine in the front and the guard's compartment at the back end, there were coaches for the unit Quarter Guard, the MI Room, the Rifle Companies, the Battalion Office, the Officers' Mess, the JCOs' Mess, and the Unit Canteen. Six railway wagons served as the company kitchens.

Communication within the train between the Battalion Headquarters and the rest was through field telephones[7] and the battalion continued to carry out its functions like it would anywhere else.

Unless there is a war on, all mail and express trains get priority over military specials; and the journey in a military special meanders slowly over time and distance. Wherever possible, the train would halt in the morning and the men would tumble out of the train for P.T.

At railway stations where the special was scheduled to halt for filling of water tanks and charging of the batteries, the men would get off the train and guards with fixed bayonets would take position in front of every carriage, all on the call of bugles. The people at the stations would stare wide-eyed at how the men quickly fell in and out of position and went about their duties with silent clockwork precision.

At these stations, the children would get hosed down with water for their baths amid much laughter and merriment. A railway journey in a military special is a break from the tough training routine for the soldier. In the evenings one could hear the singing of Nepali songs, as the beat of the *madal*[8] tried to outdo the sound of the clackety clack of the train on its tracks.

It had taken us six days to complete our journey from Thiruvananthapuram to Pathankot. Our vehicle convoy stopped at Jammu to have tea with 'Four Five', which was located there. Our new Brigade Commander had come down to Jammu and met us in the lines of 'Four Five'. He welcomed us and asked me, 'Where are the families?' It was a strange question because he had written to me that families were not permitted for the next six months! It put me in an awkward position so I said, 'But sir, I wrote to you and you said that they could not come for the next six months.'

There was an awkward pause and he covered up by saying, 'Oh yes, I forgot!' He did not seem to be happy with my reply.

It was getting dark by the time we entered the area allotted to us and we got busy settling down. I was going around the unit location, when I received a message that the Commander wished to speak with me. I went to the nearest unit phone and told the Adjutant to speak to the Brigade Major (BM)[9] to pass a message to the Commander that unless it was operationally important, I would call the Commander as soon as I was free. After an hour I phoned the Brigade Commander and asked to speak with him.

'Yes?' he said.

'Good evening sir. You wished to speak with me.'

'That was more than an hour ago.'

'Sir, I had a message passed to you through the BM that I was busy but would come immediately if it was urgent and important.'

'Understand one thing. When I call you, I expect you to answer me quickly. Is that clear?'

'Yes sir.'

I waited for him to tell me why he wanted to speak to me and what was so important.

'What is it that you wanted to tell me, sir?'

'It's too late now.' He said and put the phone down, making it quite obvious that what he wanted to tell me was neither urgent nor important. Although it would be wrong to compare one commander with another, as each officer has his own strengths and weaknesses, I could not help comparing him in my mind with Brigadier Narahari.

The next day, before first light, I went to the forward companies who were manning positions on the Line of Control to be with them before morning 'stand to' and to check whether they knew their operational tasks. After I had visited the companies in the forward area, I had got back to my office around 11 a.m. My office was in a tent.

Around that time, a runner[10] was sent to me by the Subedar Major who passed on a message to say that the Brigade Commander was moving around in the Unit Lines and could I please come.

I sent a message back to the Subedar Major through the runner that the Brigade Commander was welcome to roam around in the lines but that I would not come.

The runner ran off and gave my message to the Subedar Major.

The Brigade Commander asked the Subedar Major about

why I had not come and what I had said.

The Subedar Major gave the Commander a smart salute and said in Hindi. 'Saab, CO Saab has said that he will not come.'

I am not aware what the Brigade Commander said and I have never asked, but he drove quickly to my office and stopped in front of my tent in a cloud of dust. I saw the flag and red star plate, indicating that it was the Brigade Commander's jeep, so I put on my beret and walked up to him. He continued to sit in his jeep.

I saluted and said, 'Good morning sir. Welcome to the battalion.'

He looked at me in anger and said, 'Did you not receive a message that I was in your lines?'

'Yes sir. I did.'

'Then why did you not come?'

'Sir, if you choose to visit my unit lines without informing me, I will not come. If you wish to visit my unit, do please inform me and I will be there to receive you and take you around.'

The Brigade Commander looked at me in astonishment, 'You are the limit. I have never met anyone like you before.'

'There's always a first time sir,' I answered.

With that, the Brigade Commander drove away in disgust and I returned to my office.

I reproached myself at not having started my relationship with the Brigade Commander on the right note. It was not good for the battalion or me. However, there are certain norms in dealing with a CO and I expected to be treated as such. I was not prepared to be bullied for no reason or to be cowed down. Commanders at all levels have the appellation of '*Tiger*' and I was not prepared to degrade the office of a CO and behave like a mouse.

Those days, we trained hard and played hard. We built

short ranges in the company defended localities and a long range across the DCB (ditch-cum-bund)[11] and the men practiced firing by day and by night.

Meanwhile, the Commander of the Pakistani unit opposite us asked for a flag meeting to protest against our firing on the long range across the DCB. I asked for permission to meet him and after permission was granted, we met in his area of responsibility, across the Munawar Tawi, a small river, which meandered across both sides of the Line of Control.

The Pakistani CO objected to our firing on the long range that we had constructed forward of our DCB. He claimed that stray rounds had caused damage to his defences.

I asked, 'What damage?'

He gave some vague answer. I told him I would like to come and see for myself what damage we had caused, knowing full well that he would never allow me to come close to his defences. Of course, he protested vehemently and said in no way would he allow me to see the damage that he claimed we had caused.

I told him that I was well within my rights to train in my own area and in view of what he had said, I would take extra precautions to build wider retaining walls to prevent a stray round from crossing into his area.

'Anything else?' I asked.

He replied that in that case, he too would build a range and carry out firing in the same manner.

I said, 'You are most welcome because if we ever go to war, I would like to be faced with a worthy opponent. You are welcome to build a range but you too should ensure that your rounds should not come our way.'

Fortunately, he had a sense of humour and laughed; we had a cup of tea together and the matter ended there.

Some months later, we were informed of a test exercise for the brigade that would involve crossing a water obstacle.

I took it to be similar to crossing a DCB and we set about working out our drills, using our own DCB as a model to carry out our training. Gorkhas love to train and we applied our minds, evolving methods to cross a water obstacle in the fastest and best possible manner. While we were training, the neighbouring Battalion Commander visited us to see what we were up to. He told me not to take this exercise so seriously and that he had done a similar exercise the previous year in the same area and that from the safety point of view, we would have to cross an existing canal that was dry. I told him that I was preparing my battalion for its operational tasks and if the exercise was meant to train us for war, then I would continue to train to meet such a contingency.

The day of the exercise drew near and prior to the scheduled date, it rained incessantly for three days and three nights. The dam that fed all the canals in the region opened its sluice gates and all the canals now had water in them. The particular canal that we had to cross was about 20 feet wide, had water up to a depth of 10 feet and a current of about two to three knots.

The brigade had to undergo an approach march of about 6 kms and 'First Five' and the neighbouring battalion – the two forward battalions – hit the canal at about midnight. The exercise enemy was doing its best to prevent the crossing but the two companies of 'First Five' crossed successfully whereas the battalion on our left, which had taken the practice for crossing such an obstacle lightly, could not cross.

The Corps Commander and the Divisional Commander, who were watching the progress of the exercise, conferred with the umpires and the exercise was 'frozen' for a while until the Brigade Commander who was being tested, could work out a solution.

There was only one solution – the battalion that had

already put two companies across could be asked whether it could put two more companies across – that battalion was 'First Five'.

The Brigade Commander conferred with his staff and the umpires and came across to me to ask if I could put two more companies across the obstacle. All my companies had practiced this role and were well versed with crossing such a water obstacle.

I confirmed that my remaining two rifle companies could cross but the role of the battalions in the exercise would have to change and appropriate orders would need to be given by the brigade. This was done, and my remaining companies crossed and the exercise was able to proceed to its logical conclusion.

At that time, annual confidential reports were not shown to the officers who were reported upon. Apparently, the Brigade Commander gave me a poor report with just average marks in 'adaptability' and uncomplimentary remarks in the pen picture regarding my flexibility and maturity. I was lucky, however, that both the Corps Commander and the Divisional Commander were witness to the battalion's performance on the exercise and reports were called for, which showed that the battalion had topped almost all professional competitions and sports competitions in the division. It was also highlighted that the battalion also stood first amongst all the units of the division in firing, that too, by a huge margin. The Brigade Commander's report was set aside as being biased. I only learnt about this many years later.

Around this time, the Brigade Commander and the Divisional Commander had both changed and the new GOC of the division was from the 1st Gorkhas. He happened to be one of the instructors at the NDA from my squadron when I was a cadet. Soon after his arrival, the final of the divisional football competition was organized. One of the battalions from his regiment, the 1/1 Gorkha Rifles and our battalion the 1/5 Gorkha Rifles had qualified for the finals. 1/1 Gorkha Rifles had a strong and experienced team with players who had been part of teams at the Command and Services levels. The 1/5 Gorkha Rifles team consisted of young players who had consistently trained under Major Dewan from Thiruvananthapuram days but had no tournament experience.

The Divisional Commander was known for his wry sense of humour. He came to watch the match and before it started asked me who would win.

I said, 'Both teams are good, sir. The better team will win.'

He said, 'Are you being diplomatic?'

'Yes sir,' I answered.

'Hmm, we will see.'

I had instructed the officers to tell the men that we should not go overboard irrespective of whether we won or lost – we should be sober if we won and dignified if we lost.

The match started and our team appeared to be no match for the experienced 1/1 Gorkhas. They were the first to score and they put in one more goal a short while later. By half time, we were losing and the score was 2-0. The GOC appeared to be quietly confident that his team would win and said, 'Never mind Ian, this is an opportunity for the 5th Gorkhas to learn lessons from their seniors.'

No one had taken into consideration the fact that the 1/1 GR team consisted of veteran gladiators and the 1/5 GR team consisted of energetic young soldiers. During the second half it was clear that the opposing team had run out of steam and was slowing down whereas our team was still full of energy and vigour.

Towards the end of the second half, our team slammed in three goals one after another and we won in an exciting finish. Our Johnnies were delirious with joy and some of them were doing cartwheels on the side lines. I was embarrassed but also proud in the manner that Emmanuel and his boys had played to fashion such a brilliant victory. Emmanuel was carried off the football field by the boys and I was glad that he could savour the triumph of his hard work of the past two years.

My two-and-a-half years with the battalion ended all too soon. Command of my battalion was a dream that had come true. It is the ambition of every infantry officer to command his own battalion and I was especially lucky to be able to command the battalion where I started life in the army. Handing over of command has its own rituals and procedures and Priscilla came from Delhi to be with me at this significant moment in my life as Commanding Officer of the battalion. It was fortuitous that I was handing over to an officer of the unit who had been approved to take over from me.

Handing and taking over of the battalion starts and ends with a visit to the Unit Mandir so that the event can be blessed by the deity that presides over the unit's fortunes in war and peace. Gorkha units have Goddess Durga as the presiding deity and the battalion pandit invokes the goddess' blessings on incoming and outgoing COs.

The Indian Army is an institution where every religion is respected and units and formations that have a composition of mixed communities have a 'Dharam Sthal' – a place of worship that has a mandir, masjid, gurdwara and girja ghar in close proximity, and every important religious festival is given its due importance. In single community units however, like the Gorkhas, there is only the mandir. Sunday mornings have the rank and file in the mandir; being together in the mandir on a Sunday morning is not only a ritual but also a parade. As a Christian officer, I go to the mandir at the appointed time and then to the church in my own time, because religion is a personal matter.

Hindus, Muslims, Sikhs, Christians, and persons of every religious denomination of the Indian Army have fought shoulder to shoulder in trusting comradeship and it is this faith and trust in each other that fashions victory in war. It needs to be remembered that in the 1971 War, the Army Chief was a Parsi, the Eastern Army Commander a Sikh, the Chief of Staff who was responsible for the strategy on the Eastern front was a Jew, the Director of Military Operations was an Anglo Indian and three of the Infantry Divisional Commanders leading the assaults were Christians. It is this unity in diversity that has strengthened the bonds of Indian soldiers in all the wars that we have fought before and after Independence and have resulted in unprecedented performances of officers and men.

Whereas the first event in the handing/taking over of a unit is a visit to the mandir, the regimental dinner is the last event of the last day for the outgoing CO. In a peace station this is an elaborate affair but we were in an operational area, and so we had an informal dinner at the mess. It was a strange feeling to be a guest in my own mess where I had always been the host. It would be the last meal that I would have with the officers and families of 'First Five' as its CO. Priscilla was there also as families could be present on the occasion. It was a sentimental moment for me and the culmination of a hard struggle to command my own unit and I found it hard to accept that I would no longer be its CO.

Priscilla's last event was her visit to the Family Welfare Centre. She loved being with the Gorkha women and children. She knew the names of all the Gorkha children. She made a special effort to learn each name and even now after so many years, when we visit the unit for regimental get-togethers, she calls them by their first names and the families clap and cheer her for her recall. They are not aware, however, of the tremendous effort that is involved in making them feel so remembered.

Emmanuel Dewan was still my 2ic and, in his own inimitable way, recalled our association of past years when we were both young officers in NEFA and the days of my tenure as the CO. It was a sentimental moment for both of us as well as for Priscilla and I choked with emotion when I gave my after-dinner farewell speech. The dinner ended with my being lifted and thrown into the air to the tune of 'He's a Jolly Good Fellow' and Priscilla was worried that I would fall, but I didn't.

The next morning, we paid our last visit to the mandir – this time Priscilla and I were on our own – for the application of 'Tika' and then to mount the jeep which would be hauled by the officers and men to signal my final departure from the unit.

Although I would always belong to them and be part of the family of 'First Five', I was painfully aware that this was the end of my being so close to them. Some of the happiest days of my life in the army were spent with the officers, JCOs and men of 'First Five'. It was a wrench to leave them but we have learned to live with it and Priscilla and I visit them as often as we can. Each time we return, it continues to feel like home.

'First Five' has continued to do extremely well. It is the only infantry battalion in the Indian Army at this point of time that has been awarded the Chief's 'Unit Citation' four times.[12] This award is the equivalent of a battle honour and is given to units for outstanding performance in counter terrorism, counter insurgency and other actions in ensuring security of the nation in times 'other than war'. In the year 2020, it was awarded the distinction of being the best battalion in the division in which it serves.

Notes

1. Defence Services Officers' Institute.
2. Equipment that soldiers use when going into operations. The equipment facilitates the carriage of a weapon, ammunition and basic items required for war.
3. Intelligence Section – a small unit of men that is the unit's pathfinder, collators of information about terrain and enemy dispositions, and of assistance to the Commanding Officer and the company commanders with regard to acquisition of intelligence.
4. 'Old man' is the appellative given worldwide to commanding officers of units and formations.
5. A meal with the men when the menu is special. A barakhana is held to commemorate an event or a festival. In Gorkha battalions there would be much singing and dancing.
6. A military special is a train which carries an army unit to its destination. It carries all its personnel, its weapons and equipment less its mechanical transport.
7. A field telephone is a metal box-like contraption with a handle. When rotated, it generated an electrical impulse on a switchboard which was picked up by the switchboard operator who put the caller through to the subscriber the person wished to talk to. Speech was through a handset common to all telephones.
8. A Nepali drum that beats out the rhythm for Nepali songs and dances.
9. One of the principal staff officers to a Brigade Commander.
10. A runner is a soldier who conveys a verbal or written message when other means to communicate are not available.
11. A Ditch-cum-Bund is a man-made artificial obstacle consisting of a wide ditch with embankments (bunds) on both banks to restrict the movement of enemy armour and infantry.
12. A para commando unit – 6 Para – has won it six times and 9

Rashtriya Rifles has won it four times but being permanently located in an area where counter terrorist operations are the norm, they are always in operations; whereas infantry battalions are involved in such operations only when posted to such operational areas.

CHAPTER ELEVEN

Brigade, Division and Chief of Staff of a Corps

You have enemies? Good! That means you've stood up for something in your life.
WINSTON CHURCHILL

When I was about to complete command of 'First Five', I was approved by the promotion board for the rank of Colonel. Since my tenure in command was about to end, I requested for a posting to an operational area. Appointments for colonels during those days were not too many and the appointment of deputy commanders of brigades was something that had started a few years earlier and I was not too convinced about the usefulness of this appointment. Posting on a staff appointment in an operational area is what I was hoping for, but towards the end of 1980, I was posted as the Deputy Commander of the same brigade in which I had served as a

Battalion Commander. The brigade and the battalion were co-located.

Frankly, I felt that the appointment of 'Deputy Commander' was an incongruent appointment that interfered with the relationship between the Brigade Commander and his staff and between him and the commanding officers of the battalions. Now that I was posted into an appointment that I had considered redundant, I found it difficult to work out just how I could fit in and be part of the brigade team. I decided to keep a low profile.

The Brigade Commander apparently had been thinking about this himself and asked me to take on operational planning and training, which I was glad to accept. I had my own ideas on these two aspects but made sure that I discussed it all with the Brigade Commander and got his approval before it was passed down to the battalions. Gradually, he gave me more and more responsibilities. That was fine with me. I made sure that I did not get between him and his battalion commanders, one of whom was the officer who had taken over the battalion from me. It was not comfortable to have my own battalion to deal with and I was careful to keep my place and my distance.

However, circumstances did not allow me to keep away from decisions that involved my battalion to the detriment of both my battalion and me.

I happened to be the officiating Brigade Commander when the finals of the brigade inter-battalion boxing competition took place. 'First Five' and another battalion were tied for honours after the last bout. It was generally understood that the trophy would therefore be shared. However, having boxed at the academies, I knew that there was a rule that decided who would be declared the winner if there was a tie. The rule said that in case of a tie the team which had won more bouts in the heavier weights would be declared the winner.

Now everyone knew that Gorkhas do not have fighters in the heavier weights and I could have kept my mouth shut, but that was not possible. As the Officiating Commander, I knew I had to do what was right irrespective of the fact that my own battalion would be at a disadvantage. I asked the judges and the commanding officers to refer to the Services Sports Control Board (SSCB) book that has a rule for every possible contingency. What I knew was confirmed and the other battalion was declared the winner! This was probably the first time that 'First Five' lost a boxing competition at brigade level!

I spoke to the Commanding Officer and the Subedar Major and explained the issue to them. Gorkhas have a very strong understanding of fair play and they accepted my stand. Nevertheless, it was an uncomfortable situation which I wish could have been avoided.

As I went about learning my job as Deputy Commander, the Brigade Commander began to trust me implicitly and I honoured his trust. During the summer holidays, Priscilla and the boys joined me from Delhi and the Brigade Commander's family and mine became very close. That friendship has remained to the present day.

Another two years passed and by 1982 I had caught up with my coursemates and my board for promotion to Brigadier was held along with the rest of my batch. When the results were out, the MS, who happened to be my company commander in 'First Five', rang me up to congratulate me on my being approved for promotion to Brigadier.

I thanked him and asked him if the postings had also been decided.

He said, 'It will take some time before we decide on the postings but as far as you are concerned, we have decided to post you as Commandant of the Gorkha Recruiting Depot at Kunraghat.'

I was taken aback as I was hoping for command of a brigade if I was approved. So, I said, 'Why sir? Is it because I have only one leg?'

'Ian, don't be stupid. Existing rules do not permit disabled officers to command brigades and in any case, no precedent exists where a disabled officer has ever been given command of a brigade.'

'Sir, if I could command a battalion in peace and field, what is the problem with giving me command of a brigade?'

The MS put the phone down. He probably thought that I would be grateful that I had been approved for promotion and here was I demanding command of a brigade!

I decided to take up the matter immediately before the posting order to Kunraghat was issued. My application would have to go through proper channels and that meant it would go through the brigade, division, corps and command along with the recommendations of the commanders of these formations and finally the Army Chief and that would take time! I have a general idea of what I said in my application. I kept it short and to the point. Briefly I said something like this:

My dear Chief,

I have the honour to inform you that I have been approved for promotion to the rank of Brigadier.

It however appears that MS Branch has some issues with regard to giving me command of a brigade on account of my being physically disabled. I am a battle casualty of the 1971 Indo–Pak War.

They state that no precedent exists to give command of a brigade to a physically disabled officer.

Sir, I would like to submit that higher levels of physical fitness are required in lower ranks, and if I could command

*a battalion successfully in peace and field then there is no
reason why I cannot command a brigade.*

*I have stayed on in the army basically for the privilege
of command of troops and I request Sir, that my promotion
is not made effective, till this matter is decided. I hereby
submit an 'Adverse Career Certificate' to state that I will
not represent if in the process, officers junior to me are
promoted ahead of me.*

Yours faithfully
Colonel Ian Cardozo

Here again, I was lucky! The Army Chief was General
Krishna Rao, who was the GOC of the division under whom
'Four Five' had served during the 1971 War.

General Rao apparently saw the logic and relevance of
my application and sent for the MS. Many years later, after
both the MS and I had retired, the MS told me that the Chief
had said: 'What he says makes sense! If he can command an
infantry battalion, there is no reason why he can't command
a brigade. If there is no precedence, then create one! Where
is he now and when is he due for promotion to Brigadier's
rank?'

The MS told him that I was Deputy Commander of an
Infantry Brigade and that command of the brigade would soon
fall vacant. 'Then why can't you promote him in command of
the brigade where he is now?'

After a few months I was promoted in the same brigade. My
promotion to Brigadier in fact removed the last impediment
for promotion of all battle casualties to higher ranks.

After I got approved for promotion, Colonel 'Yogi
Sharma' who was senior to me and was at that time
Deputy Commandant of the IMA wrote me a letter that
said something like this: *'Thank you, Ian. Your promotion*

to Brigadier and approval for command of a brigade is great news! You are carrying us battle casualties on your shoulders.' He and I had been in adjoining rooms in MH Pune and had received our artificial legs from the Artificial Limb Centre around the same time. In the years to come, he was the first battle casualty to be promoted to Lieutenant General's rank and later to Army Commander. I have always had great regard for him and his words made me feel good. His promotion to Army Commander's rank was followed by Pankaj Joshi and Vijay Oberoi. Joshi retired as Director General of Mechanised Forces, and Vijay Oberoi retired as the Vice Chief of the Indian Army. However, it was my promotion to Brigadier that paved the way for promotion of battle casualties to higher ranks, and we wait for the day when a battle casualty will be promoted to Army Chief – the highest appointment in the Indian Army.

On assumption of command of the brigade, I gave out my areas of priority to the battalion commanders which included operational preparedness, physical fitness, professional competence, ability to shoot well and maintenance of our defensive infrastructure that included the DCB.

During my years in command of 'First Five' I had always taken my physical tests to remove any doubts that battle casualties would shirk from doing what was required of able-bodied officers. Now that I had assumed command of the brigade, the situation had not materially changed. Brigadiers also had to be physically fit and to be seen as such. When the time for the battalion physical tests drew near, I made it clear that I expected all to do the tests and to do them well.

One day after a conference at the Brigade Headquarters, the commanding officers of the battalions stayed behind, ostensibly for a cup of tea, and while we were chatting, they brought up the issue of the physical tests. They said that when they were young officers in their units, no CO ever did these tests, and asked me why should they be required to take them now that they had reached the same rank themselves.

I had anticipated this and was glad that they gave me an opportunity to respond. I said, 'It would be pointless, my telling you how important it is to keep physically fit. I will leave it to you to find your own way to do that. There will be plenty of opportunities for you to prove to your men that you are no less than them when it comes to endurance and that as their commanding officer you will set a personal example in physical fitness as with everything else. However, I would like you to know that I too have to a point to prove and this applies to me as well – in any case, I will be doing these tests, as I find the need to prove to myself that I am no less than anyone else. When I or anyone else inspects the battalion, I do not expect you to do the test but I do expect you to do the tests in your own time to satisfy yourself and your men that you are fit.'

My answer seemed to satisfy them. When an inspecting officer visited the unit, they needed to be seen as commanding officers. However, it was up to them to ensure that they kept themselves physically fit. They got the message. I don't think I was being unfair. Senior officers are required to be physically fit and commanding officers in particular need to set an example to their officers and men.

Two-and-a-half years in command of the brigade passed very quickly. We rehearsed our operational tasks till we knew every bit of ground of an area where our troops had fought in 1947–48, 1965 and in 1971. We trained hard, played hard, exercised and rehearsed in various contingencies, and also enjoyed doing what we did. We did well in professional competitions, and in sports and games. The brigade during my tenure had excellent battalions from the Marathas, the Madras Regiment, the Sikh Regiment, the Sikh LI and the Raj Rif with strong and valiant commanding officers.

Before I knew it, it was time to move on and I was posted in October 1984 as Dy MS (A) in MS Branch, Army Headquarters, an appointment which managed the career planning of all officers of the rank of colonels and below, except officers of the Medical and the Dental corps.

I was interviewed by the MS who told me that I should do what was right irrespective of pressure from various quarters especially when dealing with requests from senior officers. I asked him what I should do about such requests. He said that the only requests that could be entertained were those from officers in the chain of command or from the Colonel of the regiment/Colonel Commandant to which that officer belonged.

I was quite clear therefore on how to deal with such requests not realizing that I would, in the process, earn the displeasure of many senior officers.

Paradoxically, I was sometimes called by the MS to explain why I did not acquiesce to requests from senior officers and I had to remind him of his orders on the subject.

During my tenure in the MS Branch, I came up on the panel for the National Defence College. I was first on the panel. Someone, who was dealing with this matter, put up a case stating that an officer, who had been given an award, had already received the honour of being decorated and that the points that accrued from these awards should not count for his placement on the panel for the National Defence College. And so, the benefit of the points that accrued from two awards were removed and I did not go on the course.

Soon after, I was first on a panel to go as the Defence Advisor to France. Once again, another officer was selected, and I did not go.

As Dy MS (A), I did my best to do justice to those cases which had merit and tried to help all those who deserved to be helped. All cases were put up on file including those where a rule had to be broken – but the case had to be deserving and valid. I earned the displeasure of many but also the gratitude of those who were fairly treated.

Strangely, I lasted out my tenure not only with the first MS but two more! However, I had to pay for the way I carried myself in this appointment later on when I came under an officer who felt that I had been unresponsive to his requests. I had been brought up on 'doing what is right irrespective of the consequences' but sometimes it is tough to practice what you preach.

Finally, I was glad when my tenure in MS Branch ended and in early 1987, I was posted as Brigadier General Staff (BGS) XV Corps – an interesting professional appointment. The corps was responsible for areas bordering both Pakistan and China, a region important to India's strategic interests, including territories where the Indian Army had fought repeatedly in 1947–48, 1962, 1965 and 1971 and later on in 1999. It also encapsulates some of the most beautiful places in the world.

The history of Kashmir is redolent with the history of wars and battles of days gone by, and resonates with the clash of arms from generations ago to the present day. It was in these areas that Zorawar Singh, the great Dogra General led his armies to win great battles in his forays into Tibet. In this area also lies the Zanskar Valley in Kashmir which has a few villages of the 'Minaro' community, popularly known as the Brokpa tribe. Their distinct features of being tall and statuesque, with green eyes, high cheek bones and flawless skin are evidence of the fact that some of Alexander's soldiers settled here and the present inhabitants are the descendants of his army – of pure Aryan or Greek descent, untouched from those times.

It was here that 'The Great Game' was played out when Soviet Russia and Britain jockeyed to dominate the roof of the world and it was also here that the great cartographer Nain Singh mapped this uninhabited, desolate, icy wilderness, disguised as a sadhu counting the beads on his rosary when in actual fact, he was measuring and recording distances. His name remains on present-day maps acknowledging his contribution to the mapping of these unchartered wastelands. At the northwestern extremity of the corps,[1] the boundaries of India, China, Russia, Pakistan and Afghanistan are bound together by geographical contiguity in the vicinity of the great Pamir Knot and the Hindu Kush where the extension of the Western Himalayas meets the Pamirs of Soviet Russia, the Koh I Baba range of Afghanistan and the mountains of Chitral of Pakistan.

Kargil, Ladakh and areas north of the Indus and the indescribably beautiful valley of Kashmir formed part of this corps. Unfortunately, it circumscribed areas that became a bone of contention between India and Pakistan and between India and China. One of these involved the Siachen Glacier and there is a lot to be said about the background of the Siachen dispute.

I wrote about this briefly in my book *Param Vir – Our Heroes in Battle* and I think it is worth repeating here for the benefit of the reader:

> Siachen is a world apart. To those who have not been there, it would be difficult to conceive of its beauty or comprehend the brutal conditions under which men in uniform must continue to live and fight within its cold embrace. It is undoubtedly beautiful beyond words, in the pristine and primeval majesty of snow and rock and ice that caps the roof of the world.
>
> Time has carefully marked its passing in the serrations that countless centuries have etched on ancient rocks and within whose depths are concealed the fossils of fish and

plants and other aquatic organisms that were pushed from beneath the sea in the awful cataclysm that created the Himalayas millions of years ago. The snow and ice that cover these mountains – the icing of the cake, as it were – sparkle in scintillating hues of green and blue and white that make it breathtakingly beautiful. Breathtaking is apt, because at these formidable heights, there is not enough oxygen to even breathe. The Siachen Glacier is the second longest glacier in the world. Beneath the veneer of this bleak beauty lie menacing hazards that snatch away human lives if one is not careful. More lives are lost due to climate, crevasses, avalanches and altitude sickness than to war. Those who take these mountains lightly do so at their own peril.'

The Siachen area has unfortunately been a bone of contention between India and Pakistan for many years. The dispute is 'unfortunate' because it could perhaps have been avoided. The cause goes back to 1949. In the Karachi Agreement of 1949, representatives of both nations drew the Cease Fire Line across maps of Jammu and Kashmir from Munawar in the south to Khor in the north and thence 'North to the glaciers' through NJ 9842. Presumably when they came up to this glaciated wilderness of snow and ice, they stopped at NJ 9842 on the presumption that neither side would be interested in contesting an area where not a blade of grass grows and where even breathing is a problem.

Pakistan however, complicated the issue subsequently: first, by illegally ceding 5,180 square kilometres of Indian territory to China in the areas where the boundaries of India, Pakistan and China meet, thereby altering the geo-strategic importance of this area; and second by permitting and assisting a series of mountaineering and scientific expeditions in the area thus raising the issue of 'rights' in an area that did not belong to her.

Being aware of the cartographic ambiguity of 1949, the devious nature of certain powers and the turn events could take, the Indian Army became concerned at Pakistani activities in the area. Sometime in 1983, the Indian Army got wind of Pakistani plans to move physically into the area and in April 1984 took pre-emptive action and occupied the Saltoro Ridge that marks the western boundary of the glacier. Both sides now began jockeying for the occupation of an area of dominance in this harsh environment where climate, weather, ice and snow are more dangerous than enemy action.

I was fortunate to have Lieutenant General DSR Sahni and Major General Zaki as my immediate superiors. Not only were they very professional but also had outstanding character qualities. During my tenure as BGS of XV Corps, I had to frequently accompany the Corps Commander or the Chief of Staff to the Siachen Glacier. These trips to some of the posts were made by 'chopper' and were eye openers to the harsh conditions on the glacier. On one occasion, I was witness to what is known as a 'white out condition' which pilots experience because of spatial disorientation due to the terrain. One cannot distinguish between sky and ground, or the mountain sides left or right – everything white merges, and depth perception is impaired and if not for the indicators on the panels of the helicopter, one would not know whether one was flying level or otherwise!

The situation at the posts was tough. At times temperatures went as low as minus 52 degrees Celsius at heights varying from 18,000 to 21,000 feet. Eating was a problem because everything became harder than rock. Due to the ultra-violet rays of the sun, men turned several shades darker, and many suffered from snow blindness and pulmonary oedema. Without exception, every individual lost around fifteen to twenty kilograms after six months at these high-altitude posts. Oxygen at those rarified heights is low and acclimatization is necessary before anyone can be allowed to climb up to the posts. Casualties due to the effects of climate and weather when compared to the effects of warlike operations were in the ratio of 3:1. Personnel going on patrol had to be roped together because of crevasses. If an individual fell into a deep crevasse, chances of getting him out were virtually nil and the body of the soldier would gradually get sucked into the glacier and surface centuries later as the glacier moves at the infinitely slow pace of a few centimeters a year.

Pakistan repeatedly attacked our posts on the glacier and suffered very heavy losses. The bodies of those killed would get buried in snow and it was often months before the snow thawed sufficiently to allow their recovery. Bodies became blocks of ice and required about twelve of our men to carry one down the slopes on which they had been killed. Our men had to do this because we did not want the Pakistanis to come close to our defences and we handed over the frozen bodies at a point designated by us.

Frustrated by their inability to oust us from the glacier, the Pakistani President Zia-ul-Haq threatened to 'destroy India with a thousand cuts!' Four years from the date we occupied the glacier, the situation in the valley changed for the worse.

By the time I had finished two years as BGS, I was cleared for promotion to Major General. I was in need of a new leg and so I went to the ALC at Pune so that I would have no problems in assuming command of a division. As always, we had to be admitted at MH Pune, and one afternoon on my return from the ALC, the duty sister informed me that she had received a telephone call to say that I had been posted to the infantry division located at Akhnur in Jammu & Kashmir.

It appeared that I was destined to remain in the same area where I commanded a battalion and brigade.

The first sitrep (Situation Report) that I received on taking over the division in 1989, informed me that a large number of rounds of small arms ammunition had been fired that day against Pakistani positions. I was alarmed. I rang up the Col GS, the officer responsible for handling staff duties concerning operations, and the conversation ran something like this:

'What is going on? Is there a war on?' I asked.

The Col GS seemed mystified and said, 'No sir. Why do you ask?'

'I'm looking at today's sitrep which says that a large number of rounds were fired today in the division area.'

'Oh sir! That's normal. The Pakis keep firing and we have to respond.'

'Hmm, the sitrep does not reflect any casualties.'

'That's right, sir. There normally aren't any.'

'Their side or ours?'

'Both sides sir. If they had any casualties, we would know.'

'So, why do we fire?'

'Sir, the Pakis fire day in and day out. We need to respond.'

I was appalled because to me this was bad fire discipline!

'I see. Speak to me about this, first thing tomorrow morning.'

'Yes sir.'

The next day I asked for the sitreps of the past month and the ammunition expended was about the same each day.

I passed an order from that day onwards that commanders at every level would ensure that every round fired was fired for effect.

From then on though the Pakistani firing continued, we did not reply. After a while, they stopped firing and there was relative calm on the Line of Control.

I ordered all the battalions to have short ranges built at the posts and where possible a long range at the base and said that I would like to see ammunition used more constructively. My men did as I asked and I felt vindicated.

However, I had not reckoned with the warped mindset of the Pakistanis. After a couple of months of relative calm, one of our men was killed at one of our forward posts in the hill sector. It was a headshot wound and only one round was fired. It was obvious that it was the work of a sniper, and the post from which the round was fired was identified by the other sentries.

I asked for a chopper and within a couple of hours I was at the post. I asked the battalion commander to assemble all the troops who were not on essential duty. The mood appeared glum and despondent.

I explained to them the drawbacks of indiscriminate firing. Coming down to the current incident, I asked them what they intended to do about it.

The assembly was silent. Finally, a rifleman spoke up. He said, 'Saab, how can we do anything about this when you have directed that we should not fire back?'

I explained that this is not what I had said. I said that we must not fire indiscriminately and that for every round fired I wanted evidence that the round had been fired effectively. I asked him what that meant. The same rifleman asked, 'Sir, do you mean that for every round fired you want a dead Pakistani soldier?'

'Yes,' I said. 'What else could that mean?'

Explaining further, I said, 'However there has to be a reason to kill. We are not at war with Pakistan. But this behaviour is unacceptable and we must make them understand that.'

A havildar stood up and asked, 'Saab, can we raid their post?'

'No, that would involve intervention of higher headquarters and we need to find a response where we can act on our own,' I said.

Another rifleman raised his hand and said, 'Saab can we go forward?'

'Yes. However, we need to be cold and calculated in our response. They are on full alert now. We must wait and watch and choose our time and place to react. Go forward if necessary, but within our own defended area and build "hides" at night from where we can clearly observe their movements and routine. Then we need to strike. Get the best firers of your company to man those hides and I want it to be conveyed to the Pakistanis that we will take five for every one of ours that they may take.'

It was a good battalion, and it happened the way we wanted.

A day later, the opposite side asked for a flag meeting. We got permission from higher headquarter to attend.

The Pakistani officer pretending innocence asked, 'Why this sudden violence?'

Our representative explained the case of the sniper shot from the post opposite and said, 'You started it, and you need to accept the consequences. Be sure that if you start something, we will end it. We know how to play your game. If you take one of ours, we will take many more of yours because that is the only language that you understand.' The Pakistani officer understood that we meant what we said.

Whenever I had free time, I used to go around the divisional area studying the ground and talking to the locals. I used to move around in an open jonga with my driver, my runner and a radio operator, till one day the Corps Commander rang up and asked if I was going around the divisional area without an escort. When I responded in the affirmative, he said that I should stop. He had received information that the Pakistanis had information about this and might do something about it.

The division had both the International Border (IB) as well as the Line of Control within our area of responsibility. My orders were that both had to be dominated by us. In this we fully succeeded. However, one day when I returned from leave, I was told that the Pakistanis had constructed a post on the IB overnight. I checked and asked for an eight-figure grid reference[2] and was told that their post was right on the IB or one pencil point across it on a one-inch map in our area of responsibility. This I was not prepared to accept. The Brigade Commander was on leave. I went immediately to the brigade concerned and reviewed the situation.

I'm afraid I was very tough on the Deputy Commander of the brigade who was now the officiating commander. I asked for an explanation as to why this situation had arisen. He had no answer. I told him that there were only two options – one, that I order a Court of Inquiry, the outcome of which was a foregone conclusion and someone's head would roll. The other was that he did whatever I would order him to do.

The officer said he would do what I asked, although he had no idea what I had in mind. I told him that he would need to establish three posts. One post immediately in our own area, in front of the Pakistani post to distract them and to keep them engaged and occupied, and two posts behind the newly created Pakistani post.

'But sir, how can we cross the international border without orders?' he asked surprised.

'I am giving you an order and I am giving it to you in writing if that is what it takes. I want the "Pakis" to vacate this intrusion within 48 hours, otherwise you will have to answer for it. Unless, of course, you have a better solution.'

He thought about it for a full minute before agreeing to do as I said.

We sat down and worked out a plan and war gamed our responses depending on how the 'Pakis' reacted. We worked out various contingencies as we are taught in the army, except that I knew that we should also be prepared for an unforeseen contingency. After we had gone over all possible options, I left for the division headquarters. Early next morning I got a completion report that my orders had been carried out. I asked whether anti-personal mines had been laid as per my orders and been tied to allow for the possibility of a quick retrieval. It was confirmed that this also had been done. The positions across the IB were occupied by two excellent battalions of the Garhwal and Maratha regiments.

The next night I had turned in early and was woken up by a phone call around midnight. It was the Deputy Commander of the brigade. About fifteen to twenty Pakistani trucks had come close to the Pakistani defensive positions; the noise of stores being unloaded could be heard and he expected some action that night.

I now began to wonder about what I had started. Should I have reported this to the Corps Commander instead?

I decided, right or wrong, to fight my own battle. Just as I had told the Deputy Brigade Commander that he had to fight his own battle, it was now my turn to practice what I preached.

I alerted the Commander Artillery and the Squadron Commander of the armoured regiment that was in location and briefed them about the present enemy build up, told them to stand by and to be ready according to laid-down contingency plans. I asked for my jonga with the radio operator and drove quickly to the scene of action.

I reached the location just as dawn was breaking and saw two Pakistani platoons assembled forward of our two positions, threatening to assault our positions. A Pakistani officer or a JCO using a loud hailer demanded that we withdraw from our positions, failing which they would evict us.

It was a critical situation but we had anticipated this contingency. The JCO from the Garhwal battalion shouted, 'You are welcome to attack but remember that we are dug in. You are in the open and we have laid mines.' Then he shouted to his troops: 'Load!' This was followed by clatter of the loading of automatic weapons by our posts – the Garhwalis and the Marathas.

It was a tense moment, but the 'Pakis' understood that they were in a disadvantageous position and we meant business. The question was who would blink first.

The Pakistanis backed down.

A little while later a Pakistani brigadier accompanied by an officer carrying a white flag came asking for a meeting with our Brigade Commander. There was of course the Deputy Commander, officiating as the Brigade Commander, but I felt that the situation demanded my intervention before things got out of hand. I took off my badges of rank and accompanied by an escort went forward to meet the Pakistani Brigade Commander.

The Pakistani Brigade Commander saluted me and kept saying 'Sir'. I asked him why he was repeatedly calling me 'Sir'.

He replied, 'Sir, I know that you are the Divisional Commander.'

'How do you know?' I asked.

He smiled and said, 'We know!'

Getting down to business at hand, he said, 'How can we resolve this situation peacefully and quickly?'

'What do you mean "We?" You started this by building this post two days ago. Why did you do it?'

'Sir, we are commencing a very big exercise, not far from here and we just wanted to ensure that you would not have access to what was going on.'

I said, 'I know. *Zarb-i-Momin*, isn't it? This doesn't make sense! That exercise is taking place forty miles from here!'

'How do you know?'

It was now my turn to smile and say, 'We know,' and added, 'in any case, how would a post forty miles away from the exercise location help?'

'Those were my orders, sir. However, I have been directed to solve this problem and that we can demolish this post. However, will you please withdraw first?'

'That's ridiculous! You came first and you will have to go first.'

He repeated, 'These are my orders, sir.'

'Those maybe your orders. They don't apply to me!'

He considered the impasse for a while and then said, 'Can we withdraw simultaneously?'

I thought about it for a moment and thought it better to get them out rather than prolong the situation and said, 'OK, but understand that I am making a concession here and that next time, if there is one, I would not be so understanding!'

'I will have to get back to my headquarters. Do you have to consult with your higher headquarters?' he asked.

'No,' I said. 'I have the authority to deal with you on this issue.'

He left saying he would come back within an hour. But he took several hours and by the time he came back it was getting dark.

He apologized for the delay and said, 'Sorry sir. It took longer than I expected. However, my higher commanders have agreed to a simultaneous withdrawal. Can we please commence moving back to our original positions?'

'No. You have taken too much time to get a simple answer. It is now dark. We can commence withdrawing only after first light tomorrow morning,' I said, reviewing the situation.

He was surprised, and also upset. 'Sir, you gave me your word and now you are going back on your commitment. I will be in serious trouble if the withdrawal does not commence immediately!'

'I have not gone back on my word. I accepted a simultaneous withdrawal. It is you who told me that you would come back in an hour and you have taken four hours to get back. It is now dark and frankly I have no reason to trust you. Unless I see you across the Munawar Tawi, I cannot consent to do this today because it is now dark, and I will not be able to see whether you have left the area or not.'

The brigadier now got quite agitated and repeated that he would be in serious trouble if the withdrawal did not commence immediately.

I thought about it and said, 'OK, to save your skin, I will withdraw one section each from my forward troops so that you can report that the simultaneous withdrawal has commenced. However, the others will remain until I see you have gone away by first light tomorrow morning. And if you ever think of encroaching again be warned that I will have multiple posts built immediately across both the IB and the LOC.'

He thanked me, saluted and was gone. I do not remember his name. Next morning by first light we could see that they had demolished their post and had withdrawn across the Munawar Tawi, and we also commenced moving our troops back.

Just at that moment, I was told that there was a call from the Army Commander. I walked across to the field telephone. 'Yes sir. Ian Cardozo here. Good morning.'

'Hullo, Ian. Is there a problem in your area?'

'Yes sir – minor problem.'

'Minor problem? How can you say that? I have just been rung up by the Chief! He says that your division has crossed the International Border in two places. Is that true?'

'Yes sir. The Pakistanis had encroached into our area and I had to get them to go back.'

'So, what is the situation now? Do you need any help?'

'No, thank you sir. They have gone back.'

'They've gone back?'

'Yes sir, and we've also come back.'

'Good. Can I tell that to the Chief?'

'Yes sir. You can.'

'OK. Well done. However, you could have kept me informed.'

'I did, sir. Please see yesterday's sitrep.'

'OK. These guys out here did not show it to me! Good luck and take care.'

I went to the Officiating Brigade Commander and congratulated him and the troops for a job well done. I checked whether they had brought back the anti-personnel mines back and disarmed them. They confirmed that this had also been done.

I had stated in the previous evening's sitrep that Pakistan had encroached into our area across the IB and had given the grid reference on the map. I had reported that we had established three posts with the respective grid references. Having worked in MO Directorate, I knew that the duty officer would pin-point the locations on the map. When he found that we had crossed the IB, he immediately informed the GSO2 and the incident was reported rapidly from one level to another until it finally reached the Chief.

I could have reported the matter by a 'Flash' message but preferred to solve the problem on my own and I needed time to do that and fortunately, that is exactly how it happened.

On my way back, I was stopped by a DR (Despatch Rider) from the Corps HQ. He had been sent because some papers had to be signed by me. It was only then that I realized that I was the officiating Corps Commander!

The Corps Commander and the Chief of Staff were both on leave and neither of them had told me that I was the officiating Corps Commander! Anyway, it was just as well, because in any case I had acted on my own.

Some months later, the Army Commander met me at the Command Athletics meet, put his arm around my shoulder and took me to the Corps Commander saying, 'When you were away, Ian had an encroachment in his division but he resolved the problem immediately and on his own. He did a great job. I wish the other encroachments in the Command Zone could have been similarly resolved.'

The Corps Commander said, 'Yes sir, but he could also have started a war!'

It was obvious that all was not well between the Corps Commander and me, but I am not sure if the Army Commander noticed.

Based on my reports from the previous Corps Commander, I was posted as Chief of Staff of a corps in the Northeast in September 1990. I should have gone on the date I was supposed to move, but the Army Commander asked for a deferment of my posting until the passes had got snowed up. And so, I got one more report from the current Corps Commander to my detriment.

I reached the Corps Headquarters to which I was posted to on 31 December 1990 – the last day of the year. Assam was in turmoil with the ULFA (United Liberation Front of Assam) insurgence.

I met Lieutenant General Ajai Singh, the Corps Commander in his office the next day, on 01 January 1991. A kind and affable officer, he welcomed me and said, 'Ian, I am glad you have come at last. I had asked for you by name to be my Chief of Staff. You will eventually be taking over from me. Your tenure as Chief of Staff will be useful to you.

You will act on my behalf in all matters operational and administrative and come to me only when you feel the matter is beyond you. Then too, I am confident that you would have examined the issue from every angle and I will listen to what you have to say. You will always have my total support. I wish you a very happy stay as a member of my team.'

General Ajai Singh was in fact laying the groundwork on how I should conduct myself as his Chief of Staff. He believed in delegation of authority and in 'management by exception'. During the Indo–Pak War of 1971, he functioned as the regiment's 2ic as well as a Squadron Commander in the Battle of Basantar, where his unit, the Poona Horse, did exceptionally well under the command of Lieutenant Colonel Hanut Singh, who went on to become a famed and revered general. It was in this battle that Second Lieutenant Arun Khetarpal was awarded the Param Vir Chakra, India's highest award for courage in battle. General Ajai kept his finger on the pulse of his command and always knew exactly what was happening and intervened only when essential. Everyone responded to the trust that he reposed in them, and it was a pleasure to serve with him. He knew every officer by his first name and was a loved and respected Corps Commander.

The corps was responsible for the border with China and internal security of the whole of Assam. Luckily, at that time, the border with China was quiet and the focus was the control of the ULFA insurgency. The corps was fortunate to have Brigadier Vasant Srivastava as the Brigadier General Staff (BGS) and Colonel Rakesh Kumar Chaturvedi as the General Staff Officer (Operations) handling operations against the ULFA – both very capable, committed and efficient officers, leaving me with little to worry about.

The problem of the insurgency in Assam was the crisis caused by the illegal migration from East Pakistan and later from Bangladesh. The ULFA, who claimed to be the voice of the people of Assam, declared that this invasion from across the border had upset the demography of the state. They demanded the detection of these illegal migrants, their deletion from the voter's list and their deportation to where they came from.

The United Liberation Front of Assam was established at Sibsagar on 7 April 1979. While secession from India was its declared goal, the organization adopted the anti-foreigner plank as the means to achieve its aim. Whereas the cause had some relevance, the ULFA's brazen acts of kidnappings, killings, extortion and declaration to secede were not acceptable. Unfortunately, electoral politics kept the pot boiling. By 1990, the situation had reached rock bottom and the Central government dismissed the state government, declared President's Rule on 28 November 1990 and launched 'Operation Bajrang'. Unfortunately, sympathizers leaked the information to the ULFA. When the army hit their camps, they found that the ULFA members had escaped and dispersed across all the districts of Assam and to the jungles of Bhutan. It was now left to the army to seek them out, apprehend them and put them behind bars.

It was during this phase of 'Operation Bajrang' that my battalion, the 1st Battalion the 5th Gorkha Rifles (FF) with Lieutenant Colonel Hari Babu Vadde as the CO entered the area of operations and was deployed in the district of Dibrugarh. The ULFA in Dibrugarh had a hard time. The battalion, unorthodox as always, achieved outstanding results. Besides capturing a large number of hardcore ULFA terrorists, the battalion captured the district commander of Dibrugarh district and the treasurer and finance secretary of the ULFA with three crores of Indian currency. Lieutenant Colonel Vadde had a 'nose' for good leads and the battalion continued to operate night and day with success, resulting in the cleanup of the Dibrugarh ULFA outfit and their assets in terms of weapons, money, sophisticated communication equipment, fiberglass boats, high-powered OBMs, telescopic rifles, early warning systems and one and a half crore more of Indian money. Within four months, the battalion had broken the back of the ULFA in Dibrugarh. The battalion was pleased to receive congratulations from Army Headquarters and from the Prime Minister's Office. Unfortunately, politics once again took control and by June 1991 the army was ordered back to the barracks due to impending elections. Hiteshwar Saikia, the chief minister, ordered a general amnesty to all the captured ULFA cadre detainees and they were set free.

The ULFA, however, failed to honour its commitment to the amnesty given by the government and went on a rampage of killing and kidnapping, forcing the government to once again call in the army to restore peace and order.

'Operation Rhino' was launched by the Indian Army on 15 September 1991. This time, the security of information was maintained and several top- and middle-ranking ULFA leaders were captured in addition to the lower rank and file.

One of the pathbreaking steps we took at that time was the institution of '*Wolf Packs*'. We selected young, competent, energetic officers and allowed them to select their teams of just a few competent individuals. Each team had a free run across the Corps Zone and across inter-divisional boundaries to hunt down the key leaders of the ULFA. These operations met with unprecedented success because the insurgents could no longer find safety by crossing divisional boundaries.

Within a short period of time, we had captured Aurobindo Rajkhowa, the ULFA president; the Vice Chief Saurabh Gogoi; Anup Chetia, their finance minister, along with most of the key appointees of the ULFA cadre. The corps had literally run the ULFA into the ground. The only person we failed to capture was Paresh Barua, their chief.

We also set up our own systems to acquire intelligence and information. We learnt that Barua's sister was to get married and set up an elaborate system to trap him. He seemed to sense that we would use this occasion to snare him – he did not attend the wedding. But most of the top cadre of the ULFA had been apprehended resulting in the reduction of hostilities and in order to win over the demoralized ULFA cadres, Chief Minister Saikia once again announced clemency – Operation Rhino was temporarily suspended. Talks were held in January 1992 with top ULFA leaders and it was agreed that the best way forward to find a solution to the Assam problem was within the Constitution of India. It was also agreed that the ULFA would cease violence and surrender all arms. Some of the hardliners, however, refused to accept the terms of agreement and this resulted in a rift within the ULFA, and that aspect of the issue remained unresolved.

It was during the summer of 1992, while I was on a visit to the forward areas ahead of Tawang on the Sino–Indian border, that I received a signal from Lieutenant General F.N. Bilimoria that I had been appointed to take over from him as Colonel of the regiment. General Bilimoria was the Army Commander of Central Command at Lucknow.

Being appointed as Colonel of the regiment is a great honour. It signifies that the person selected has been found most suitable to handle the affairs of the regiment from among all the senior regimental officers. Considered to be the 'Father of the Regiment', it is his role to look after the interests of the regiment and find informal solutions to regimental issues, if any. It is an informal appointment, and the concerned officer carries out his functions from wherever he is posted.

Priscilla was with me and the road back from Tawang to Tezpur had caved in so, we had to walk across a landslide that

The artist's impression of 'Operation Bajrang' where the ongoing situation was clearly in favour of the ULFA.

'Operation Rhino' in progress with a solitary soldier facing the wrath of the ULFA, riding on the back of a rhino.

The symbol of IV Corps is a 'charging elephant'. This picture shows the elephant getting increasingly irritated by the restrictions imposed on it to carry out its tasks.

was still rumbling and moving but we managed to get across safely to where transport from the Corps Headquarters was waiting to pick us up.

My first task as Colonel of the regiment concerned the regimental medical officer (RMO) from the 3rd Battalion of the regiment. Captain Leena, the RMO had volunteered to accompany the battalion to a combat zone in the Kashmir Valley but the brigade, divisional and Corps Commander had turned

---

These three caricatures were done by Arun Cardozo, the author's son, when he visited Tezpur on a holiday. He was then studying at St. John's Medical College, Bangalore.

her request down on grounds that the Valley was no place for a lady doctor, listing out a number of reasons to support their stand. With some amount of logic, we managed to persuade the military hierarchy in the chain of command which included the Medical Directorate at Army Headquarters, to change their decision. Leena went on to do a brilliant job as a doctor and went on to create history by becoming the first woman of the Indian Army to be awarded a gallantry award.[3]

Around this time, I met Khushwant Singh, the well-known journalist and author at a party hosted by doctors Robin and Lakshmi Goswami who lived in a bungalow close to ours at Tezpur. Khushwant Singh made me sit next to him and said that he had heard that I had led an interesting life and that he would like to write my story in one of his syndicated columns 'THIS ABOVE ALL'.

We had been brought up those days on the precept 'Do not blow your own trumpet or beat your own drum'. So, I thanked him and said that there was no story to tell. He was surprised and said, 'General Saab, you are a strange man. People in Delhi keep running after me to include them in my columns and you are saying no?'

I kept quiet.

He then said, 'Does that mean "No?"'

I said, 'Yes.'

'I will write your story in any case,' he said, adding 'and if there are any inaccuracies, you will be the one to blame.'

I said, 'That's OK,' and we proceeded to drink a couple of whiskies together and to talk about the insurgency in Assam. I forgot about the incident until I received copies of his article from a number of well-wishers. I realized then that it would have been better had I given him the information he wanted, because neither did I like the headline nor was the article accurate.[4]

By this time my board for promotion to Lieutenant

General was held and I did not make it. I was disappointed but accepted it with grace. The army teaches us to take the good and bad without breaking one's stride and I decided to do likewise.

The last week of August 1993 was my last week in uniform. It was heartbreaking to be leaving the life I loved but all good things had to come to an end. On the eve of my retirement, after handing over my appointment as COS at the Corps Headquarters, I was permitted to move to the Regimental Centre at Shillong to hand over Colonelcy of the regiment and to spend my last days in the army with the Regimental Centre. However, the 4th Battalion the 5th Gorkha Rifles (FF) had moved down from the China border and was waiting for their special train to take them to their new posting. I preferred to spend 31 August 1993, my last day and night in uniform with my battalion right there at Rangiya Railway Station.

We spent the night talking about the good old days and early next morning, I left for the airport at Guwahati. Despite the protestations of the Battalion Commander, I had my flag and star plates removed as I was no longer a serving officer. A new chapter in my life was going to begin and once again, I had no idea where destiny would take me. But I was full of hope and also glad that I would have more time to spend with my family.

Notes

1. The boundaries of the corps may have now changed.
2. A map is a representation of the ground on a chart which is divided into lines of longitude and latitude and numbered. A position on the ground therefore can be pinpointed on a map numerically which allows supporting weapons to align

themselves on the position on the ground and to fire on them. An eight-figure grid reference enhances the accuracy of the reading.

3. Captain Leena was awarded the Sena Medal for gallantry on 15 January 1995. The award was given to her by General Roy Chaudhury, the then Army Chief who was in fact the Corps Commander who allowed her to accompany the 3rd Battalion the 5th Gorkha Rifles (FF) to the Valley. Her story is also part of my book of short stories, 'Captain Leena Goes to War'.

4. Please see Appendix 'E' (p. 401) for the article.

CHAPTER TWELVE

Fear, Responsibility and Accountability

A hero is no braver than an ordinary man,
but he is braver five minutes longer.
RALPH WALDO EMERSON

I felt that this story would be incomplete if it did not address the issue of fear and its outcomes.

Field Marshal Sam Manekshaw has made it very clear to all of us that 'fear is something felt by all human beings and that anyone who says he has not known fear is a liar or a Gorkha.'

Common to all human beings, the reaction to fear could be – 'Fight or Flight'. In the profession of arms, it is imperative to fight fear and not run away from it. Fear and courage are opposite sides of the same coin. Courage is not the absence of fear; it is the conquest of fear! If a leader is fearful then his followers would be fearful because fear is contagious. However, if a leader is courageous then his subordinates will also be courageous because like fear, courage is also contagious. It is said that 'A *herd of sheep led by a lion will do better than a pride of lions led by a sheep.*' The Indian Army is not afraid to take calculated risks in war to obtain decisive outcomes. Taking risks is a part of its calculus in decision making.

Lieutenant General Sagat Singh, General Officer Commanding (GOC) IV Corps was not afraid to take big risks to ensure outstanding outcomes in the Indo–Pak War of 1971.

He took an enormous risk in sending an under-strength battalion to capture Sylhet. He was however, lucky to have a Commanding Officer like Lieutenant Colonel Arun Harolikar in command of the 4th Battalion the 5th Gorkhas. He and his battalion went beyond the call of duty to deliver outstanding results in tying down two Pakistani infantry brigades and the Sylhet Garrison. He was lucky to have an equally brave Indian Air Force colleague in Group Captain Chandan Singh, who took the enormous risk to send unarmed helicopters without armor plating to heli-land the Gorkhas against enormous enemy fire. But the fact is that these three officers put fear aside in the execution of extremely difficult and challenging tasks.

We were taught at the IMA that fear originated in the mind and it was there that it had to be faced and put to rest. One of our platoon commanders at that venerable institution – Captain Desmond Hayde, dinned into our heads that 'Battles are won or lost in the mind before they are won or lost on the ground' and he proved this many years later at the Battle of Dograi.

There are many kinds of fear and everyone is afraid of something or the other. Each of us has our own experience of fear and each one's fear is different depending on our own thoughts, particular situation and background.

It would perhaps not be true to say that during war fear is not part of the psyche of those involved in combat. It is definitely there but it is pushed aside by more important things like defeating the enemy and the desire by the group to survive. Survival is a strong human instinct and it devolves on the officer to ensure the compulsion to survive by accomplishing the task in hand. Those who have been in battle would perhaps agree that as an officer, one is so obsessed with the job in hand and there is so much to do to capture an objective, to break out of an ambush, to raid an enemy post or to beat back an enemy attack that there is no time to be afraid; there is only time to act.

Perhaps the key to overcoming fear therefore is the opportunity and the ability to react responsibly and positively to what could be the cause for fear. There is also the saying '*You will die only by a bullet that has your name on it*', which most soldiers like to believe.

As mentioned earlier, fear and courage are opposite sides of the same coin and both are contagious. The Indian Army officer therefore leads from the front. He does not say '*Go ahead, I'm coming.*' He shouts instead '*Follow me!*' and Indian soldiers – the best soldiers in the world – follow him, unquestioningly because they know that their 'saab' is right out there in front facing the brunt of the enemy's onslaught and that they have to keep up with him in order to complete their mission. And sometimes, when the officer is killed, it is the JCO or NCO or a senior soldier who takes the lead to fulfil the mission. This has happened in every war that India has had to fight and there are numerous examples to prove it.

In the Kargil War, Lieutenant Manoj Pandey, a young officer said, '*If death strikes before I prove my blood, I swear I will kill death.*' He continued to lead his men in one battle after another, until he was killed leading his men in a final assault. His last words were, '*I regret that I only have one life to give up for my country.'* He was awarded India's highest award for courage on the battlefield, the Param Vir Chakra. The other example is that of Captain Vikram Batra who said, *'Either I will come back after hoisting the tricolour, or I will come back wrapped in it, but I will come back for sure.'* Prophetic words because that was exactly what happened. His men nicknamed him *'Sher Shah'* and even the enemy addressed him as such above the fire and tumult of battle. He too was awarded the Param Vir Chakra. It is leaders like these that fire up the men and blow away their fears. In both these examples it was the JCOs and the NCOs who took inspiration from their officers and led their men to carry on and complete their mission after these young tigers were killed.

In the 1965 Indo–Pak War, Lieutenant Colonel Desmond Hayde led his battalion, 3 Jat across the Ichhogil Canal to capture Dograi, a town in the vicinity of Lahore, in Pakistan. Dograi was captured but many died in this attack and many more were wounded. Unfortunately, the brigade could not link up and the Jat Battalion was ordered to come back. After a while, the brigade was ordered to capture Dograi again. 3 Jat had considered it a slur to their honour that they were ordered to come back. They volunteered to be in the vanguard of the assaulting force once again. But by now, Dograi had been reinforced by enemy armour and infantry. In order to motivate the soldiers who would have been tired after a long battle and also grieving at having lost so many of their friends, Lieutenant Colonel Hayde spoke to his men in Haryanvi and fired them up to achieve the virtually impossible. He told them that the battalion had to retrieve its honour by capturing Dograi once again and he made no bones about the fact that many more would die and many more would be wounded. He added that he would be leading them once again and that if he, as their CO was killed, they would have to carry his body to Dograi because that is where he wanted to be the next morning after the capture of Dograi – dead or alive!

He then asked the men, 'Where will we be tomorrow morning?' and the men roared, 'In Dograi!'

Dograi was captured again, but at a great cost. However, it was the inspirational leadership of the CO that was taken forward by his officers and JCOs that demolished all aspects of fear and succeeded in fulfilling an almost impossible mission.

The Sino–Indian War of 1962 is an example of decision making by our politicians and bureaucrats going haywire due to the warped thinking of the government on how to deal with China and the inability of the military to stand up to unreasonable pressures from Prime Minister Nehru and the Defence Minister Krishna Menon.

Prime Minister Nehru's supine reaction to China's takeover of Tibet in the early 1950s was the first indication that it was not historical linkages that governed his attitude. A continued policy of appeasement and making unwarranted excuses for Chinese aggression ultimately resulted in the debacle that followed.

The above examples are indicators that although the armed forces are subordinate to the government, the politician and the bureaucrat need to understand that there are limits to their omniscient knowledge and that they need to pay heed to the advice of the military on matters that the military are more competent to deal with.

The military, on the other hand, need to understand that it is imperative to stand up to wrong directions by the civil or military hierarchy keeping in mind – 'Country first, soldiers next and self, last'.

There has been a concerted effort in recent times by some bureaucrats in the government who are doing their best to denigrate and diminish the armed forces, fueled perhaps by an irrational fear of them. I find it difficult to rationalize this fear. The role and function of the bureaucrat is totally different from the armed forces and yet they act as if we are in competition with them. It is, in my opinion, the fear that they will lose their power and standing if they don't keep the armed forces clamped down. Being close to the politician, they have fueled an irrational fear in the minds of the politician that unless the Indian Army is kept in its place, they will take over the country. In the last seventy years, they have succeeded, to a large extent, in increasing their own status and perks while denying them to the armed forces because they are the ones who make the rules. Examples are many but this perhaps is not the place to discuss them.

Courage is the antithesis of fear and can be of two kinds – physical and moral.

During the 1971 War, the 1st Battalion the 5th Gorkha Rifles (FF) was tasked to carry out an offensive in Punjab. They were tasked to eliminate the 'Sehjra Bulge'. It was from here that Pakistan had come across the international border during the 1965 Indo–Pak War and allowed its villagers to loot Indian villages, homesteads and a gurdwara. Amongst other articles that they looted, they uprooted the gates of the gurdwara at Rattoke and made off with them along with furniture and belongings of the villagers.

The Sehjra Bulge gave easy access to the Pakistanis to enter Indian territory. It was decided during the 1971 War to eliminate this bulge.

The enemy defensive position at Sehjra was located on an escarpment and held by a Pakistani battalion supported by artillery, mortars, medium machine guns and small arms. There were two possible approaches to the enemy defences at Sehjra – eastern and western. The western approach was protected by a river and so it was decided to use the eastern approach. The Pakistani defences at Sehjra were protected by minefields and barbed wire and defensive fire from artillery, mortars, medium machine guns and small arms fire. However, repeated reconnaissance by elements of our artillery, armour, engineers and the supporting arms and services confirmed the Pakistani assessment that Sehjra would be assaulted from the east. So, the Pakistanis redoubled their efforts to make the Sehjra defences impregnable along the eastern approach. They also commenced digging a deep ditch forward of their defences along this approach and strengthened the mine fields and wire obstacles. The diggers and tractors which were digging the ditch could be clearly seen from our defence localities.

This attack had been planned by the Indian Army a couple of months earlier as a contingency plan in case the two countries went to war. Towards the latter part of the year, the President of Pakistan, General Yahya Khan made it clear that war was imminent. This caused the recces of our troops to double despite the protests of Lieutenant Colonel Suresh Gupta, the Battalion Commander of 'First Five' that the continued recce by our troops would give away our intention to attack along the eastern approach.

After a while, it became increasingly clear to Lieutenant Colonel Gupta that if 'First Five' attacked along the eastern approach not only would he fail to capture Sehjra but his troops would be slaughtered due to the excessive defence preparations by the Pakistanis along the eastern approach.

Earlier recces of the western approach in September had revealed that the width and depth of the river that ran in front of the objective made it very difficult, if not impossible, to attack along the western approach. But that was soon after the monsoon. It was now the third week of November and the water could have receded.

A recce at night confirmed the CO's belief that the river was now crossable, even by Gorkhas who are shorter than other troops. Lieutenant Colonel Gupta knew that the route to success lay on his assaulting Sehjra across the river along the western approach.

But the trouble lay in the fact that a great deal of time and effort had gone into the plan to attack along the eastern approach and the plan had been approved and confirmed by brigade, division, corps and command. Also, each of the supporting arms and services had made their detailed plans which were dovetailed into the overall plan and they were allergic to the suggestion that the attack plan could change because that would mean that they would have to re-work their plans and that too on the eve of a war that could break out at any time.

It was in these circumstances that Lieutenant Colonel Gupta had to make his case for attacking along a different approach against the views of all in the military hierarchy. All the formation commanders and the heads of the arms and services stated that it was not possible to accept a major change at this late stage of the war, just before the attack was to go in.

It was here that the issue of moral courage surfaced when Lieutenant Colonel Gupta had to face the opposition and disparaging remarks of all the commanders' brigade upwards as well as from the commanders of the supporting arms and services and the staff at brigade, division and corps headquarters. He, however, stuck to his guns and asked for a sand model discussion to prove his point.

It was like a scene in a court room with Lieutenant Colonel Gupta as the defendant, against the prosecution by everyone else. In his opening address, he said the following:

(a) That he had recced the river and found crossing places for his troops.

(b) That there should be no change in the supporting

fire of our artillery. The artillery should continue to fire on the eastern approach, which would serve as a diversion to lead them to believe that we would be attacking along the eastern approach while he would be attacking across the river to the west. The artillery Forward Observation Officers who would be accompanying the assaulting companies could in any case take on 'opportunity targets'.

(c) There would be no change in the reorganization plan as this would commence along the same vehicle safe lanes only after the objective was captured.

(d) That he could guarantee success if he was allowed to attack along the western approach and the Brigade, Division and Corps Commander were invited to have breakfast with him on the objective after the enemy opposition had been mopped up, which would be latest by 11a.m.

(e) That if it was still insisted that he attack along the eastern approach he could not guarantee success but his life and those of his men would likely be sacrificed on the altar of a plan that was inflexible and unworkable.

The artillery and supporting arm commanders now had no grounds to oppose the plan as Lieutenant Colonel Gupta had insisted that their plans should not change as it would work as an excellent deception plan. The opposition gave in because the plan was logical. It was accepted but with several misgivings.

'First Five' attacked along the western approach and Sehjra was captured with minimum casualties. The *NEWSWEEK* magazine published a picture of the Pakistani Commanding Officer's trousers that were left behind in the panic of withdrawal.

A huge amount of ammunition and arms were captured

that included anti-tank guns, mortars, medium machine guns, light machine guns, hundreds of rifles and three truckloads of ammunition and mines.

The Corps Commander, the Divisional Commander and the Brigade Commander were able to have tea on the objective at Sehjra after it was captured.

All this happened because a battalion commander had the moral courage to overcome his fear of standing up against all opposition to produce a brilliant plan and outstanding results.

The Corps Commander presented 'First Five' with a silver cup for the most outstanding results in the Indo–Pak War of 1971 in the Corps Zone.

There is no end to stories of how men overcome fear with courage and produce outstanding results in war. However, there is a finality to this story and I will end this chapter here with a postscript taken from a Pakistani book of naval war stories titled *Bubbles of Water* that I had come across during my research for my earlier book, *The Sinking of INS Khukri*. I don't remember the exact words but it is an amusing anecdote on fear and it ran something like this:

A company commander of a Pakistani infantry battalion was going round his defences during war when he noticed a JCO running from place to place and taking cover every now and then from the bullets that were whizzing past. He admonished the JCO saying: 'Why are you running around like this and taking cover? Don't you know that you can only be killed with a bullet that has your name on it?'

The terrified JCO said, 'That's all-right sir, but how about the bullet that is inscribed with the words "To whomsoever it may concern!"'

CHAPTER THIRTEEN

Retirement and Working for Persons with Disability

*Life is a succession of lessons which must
be lived to be understood.*
HELEN KELLER

I looked at the file in front of me. The subject in block letters on the cover read 'PLANS FOR RETIREMENT'. Inside was a paper written by me a few years earlier and it outlined just how I would embark on a second career. Army personnel retire early. As a Major General I retired at the age of fifty-six.

The file included a bucket list of all the places I had always wanted to visit but never had the money or the opportunity to see and all the things I wanted to do but never had the time. As a career, life in the army has no equal; however, getting permission to go abroad was always a big hassle.

Field postings meant maintenance of multiple homes

as a family, especially when the children went in for higher education. This took a heavy toll on one's savings. At one point of time, all five of us, Priscilla, I and our three sons, were at five different places. A vehicle and a roof over our heads had become a necessity rather than a luxury. The instalments to pay for the loan that I had taken for a flat took a long time to clear, until I could finally say that the flat was ours. If we own this home in Delhi it is entirely due to the generosity of my coursemate Brigadier Kulvender Singh, who pushed me to apply for the flat and loaned me the money to make the initial deposit that accompanied the application. When I thanked him, he replied, 'Ian, what are coursemates for?' He too is a battle casualty due to a machine gun burst on his right arm.

After I retired, I decided that whatever I had saved needed to be invested, so I set out with my file that contained the list of my savings to meet an ex-Air Force officer who was helping service officers with their investments. He looked at the page that outlined my savings. He didn't seem to be impressed and asked me if I had any commitments.

'Yes,' I said. 'I have to buy a car.'

He closed my file and said, 'I am sorry, sir, but you have no money to invest.'

'What do you mean?' I said indignant that he had such a poor opinion of my life's savings.

He looked at me with concern and said, 'Sir, if you buy a Maruti 800, it will cost at least two and a half lakhs; that just leaves an equal amount left over. I don't know how and where you have spent your money but I would advise that after you buy your car, you should invest whatever is left over in fixed deposits so that you will have access to the money whenever you need it again.

I was disappointed but I realized that he was right and I would have to land a good job if my bucket list had to have any meaning. However, I was confident that I would be able to land a good job in the corporate sector. I had earned multiple degrees and diplomas many years earlier when I had felt that I would be forced to leave the army on account of my being disabled. Those diplomas and degrees would surely be useful now? I was now '*Major General (Retd) Ian Cardozo, AVSM, SM, DPM, B. Com, MBA, MSc*'. It sounded impressive and I hoped I would earn a nice fat salary.

I applied to a number of corporate houses and business organizations and went through a number of interviews. The interviews went off very well and the interactions were very polite and the CEOs seemed genuinely impressed. 'We will call you, sir,' they said. Months passed but surprisingly no one called. I wondered why a person with my qualifications and experience was not able to land a job in the business world, whereas officers in the rank of colonel were being snapped up as soon as they retired – prematurely or otherwise. I finally came to the conclusion that I was probably too senior; or that being an infantry officer, I had no 'hands on' experience in matters related to the corporate sector like officers from the technical arms and services. Younger officers were trainable. It appeared that I was too old and too senior and therefore not trainable! Also, I had no contacts!

I had fought three wars, and managed forces of over 20,000 men. If my experience in war and counter insurgency meant nothing to them, then surely my abilities as a leader and in human resource development and lateral decision making counted for something? Also, I had reasonable qualifications in management and human resource development.

Unfortunately, nothing materialized and no one called. All the qualifications that I had earned and the effort that went into getting them seemed to be a waste of time. General Dick Dias, a friend and colleague from MO Directorate days, spoke to Walter Viera, a friend of his and a colleague from my school days, who in turn spoke to his contacts and I was offered a job working for disabled children in Delhi.

The interview with the Spastics Society of Northern India (SSNI) included a meeting with children with disabilities. One look at them and my mind was made up. I understood the challenges that they had to face and I felt that together we could make the world a better place for all of us.

Salary-wise it wasn't much, but it meant working for a cause and the values were good – very similar to those of the armed forces. Mrs Mita Nandi, Dr Meenu Jalan and some other likeminded women were the founders of the SSNI and they were dynamic, energetic, full of dreams and irrepressible. There was leadership here of a very high order and the work they were doing was laudable and meaningful and I felt that I had found my niche.

Although the values were similar to those of the Indian Army, the work and the ambience were quite different. In the army, the day began with loud words of command, the crash of boots on the parade ground, the firing of rifles and machine guns on the range in sharp contrast to was happening at this NGO. Here the day started with the soft cadence of the aarti and it progressed with the children reciting tables and rhymes and the pleasing sound of their laughter on the playground. It was very restful and so different to the rough and tough army routine. Mita Nandi was supported by an excellent team of qualified professionals working in the field of disability and the children did extremely well in their studies, in art work and in extracurricular activities. Although the SSNI was in effect a 'special school', it attempted to bring learning and living as close to the non-disabled environment as possible by being as inclusive as possible.

It was here that I met Javed Abidi for the first time. Javed was a person with a disability – an outstanding and fiery activist fighting for the rights of persons with disabilities in

India. He was in a wheelchair, but that did not deter him from his aim to make India disabled friendly in every walk of life and in every field of endeavour. What he did in his short life for disability in India no one has been able to replicate. This does not diminish the great work of other disabled persons working in specific fields of disability, but Javed had a bigger canvas and his work cut across all disabilities. He was 'politically savvy', he had an aim and a strategy and most important of all, he had the determination and the will to succeed.

At the time I joined the social sector, India had little time, care or consideration for persons with disability. Persons with disabilities were undermined, pushed aside and excluded. Although other pioneers in the field of disability have done great work in their respective fields, very few had the courage to take on the government head-on to make them do what they were required to. Javed had that spark and that ability. He understood the lethargic mindset of the bureaucrat and the politician. He was an opportunist and his sense of timing was perfect. His strategy, timing, as well as his tactics would have made him a great general had he been in the army.

'Disability Rights Group', founded by Javed in 1994, was his little army that executed his plans. I was enrolled and was happy to belong because at heart I am very much an activist myself and I was happy to join persons with disabilities in their struggle to get what was rightfully theirs. After all, wasn't I disabled myself? And hadn't I fought for my rights and won?

At that time, there were a number of issues that the disability sector had to face. Firstly, the world in general and the government in particular had no time for persons with disability. They preferred to believe that we did not exist and that convinced us more than ever to ensure that we could not be ignored. The media was with us and looked forward to any opportunity to report when we locked horns with the government.

Javed's strategy was what we in the army would call '*the strategy of graduated response*'. He would first focus on a current right that was being denied to us by the government by writing a letter to the ministry concerned and he would gradually build up the tempo by following-up with two or three reminders. Usually, the concerned ministry would not respond and Javed would request for a meeting with the minister. At the meeting, the standard reply from the government used to be 'We will look into the matter.' After a number of reminders and no response, we would then take our battle to the streets and get the media on board to take our cause to the people. A hand-out was given to the media so that they remained on track to get the response we desired. We worked within the ambit of the law. First, we would inform the Delhi Police of our intention to stage a dharna along with time and place. Then, the media would be informed and they would come with their cameras, TV crews and reporters and we would get the excellent media coverage that we needed.

The first time I was part of this kind of protest, Javed was not there and I was the senior-most person present. We had camped in front of the office of the minister dealing with disability under a colourful *shamiana*[1] to shelter the children from the sun. We had children singing bhajans accompanied by a harmonium and tablas with banners in the background relating to the issue in hand.

After three hours the police arrived and told us that we had protested enough and it was now time to leave. We said that we had requested for a meeting with the minister and we would not leave until we had met him. The matter was referred to a sub-inspector who came along looking very officious and stern. He softened a bit when he saw the disabled children and that we were very peaceful and not noisy at all.

He asked who was in charge. I stepped forward and said that I was in charge. He repeated that we had had enough time to state our case and that we should now go back to wherever we had come from. I told him that we would not leave unless the minister met some of us to listen to our plea.

'In that case I will have to place you under arrest for disturbing the peace,' he said.

'This is a peaceful protest. However, what do I need to do to qualify to be put under arrest for disturbing the peace?'

'You will have to cross over this rope.'

A rope was produced and placed on the ground and I stepped over it and I was told that I had broken the peace and I was now under arrest! Some of the lady teachers protested that this was unfair but their protests went unheeded and I was led away to a big black van close by that had brought the posse of police.

I was made to sit down and was asked,

'Sir, what is your name?'

'Major General Ian Cardozo,' I replied.

'Major General? Indian Army?'

'Yes,' I said. 'Retired.'

He scratched his head and decided that this was too much for him to handle and he needed to consult his superior. So he got on to his radio set and spoke to his officer and conveyed to him that he was at the site of the protest by children with disabilities and that he had 'got an army general in the bag!'

After a while, a police Gypsy came to the site and a police officer got out and approached the van. He saluted me and said, 'Good morning, Sir. Are you part of this group?'

I said yes, I was.

'My inspector tells me that you have already been here for three hours. What is it that you want?'

'We would like to meet the minister and to hand over our written request,' I said.

'Is that all? That should not be a problem. I can go and speak with him and tell him to meet some of you as it would be good policy to meet you instead of getting bad publicity.'

He was as good as his word. He went and spoke to the minister who agreed to meet some of us. The officer said that about three of us could go and meet the minister and to hand over our request.

He led the way to the minister's office. The minister being the politician that he was, gave us a long lecture about how hard he was working for the cause of disability and we should be grateful to him and his ministry for all that they were doing instead of launching protests. I let one of the senior lady professionals respond to him who knew how to handle such issues and she explained to him very politely but firmly, that on the contrary, the situation was quite different from what he said, otherwise we would not be protesting. The lady then proceeded to brief him about the issue about which the disability sector was unhappy about. He was not very happy either, but he knew that what we said had merit. He accepted the written request and we left.

Nothing happened immediately and it required many more *dharnas* to finally get what we wanted.

The issue we were highlighting was the lack of access to buses, trains and aircraft. There had been some improvement with regard to access to aircraft because that issue had become international and progress abroad in this area had rubbed off to Indian airports and airlines operating in India but much more needed to be done particularly with regard to surface transport.

We launched many more protests and the Delhi police were quite reasonable in the way they handled the disability sector compared to the way they handle other protests. Perhaps that was because we were always peaceful and apolitical.

Of the many issues addressed were access to education in schools, colleges and universities, access to public buildings, public places and places of entertainment, access to information in its various and different forms, access to employment in the government and outside of it, including the Indian Administrative Services, access to healthcare and government hospitals, making elections more accessible to persons with disabilities, making the census more accessible and inclusive, inclusive education, inclusion in better funding as part of budgetary allocations in government financial planning, institution of a legal framework to make better and more responsive legislation which resulted in the Disability Act of 1995 and its replacement by a new law in 2016, and many more issues, all of which had excellent outcomes for persons with disabilities.

The government gradually began to understand the power of the disability sector and Javed switched over from activism to engaging with the government through discussion when he found that they were prepared to listen to our pleas for better management in matters concerning the disabled.

The problem with the disability sector is that it continues to be a fragmented and fractured group with each category of disability trying to corner best outcomes for their own disability. In this, the Blind and Vision Impaired are the strongest. It had been Javed's aim to bring all the disability groups under one umbrella so that we could have a stronger platform to engage with the government. Javed and the Disability Rights Group played a major role in ensuring better legislation for the disabled. In the Disability Act of 1995 only seven disabilities were recognized. However, with the concerted effort of the sector, a new Act was promulgated in 2016 and the number of recognized disabilities has risen to twenty-one.[2]

Sometime in April 2005 after working five years with the Spastics Society, I got a call from Pulok Chatterjee, the then

Private Secretary (PS) to Prime Minister Dr Manmohan Singh. The call was put through to me from the telephone exchange of SSNI. I wondered what the PS to the prime minister would want with me.

He said, 'This is Pulok Chatterjee here. The Prime Minister would like to know whether you will accept being appointed as the Chairman of the Rehabilitation Council of India.'

Surprised, I asked, 'Why me? There are many persons working in the Disability Sector who are more qualified than me.'

'The Prime Minister would like a "Yes" or "No" answer,' he said.

'I will have to speak to my own minister,' I replied.

'Who's that?'

'My wife,' I said.

'Do that,' he said with a laugh. 'But let me know your decision by tomorrow.'

That evening I spoke with Priscilla and she said, 'Go ahead. I hope it will be good for you.' She knew that this is what I wanted to do and she was fine with it if it made me happy.

On 27 April 2005, I took over as the Chairman of the Rehabilitation Council of India. I remember the date because it was a day after our 39th wedding anniversary.

My appointment as Chairman of the Rehabilitation Council of India was equivalent to the status of a Secretary, Government of India. This made me feel good and I seemed to be coming close to the bucket list I had always dreamed of. There were two other institutions that worked for the Ministry of Social Justice and Empowerment – the National Trust and the Commissioner for Persons with Disability. The heads of both these institutions were also equated in status with that of a Secretary of the Government of India and they received equivalent salaries. I therefore presumed that since my appointment was equivalent to a Secretary of the Government of India, I would get an equivalent salary. After I signed the agreement, I was told that there would be no salary or allowances of any kind for this appointment. Pulok Chatterjee had not told me that this was an unpaid job. I should have asked but felt embarrassed to do so and paid for it. I made it clear, however, that I would like to be given an independent hand to carry out my work.

The ministry did allow me to do my work without interference. Perhaps they knew that no one else would want to work in an unpaid capacity and that I would resign if interfered with. However, they took their pound of flesh in that they were more than mean by not allowing me to even draw a 'sitting allowance' as was admissible to all Honorary Chairmen of institutions for every conference that they chaired. I was told that I was not an Honorary Chairman and so I lost out financially in every way.

My work as the Chairman of the Rehabilitation Council of India involved the management and supervision of institutions training professionals working for the disabled, regulating the conduct of their training, the evolution of criteria for the employment of professionals working in the field of disability, liaising between universities and institutions accredited to such universities, the inspection of institutions working for the disabled, the holding of examinations, etc. The job was interesting in that it allowed me to examine the manner in which institutions were training professionals working in the field of disability and because it gave me a better insight into issues across all disabilities.

A year-and-a-half after I had taken over as the chairman, I received an offer to head 'HelpAge', an institution that takes care of the aged and elderly disabled. It was a paid job. I could have resigned from RCI and accepted the offer but I had given my word to the government and I felt that my word as an officer of the Indian Army was more important than any written agreement. Doing the right thing is never defined by formal agreements or written contracts. Army officers work on the basis of trust and I felt I should live up to the values of the Indian Army for which I had worked for the greater part of my life. I recommended Major General Inderjit Singh Dhillon, a competent colleague who had worked with me in Assam. He got the job, and 'HelpAge' and I were happy to have him working for them.

After working nine years without pay or allowances of any kind from the Government of India, I demitted office on 21 February 2014. My successor asked for a salary prior to being appointed and got it, although it was not the equivalent to the salary given to a Secretary, Government of India. Those nine years gave me a fairly good understanding of the workings of the bureaucracy and politicians.

The problem with most bureaucrats and the politicians who hold office in ministries is that they move from one ministry to another with little understanding of the work they need to do in their next assignment, and when they do get a grasp of what they ought to be doing they are moved to another ministry. To me, their aim appeared to be to keep on the right side of the minister, to keep files moving without taking decisions – '*to pass the buck without biting the bullet.*'

• • •

Javed Abidi passed away in March 2018, marking the end of an era in the struggle for the rights of persons with disability. The voices of the disabled are diminished now after the disability sector lost its champion. Individual groups continue to make attempts to be heard but the person who unified them and ensured that they were heard is gone.

After I had hung up my boots for the second time, I finally had time to go down memory lane. With some amount of satisfaction, I could look back at how far this little boy from Bombay had travelled.

Notes

1. A colourful tent-like structure that gives protection from the sun.
2. Twenty-one disabilities are: Blindness, Low vision, Leprosy cured person, Hearing disability (deaf and hard of hearing), Orthopedic disability, Dwarfism, Intellectual disability, Mental illness, Autism spectrum disorder, Cerebral palsy, Muscular dystrophy, Chronic neurological condition, Specific learning disability, Multiple sclerosis, Speech and language disability, Thalassemia, Hemophilia, Sickle cell disease, Multiple disabilities including Deaf blindness, Acid attack survivors, and Parkinson's disease.

CHAPTER FOURTEEN

Looking Back

We stayed at a place called Colaba,
a place quite close to the sea
My mum and my dad and my brother,
and of course there was also me.
AUTHOR

The early years of my life were spent at Colaba, Bombay. Our dining room overlooked a vast open space called the Gun Carriage Factory used during the years of the Second World War as a camping ground for troops going overseas. This is where I got my first glimpse of military life. Tented camps would spring up overnight on the ground when an army unit arrived and would disappear as suddenly when they left for the front. The huge gun at the entrance of the Prince of Wales Museum, now called the Chhatrapati Shivaji Museum, was unearthed here and the first Air Defence Regiment of the Indian Army was raised on this ground.

Life at these camps was regulated by bugle calls and their routine included arms drill, weapon training and physical training, and in the evenings, they would often get together at campfires and sing songs. Suddenly one morning they were gone to fight on some distant front in Europe, Burma or the Middle East, to be replaced by another lot who followed more or less the same routine. I found their lives fascinating but their songs had something poignant about them, full of hope that they would one day return home. I was impressed by their discipline and behaviour and decided that one day I too would join the army and have a gun and a tent of my own.

In those days, the street lamps used to be powered by gas and I remember a lamplighter used to come to our street at dusk with a long pole with a hook at the end, and ignite the lamp by pulling a lever inside the lamp.

My school in Bombay, St. Xavier's, was a Jesuit institution and in addition to academic excellence, the focus was on all round development with an emphasis on the building of character. We had boys from every walk of life and every religion with no discrimination. We were taught not to lie, cheat or steal, to be respectful to our elders, to work hard and to be the best and to do what was right irrespective of the consequences.

Corporal punishment was not an issue then, as it is today, and we learnt to take our punishment like a cane on our palms or a twist of the ear, if we did something wrong. The school has just celebrated one hundred and fifty years of its existence and has produced persons of eminence in every possible field of endeavour – doctors and surgeons, engineers and architects, professors and teachers, artists and artisans, judges and lawyers, scientists and technicians, journalists and photographers, poets and authors, national and international sportsmen in athletics, cricket, hockey and football, industrialists and philanthropists, priests and religious heads of many faiths, actors, playwrights and dramatists, bureaucrats and members of legislative assemblies, officers in the army, navy and the air force, including an Army Chief.[1]

I don't remember ever being overburdened with homework and the priority of our young minds was on games and sports, except at examination time when we had to catch up on our studies. I learnt Latin which helped me understand English grammar and strangely enough facilitated my learning of Nepali.[2]

We used to go to the school by tram as did my father and grandfather. These used to run on rails and were powered by electricity that came from electric cables that ran above the tram rails. As soon as we reached home from school, we would down a glass of milk, grab our hockey sticks and would head for the Oval, hitting the ball to each other across the road till we reached. There were very few cars on the roads those days and Badhwar Park did not exist. Instead, just where Badhwar Park is now, there were Air Force barracks that housed air force stores during the Second World War and before that it was the location of the Colaba Railway Station. Alongside was what is now known as a 'flyover' and along its slope were wooden benches overlooking the sea. Below this flyover was a siding of an ancient railway line. We would run past Cuffe Parade, Wellingdon Mews, Wellingdon Club, the Cooperage and the Bandstand and at last reach the Oval.

We played with sportsmen like Anthony Braganza, James D'Costa, John Charles, Neville DeSouza and his brother Derrick DeSouza, all of whom reached national and international fame. Neville made history when he scored a hat-trick for India in football during the Olympic Games in Melbourne. A question on this feat at the Amitabh Bachchan *'Kaun Banega Crorepati'* show would have got a contestant a crore of rupees but he did not know the answer!

Swimming was learnt in the sea at the beach at Cuffe Parade – a beautiful promenade that could match any walkway in the world. It ran for more than a mile about ten feet above the road. It started from the beach adjacent to what is now Badhwar Park and finished at the military area. That beautiful promenade has now been destroyed on the altar of political expediency and the beach has been converted into a messy fishing village.

At that time there were only four swimming pools in Bombay that we knew of. They were the Golwalla Baths, the Backbay Baths and the Mafatlal and Breach Candy swimming pools. We did not have access to any of these pools as each was meant for a specific community and so we took to the sea at Cuffe Parade. Underwater swimming was the order of the day. We learnt to swim under one canoe, then two and three and more till we became really good at it. The penalty if one surfaced early was a back scraped by the barnacles lining the underside of the canoes, so we learnt the hard way. A few years later I broke the record at the NDA by swimming a length and a quarter of the Olympic-size pool at Khadakvasla underwater. My joy was short lived – another cadet, Jim Agnihotri, broke my record the next day by swimming a few inches more!

We grew up during the war years on a staple diet of Commando and Champion Comics that figured heroes like Rockfist Rogan of the RAF and Biggles. We watched in silent awe as Tiger Moths, the fighter biplanes of that era droned lazily over Bombay skies or engaged in mock battles and gazed in wonderment at the barrage balloons that peppered the sky over the harbour to dissuade an air attack by the Japanese on Allied ships and harbour installations. Although the barrage balloon seemed small in the sky, it was gigantic on the ground. One of them was garaged under a huge hangar at a corner of the Oval and we looked like dwarfs before it.

It was 14 April 1944 that the Great Explosion took place in Bombay. I was in Preparatory 'D', the junior-most class – the lower kindergarten of today. Just before school finished at around 4.15 p.m. there was a tremendous blast that shattered every glass window of the school. My classroom was separated from the next class by a wall which had an archway of glass panes and every pane broke with the sound that only glass can make when it breaks. We were little tykes then and we wondered what was happening. But there was no fear, just surprise and wonderment! Our teacher, Sheila Fernandes, took charge and told us to pack our bags and wait for someone to take us home. Our classroom was beneath the chapel and a great piece of red-hot metal crash-landed on the ground just short of the chapel and close to our class. It was about a foot-and-a-half thick and approximately two-and-a-half-feet in jagged diameter and it sizzled for days before it finally cooled down. We learnt later that it was part of a propeller of one of the ships that had been blown out of the sea. After a couple of minutes there was a second explosion. This time there was no glass to break but it was followed by a strong gust of hot wind that blasted through the open doors and windows. Our school was perhaps a couple of miles from the epicenter of the explosion and fires were burning and black smoke spewing from the areas near the docks.

My cousin John came looking for me and we both boarded a tram that was making its way to Victoria Terminus. The tram however was overcrowded and leaning at an angle of nearly thirty degrees, so we jumped off and set off on foot amongst a vast concourse of people moving in different directions. Nobody was talking and everyone seemed to be in silent contemplation about what had happened. We walked past Azad Maidan, Bombay Gymkhana, the High Court, Flora Fountain, and Museum, Regal, Colaba Causeway and reached home around the same time that my dad reached home. He had been to the school and found that I was not there and hurried home, relieved to find that we had reached home safely. Home was closer to the site of the explosion and my brother Colin was looking out of the window of the sitting room when the explosion took place and the window banged shut and he ran inside saying, 'Mummy, the Japs have arrived!'

Dad took us to the bunder[3] later that evening and we could see the docks on fire and a number of red-hot ships that had been towed out to sea. These were strange sights but we were too young to understand the implications of the incident.

Later we learnt that 1,300 persons had been killed and over 3,000 had been injured. A ship, the *SS Stryknene* that was carrying bales of cotton, gold and over a thousand tons of explosives blew up in the docks causing fires and explosions on four other ships. Gold bars literally rained over the area of the docks. Most were recovered but quite a few have yet to be found, waiting to be unearthed from wherever they lie undiscovered.

We lived with the sea on both sides of Colaba Causeway, closer to the bay which probably gave Bombay its name. Along the stretch after the Gateway of India were a number of small harbour inlets colloquially called bunders. The biggest one was of course the Apollo Bunder which gave access to the Gateway of India and the boats of the Yacht Club, followed sequentially by Arthur Bunder, Sassoon Dock Bunder and Pilot Bunder. These little harbour inlets gave access to sea going yachts, fishing dhows and small craft of various sizes. During the war years, Arthur Bunder was used to build the huge floating docks that served the Allied navies in the Pacific Ocean.

The floating docks worked on the Archimedes principle that if you fill a hollow object with water, it will sink and if you remove that water, it will rise. The sinking or rising would depend upon the amount of water in the huge tanks that took in the water or let it out. The floating docks consisted of two huge, hollow metal rectangular canisters, each as big as a two-storied building connected by a steel floor. When sea water was pumped simultaneously into these two rectangular buildings that served as tanks, the whole floating dock would sink, allowing a ship to enter the space in between. Once in, the water was pumped out, allowing the dock to rise and the space in between to be used by workmen to repair the ship. The floating docks were built by Pathans from the North West Frontier and the way to the floating docks was via our home. At 5 in the evening when a siren sounded that work was done, our street would be flooded with a torrential mass of Pathans in oil-stained clothes, running, shoving, and shouting in Pushto and scrambling to catch the tram that would take them home. All of us kept away from the street at that time.

These floating docks rendered valuable service to Allied shipping in the Pacific. They were however vulnerable to enemy action at sea. Two were built at Arthur Bunder and both were sunk by the Japanese towards the end of the war in the Pacific Ocean but no one has written their story.

The Brits were still around during our early days at school. Fortunately, the whites had their own schools – and we only met them in public places. Interaction with them was never comfortable. My dad's office was a Greek firm. There, and in many public places like stadiums, clubs and hotels, staircases and toilets were separate for the whites and separate for us. These and other forms of manmade discrimination were disgusting. It was something I could neither understand nor digest, resulting sometimes in unpleasant experiences. It amazed me that people could treat people differently based on the colour of their skin.

Our House in Goa – Candolim – 1953

The roots of the Cardozo family lie in Candolim, a village by the sea in north Goa. It is from here that my great grandfather migrated to Mhow and he lies buried in the graveyard behind the old Scottish kirk of St. Andrew. His son, Dr Vincent Cardozo, went on to become a distinguished medical practitioner, and a ward has been named after him in the Municipal Hospital at Mhow. Other members of the family moved on to Bombay and Jodhpur and today they are all over the world.

While the British were ruling India, the Portuguese were in control in Goa, Daman and Diu. Notwithstanding all the damage that the British wreaked on India, they did offer better opportunities for employment. As a consequence, most Goans left their ancestral homes in search of better employment outside of Goa.

Whereas the British had the good sense to leave when they realized that with independent India, they could no longer rely on the armed forces to do their bidding, the Portuguese hung on, despite being repeatedly requested to leave with dignity. They were finally evicted by the Indian armed forces in 1961.

The language we Goans speak is Konkani because Goa is part of the Konkan coast. Konkani is also spoken by some communities from Mangalore, Karwar and Malwan. Goan villages are divided into vados. Ours was Bamon Vado and our house was called '*Motto Curis*', which means 'Big Cross'.

Whenever we could, we would spend our summer holidays at our ancestral home which was right on the beach. At night, we could hear the waves crashing on the shore. We would run every morning in our swimming trunks to the scintillating white sands beyond the house and play on the beach. Sometimes the waves would throw sardines onto the shore and they would be jumping and flipping on the sand and all we needed to do was to run along the shore and pick them up before the next wave took them back into the sea. Fish those days was so plentiful that some of what could not be consumed was used as manure.

We entered our house through what was called a *balcaon* – a cross between a 'sit out and a balcony', which led to a sitting room with furniture that would today qualify as being 'antique'. A passage took off from the sitting room on either side of which were bedrooms and then a long dining room on one side with a big kitchen on the other. The kitchen also housed the bathroom. During those days there was no electricity or plumbing and cooking was done on wood fires, the smoke of which enhanced the taste of our food. Water was drawn from a well, half of it was part of the bathroom and the other half was outside the house. The toilets were outside of our house in the backgarden.

Ancestral homes of those who had left Goa were normally looked after by a relative or as in our case by Marianne, a lady who was adopted by our family. Marianne was an excellent cook and she would stock her mouth-watering Goan dishes before we arrived. Meat and fish surplus was salted and stored in clay pots that hung from rafters in a number of store rooms that ran the length of the back garden, there being no refrigerators in those days.

What resonates in my mind are the smells of the Goa of those days – the smell of wood fires, of the oil from the *pontis* (lamps) at night, of coconuts and cashew kernels left to dry in the store rooms before being de-husked, of the pickles of *khara*[4] and *para*[5] that hung in clay pots from the rafters of the store rooms at the back of the house, of ripe Alfonse mangoes that Goa is famous for and the smell of earth with the first rains of the monsoon.

The sounds too echo in my memory of those days – the waves crashing on the shore, of the breeze through the fronds of the coconut trees, the *pom pom* of the bulbous horn of the *poder's*, or the baker's boy who brought bread to the house, the shouts of the fishermen as they pulled in the catch from the sea, the sound of the *rebecs*, the violin at funerals and weddings and even the squealing of the unfortunate pig being carried away to be slaughtered.

The kitchen was a magical place filled with the aromatic fragrance of Marianne's excellent cooking. It was here that she concocted exquisite dishes from ancient family recipes – *vindaloo, caldeen, cafreal, shakuti, sorpotel, baffad, rechad, sanna, coconut rice, mole* and some others whose names I don't remember. All of our food was eaten with rice or with sannas.[6] Coconut water and the coconut kernel formed an intrinsic ingredient of Goan dishes, as also Goa vinegar which contributes to its distinctive taste. Huge cakes of *mangad*[7] and *bibinca*[8], exotic Goan sweet dishes, would be prepared for us when we came for our holidays. Chapattis, parathas and puris as far as I know, did not form part of Goan cuisine.

Besides Goan cuisine, Goans are also well known for their love of music and their songs and dances are imitated by Bollywood. My uncle, Professor Antsher Lobo, founded 'The Goan Folksong and Choral Society' that made Goan song and dance popular in India during the war years. The music for the military march *Sare Jahan se Achha* has been composed by him and his name appears on all the band programmes issued at the Beating of the Retreat every year during the Republic Day celebrations.

Goans, in general, are content with their lot and are not overambitious. They are generally happy and peaceful. What cannot be done today can be done the next day or the day after that or whenever! The laidback philosophy here is that if you have to work hard to be rich and that being rich means living a relaxed life, then what is the point in working hard for it, when living a relaxed life is what they already have, without having to work for it?

I remember during those days in the months of April and May, Goans from all over the world would congregate in Goa to spend summer in the land of their ancestors. For us, this journey was made by steamer. It was prohibition time in Bombay those days and when the steamer left Bombay harbour, liquor of all varieties would emerge from hidden places. Along with the liquor, violins, guitars and mandolins would also appear and the sea voyage would be a song fest that drowned out the noise of the ship's engines and music would continue till it was time to sleep. Next morning as the grey of dawn gave way to light, the old timers would gather at the bow of the ship to sniff the air and catch the first glimpse of the land they loved.

On docking at Panjim harbour, the customs would make a search for contraband liquor but all of it would have been consumed and so no one had anything to declare. There was no bridge over the Mandovi River at that time and we had to use the ferry. Goans had quaint names for river and sea craft. The ship that brought us was called the *aagboat*[9] and the ferry was called the *gasleen*.[10]

The beach at Candolim extends on one side to Fort Aguada and on the other to the beaches of Calangute and Baga. It was on this wide expanse of white sand that Goans from all parts of the world would congregate in the evening to renew old acquaintances and mothers would eye suitable boys and girls and make matches for their children.

Breakfast would be eaten after we returned from our sojourn at the beach. Goan breakfasts were quite different from breakfasts eaten by the rest of the world and one had to develop a taste for it. It consisted of *kanjee* or *pez* which was actually a kind of soup made of rice and eaten with pickle. Not very appetizing for us children from Bombay, but we were told to eat it quietly because it was good for us.

After this typical Goan breakfast most of us would move to the *tinto* – the village marketplace. One thing the Portuguese did to keep the Goans happy was making Goa a duty-free port. So, liquor and chocolates and all imported goods were freely available and were very cheap. At the tinto the men would be buying liquor or discussing politics, the women would also be shopping and gossiping and at the same time trying to matchmake, some of the elder boys and girls would be flirting and we, the younger lot, would be playing games till it was time to go home for lunch.

Lunch was always heavy and then it would be time for the elders to have their *siesta* and for us to play indoor games and then return to the beach, the centre of all our activities.

The idyllic days spent in the Goa that I knew are no more. Buildings and hotels have pushed out the cottages and bungalows, pubs have pushed out the tavernas, the beaches have been taken over by shacks of every description, the white and golden sands are covered by deck chairs to cater to the hordes of tourists that descend upon Goa from every corner of India and the world. Goa is no exception to the destruction of some of India's finest beaches – all in the name of development, money and progress!

I feel blessed that I had the childhood that I had – a close family, good school, friends and a simple life. Games and playtime figured largely in the early part of our lives. That is how it should be. The life of a serious student and career goals would come later. My mom and dad are no more, but the memory of their kindness and the clarity with which we were taught our values remains firmly etched in my mind. Character building played a major part in our upbringing and that helped my brother Colin and I face the difficult challenges that would come later on in our respective lives.

My mother was gentle by nature. She believed in making sure that her children understood the meaning of character and values. Her name was Diana, which according to Roman mythology is the goddess of chastity, the huntress and the moon. She was a good listener and women from all walks of life would come to her with their problems. She would listen to them carefully and patiently and render sound advice. This made her a well-loved lady in the neighbourhod. Convinced of the rightness of a cause, she would follow a course of action and she never gave up. Mom's bedtime stories always had lessons to be learnt and I was glad to hear them being repeated by one of my sons to his children last year and one hopes that those stories will continue to be repeated to future generations of the Cardozo family, now in faraway lands.

My father inculcated in me a love for sports and books. He exercised daily, even in his later years. He had very strong and well-developed biceps and what today is called a six-pack. His favourite game was hockey and he played outside left for the Lusitanians – a very famous hockey team of those days. Once he got the ball, he was difficult to stop and his strong left flick made him an asset to the team. Dad encouraged me to read and introduced me to the magical world of books. He was a member of the exclusive J.B. Petit Library and brought books for me to read by Rider Haggard, Edgar Allan Poe, Rabindranath Tagore, G.K. Chesterton, P.G. Wodehouse, Agatha Christie and poetry by Keats, Tennyson, Sarojini Naidu, Rupert Brooke, David Sassoon, Harindranath Chattopadhyay and a host of other authors and poets. I was a voracious reader and would read into the late hours of the night till he would gently shepherd me to bed, saying there would be plenty of time to read later. It was perhaps his scrapbooks that contained newspaper cuttings and pictures of the Second World War from the day war was declared on 3 September 1939 to the surrender of the Axis powers in August 1945 that kindled in me an interest in a life in the Armed Forces.

My brother Colin and I inherited the values and character qualities of our parents. Both of us developed a love for hockey and both of us played hockey for St. Xavier's School. Colin followed my dad into the corporate sector and worked for a branch of Ralli Brothers. It was there that he met Neena, his future life-partner and he is happily married with two lovely daughters. He has a very happy disposition and is much loved by all who know him.

It was a blissful childhood until life took me into the army and to places miles away from home to a different life altogether. But it was perhaps this magical world of stories and experiences of my early years that motivated me to become a storyteller myself.

Notes

1.   General Sunith Rodrigues, PVSM, AVSM.

2. Latin is the root of most European languages and Sanskrit the root of most Indian languages. I found the declension of nouns and conjugation of verbs to be very similar.

3. A small harbour that allows fishing vessels and small boats to dock.

4. Khara – dry salt fish.

5. Para – a salt fish pickle.

6. Something like an idli but much bigger and made with rice flour and toddy (fermented coconut juice).

7. A dry jam made from ripe mangoes.

8. A sweet dish made from eggs, sugar and flour, cooked layer by layer painstakingly for hours over a slow fire.

9. Literally a 'fireboat' because of the fire that fueled the ship's engines and because of the smoke that it emitted from its funnel.

10. A river raft that served as a ferry and the fuel used was gasoline.

CHAPTER FIFTEEN

Writing and Reflecting

Write what should not be forgotten.
ISABEL ALLENDE

As a young boy I always wanted to write. When I joined the army, writing had to take a back seat. The perception at that time was that writers were dreamers and writing was not for men of action. Outdoor sports and hobbies were the 'done thing'. Writing on matters that were not professional was frowned upon. I am not saying that this was right, but this was what we were made to believe. However, I knew in my heart of hearts, that I would one day write, and I followed the example of Vikram, my youngest son, who at the age of eight started a notebook which he called '*My Book of Dreams*'. So, I created a similar book in which I made notes of whatever I thought would be useful for my writing in later years.

As I walked through life, I used to take note of interesting characters and dramatic incidents that I came across, noting them down under different headings for future use. Of particular interest to me were incidents that had a strange or bizarre ending. Phrases that sounded good would also find place in my book of dreams because I hoped that one day, I would weave wondrous images with the 'magic of words'. In time, I developed my own style of writing and my dictionary of the past became my vocabulary of the present.

However, breaking into the publishing world was not easy. Other than articles that I wrote for magazines, I failed to get published. Seven years into retirement, a lucky break came my way. Pramod Kapoor, publisher and owner of Roli Books, approached Lieutenant General Satish Nambiar, who was the Director of the United Service Institution of India at that time, and asked him to suggest someone who could write a book on the Param Vir Chakra, India's highest award for gallantry in battle. General Nambiar suggested my name. I welcomed the offer and set about making the best of this opportunity. It took me two-and-a-half years to research and write the twenty-one stories. I wrote to units, regimental centres, relations and friends of the awardees. I met those who were alive and the relatives of those who had been killed in action or passed away. I wrote the story in running hand between the year 2000 and 2003 when laptops were relatively new and I re-wrote it five times in my quest for perfection. I knew that I was no great author, but I remembered the lesson that I had learnt at the NDA, that what you lack in talent you may sometimes be able to overcome by hard work and I put my heart and soul into the book. However, as many times as I revised the script, I felt that it was not perfect. Finally, I surrendered the manuscript to my publisher as I could hold on to it no longer.

The book turned out to be an astonishing success and it remained a bestseller on the non-fiction chart for nearly a year. Nobody was more surprised than I but when I re-read the book even today, I am sometimes filled with wonderment that it is I who actually wrote it! The book has been reprinted fourteen times.

Offers to write followed one after another and I have written seven books thereafter, including books on wars, military history, regimental history, a biography, a book of poems on war and twelve illustrated stories on the PVC awardees along with a friend, Rishi Kumar, who does the illustrations.

I have also taken to writing short stories and commenced writing a novel. I find writing fiction absolutely fascinating! During my life in the army, I had a certain amount of control over the lives of others but I was responsible and accountable for those lives and I had to balance the safety and security of my men against the objectives of the task in hand. In writing fiction, I felt that I had total control over the lives of the characters that originated in my mind. Characters in my stories lived lives the way I wanted them to. They lived and loved, triumphed or succumbed, fought or died based on my imagination. I had the power of life and death over the characters and I could end my stories the way I wanted. The normal way was to end a story with a happy ending, but I came to realize that happy endings resulted in the story never being recalled, whereas if the hero lost out dramatically or died, that story was likely to be remembered.

I also gathered that it is easier to tell a story than to write it. While orally recounting a story one can watch the reaction of the listeners by looking at their facial expressions and continue to improvize and innovate to make the story more interesting. In the writing of a story there is no such interaction. A written response is equally important but then one has to send the written story to people in order to get feedback. I do seek the advice and suggestions from persons whose opinion and judgement I trust. Whereas I tend to bask in their praise, I have learned to pay greater attention to their comments on what is 'wrong' rather than what is right.

As I reflect on the years of my life from where most of my stories come from, fighting battles on and off the battlefield, I marvel at how well Priscilla brought up the children, almost on her own when I was mostly away on postings to operational areas. Handling three naughty boys when they were growing up must not have been easy but she did it well. She learned to drive and took the boys swimming every day before school and all three blossomed into great swimmers. As they grew, she joined them in their games and learned to appreciate the music that they listened to and their friends used to call her 'Hard Rock Mom'. She was often believed to be their sister because of how young she looked. As I became senior, I was called the 'old man' as most commanders are. To my chagrin, I was one day told by an NCO at Tezpur that my sons and daughter were waiting for me by the swimming pool. Priscilla found that amusing.

She made sure our children understood the meaning of duty, discipline and care and concern for others and that privileges had to be earned. What they are today is entirely because of her. Sunith followed me into the regiment and my battalion. Arun has become a surgeon and has settled down in the United Kingdom and Vikram works in the corporate sector.

Priscilla worked for thirty-one years as a teacher at St. Columbas School and her students still communicate with her. Teaching has given her great satisfaction. Now she has only one student and that is me! I still try to live up to her values and standards. It is difficult to 'teach an old dog new tricks', but she does try and so do I. Nowadays, I am even more into writing and she supports me in this too, although it keeps me away from her in the evening of our lives.

Even as I write, my thoughts go back to the long journey that began at the NDA where we were taught that destiny is not a matter of chance but a matter of choice and that we were the masters of our fate. Could we have shaped our lives differently? In hindsight, perhaps we could, but at that time we played our hand with the cards that were given to us and I think we did not do too badly!

All in all, I feel that I have been more than fortunate to have lived through exciting times and have been blessed by luck or good fortune to have come out alive. Perhaps it was my wife's and mother's prayers and the 'Hand of God' that brought me through it all, and for this I am eternally grateful.

God wishes us to be happy and it is up to us to make best use of the resources that He has given us to make the world a better place for us and for future generations. For this, enlightened leadership is crucial but we also need to understand that each and every one of us also have our own part to play. In this regard, I will always remember the wisdom of a twelve-year-old boy. I was talking at a school about leadership and management and I had said that if we used our resources well, India could be the most powerful country in the world and this young boy said, 'Sir, should we aim to be the most powerful country in the world or the best country in the world?' This is a question that needs introspection by our leaders and each and every one of us.

Loss of a leg changed the course of my life and made me learn a lot about myself and brought me closer to my wife and children and many others. If I was asked whether I'd be happy if I was given my leg back – I'd respond with a resounding 'No!' Losing a leg has made me what I am today and this would probably be the answer of most amputees, who have had to fight bias, discrimination, exclusion and an unjust world and in the end, still manage to come out on top.

Epilogue

You've never lived unless you've almost died. For those who have fought for it, life has a flavour the protected shall never know.
Guy de Maupassant

Some time ago, on the 47th Anniversary of the Indo–Pak War of 1971, I was asked by a newspaper correspondent whether in hindsight, I had any regrets about joining the army, particularly because of the disability that the war had caused and if I had the opportunity to live my life all over again, would I join the army? And whether I had a message for his readers.

In that brief moment, my entire life in uniform flashed before my eyes in a montage – the three wars I had participated in, the counter insurgencies initiated in the Northeast as part of a team, the raid across the border that I had led in what is today euphemistically termed as a 'surgical strike', the attacks against enemy positions, the ambushes that I had laid and the ambush that I had been caught in, a war that I had nearly re-started, my being wounded in battle in East Pakistan, the nine months in military hospital and the Artificial Limb

Centre along with hundreds of other amputees living as if there was no tomorrow. I looked back at going back to school to equip myself academically because we were told that the army would not keep us on our terms, the battles with the mandarins at Army Headquarters for seven long years to change their attitude and prejudice towards battle-casualties, working with children with disabilities after retirement and being chosen by the Government of India to head the Rehabilitation Council of India, entering the world of writing more by accident than design, my marriage to a wonderful woman who stood by me all through those years, who allowed me to pursue my dreams and who supports me even today in whatever I want to do, and my three sons, who were brought up single-handedly by her because I was never around and the life we lead together today in the evening of our lives, accepting every challenge as an opportunity. In short, life has been full and never boring.

The reporter was waiting for me to answer and I replied that I would, without doubt, join the army again because despite the joys and the sorrows, the partings and the reunions, the ups and downs, it was a wonderful and vibrant way of life – a life that has no equal!

As to whether I had a message for the readers, I said that his readers should learn from the lives of the soldiers of the Indian Army to put country first and self last, to do what is right irrespective of the consequences, to believe in God, to do what we love, to love what we do, to never be afraid and to never give up.

Finally, I reminded him of what Abraham Lincoln said: 'Ultimately it is not the years in your that life matter, but the life in those years.' And the words of Helen Keller that my life imbibed, 'Life is a great adventure or it is nothing!'

Comments by Vice Admiral Pradeep Kaushiva on my notings on file as the Academy Cadet Captain on the Honour Code

Academy Cadet Captain Cardozo – A General in the Making*

Sometime in mid 1989, when I was Director Training at the National Defence Academy, a proposal was received from the Director General Military Training to introduce Honour Code for cadets and the Academy's views were sought. It was a very well drafted epistle which made a compelling recommendation in favour and also left adequate room for arguments against.

Since the Academy was about forty years old at that stage, I was reasonably certain that this could not have been the first time that the issue had come up for consideration. So, I dug through the files to see the record of earlier discussions. And, sure enough, the subject had indeed been surfacing from time to time and differing

---

* By Vice Admiral Pradeep Kaushiva (Retd) 15 October 2019

views had been forwarded during different administrations which was fair enough, given the nature of the subject.

In this research, two issues caught my eye. Firstly, the earliest record of this discussion had dated as far back as 1956 i.e. this issue had already been discussed for more than thirty years! And secondly, at that stage, the views of the Academy Cadet Captain had also been sought, taken on record and factored in while firming up the Academy's stand. During that tenure or even a decade later as Deputy Commandant, I did not come across any other instance of a cadet's noting being taken on record in the Academy files.

What was even more remarkable however, was the sheer quality of the noting penned by Academy Cadet Captain Ian Cardozo. It was not just the power of expression, command of the language or even writing skills that were impressive. The maturity of outlook, clarity of thought and logic of arguments of the nineteen-year-old cadet who would in a few months go on to win the President's Gold Medal as well as the Silver Medal, led me to record that I would have been proud of that noting if I had authored it with the experience of more than twenty year's service as I had then!

I had not met the illustrious General or known details of his most distinguished career profile at that stage in 1989. A couple of decades were to pass before I would have the honour of meeting this living legend and role model for generations of soldiers to come. And when I did so, long after he had hung up his boots and I had also swallowed the anchor, I could not resist the temptation to narrate the above to General Cardozo. I suspect he was pleased with his own much younger self because with an amused glint in his eyes, he asked me if I would repeat the nugget to Mrs. Priscilla Cardozo who also happened to be a former colleague of my wife. Of course, it was my privilege to do so.

Citation for the Victoria Cross – Rifleman Thaman Gurung

Prelude

An important objective for the Allies in Italy during World War II was Monte San Bartolo. The position was important because it was the hinge between the Eighth and Fifth Armies on which the Eighth Army was to pivot. Since both the armies considered this objective to be important, the Commander-in-Chief, Field Marshal Sir Harold Alexander asked for its speedy capture. The task for its capture was allotted to 8 Indian Infantry Division who allotted it to 17 Infantry Brigade who in turn tasked 1/5 Royal Gurkha Rifles (FF) to ensure its capture.

The first step was to discover the enemy dispositions and patrols were sent out for this purpose on 11 November, 1944. The first patrol drew heavy fire and was forced to withdraw with four casualties. A second patrol failed to reach its objective but won for the Battalion the posthumous award of the Victoria Cross to

Rifleman Thaman Gurung. The action is best described by the words of the citation:

Citation

'On 11 November, 1944, 'A' Company of 1/5 Royal Gurkha Rifles (FF) was ordered to send a fighting patrol of one platoon onto Monte San Bartolo, which was the objective of a future attack. The objective of this attack was a high intermediate bluff devoid of cover with steep and precipitous approaches joined to the main feature held by the Battalion by a narrow almost knife like saddle. It was known that this position was occupied by the enemy and the approaches to it by a number of machine gun posts.

'Rifleman Thaman Gurung was one of the two scouts of the patrol. By skillful stalking they managed to reach the base of the bluff undetected. He then started to work his way to the summit, but suddenly the second scout attracted his attention to two Germans in a trench just below the crest. They were preparing to fire with their machine gun on to the second scout and the leading section some distance to the rear. Realising that if the Germans succeeding in opening fire the section would certainly sustain heavy casualties, Rifleman Thaman Gurung, although well inside the enemy position, leapt to his feet and charged them. Completely taken by surprise, the Germans surrendered without opening fire.

'After handing over the prisoners to the second scout, Rifleman Thaman Gurung crept forward to the summit of the position. On arrival he saw a party of Germans well dug-in on the reverse slopes preparing to throw grenades over the bluff at the leading section. Although the skyline was devoid of cover and under accurate machine-gun fire at close range, Rifleman Thaman Gurung immediately crossed it and opened fire on the German position with his tommy-gun. This unexpected attack allowed the forward section to reach the bluff. By this time the enemy, thoroughly roused, opened intense and accurate mortar and machine-gun fire from both flanks and from Monte San Bartolo itself on the remainder of the platoon which was then crossing the saddle and pinned it to the ground.

'The company commander, appreciating that it would be impossible to capture or hold the bluff against such opposition while the enemy machine-guns were still active, ordered the platoon to withdraw.

'Fully realising the difficulty of the operation, particularly as the platoon was now being sniped and fired at with Schmaesers and rifle grenades by Germans dug in under the slopes of the bluff, Rifleman Thaman Gurung left his section and once more alone crossed the skyline to a postion from which he could deal with the enemy. He first methodically, though in full view of the enemy, and constantly exposed to heavy fire at short range, put burst after burst of tommy-gun fire into the German slit trenches until his ammunition ran out, and threw two grenades that he had on him. Although all this while he was the target of numerous German machine guns and snipers, he succeeded in rejoining the section unscathed. As his platoon still appeared to be in difficulties, Rifleman Thaman Gurung collected two more grenades and for the second time doubled up across the bullet-swept crest of the hillock and hurled his grenades at the remaining Germans. This diversion enabled the two rear sections to get clear without further loss.

'Meanwhile the leading section, which had remained behind in order to assist the withdrawal of the remainder of the platoon, was still on the bluff forward of the saddle. Rifleman Thaman Gurung, however, rushed to the Bren No. 1 and, at the same time shouting to the section to withdraw seized the gun and a number of magazines.

'He then ran to the top of the hill, and although he knew that his action meant certain death, he stood up on the bullet swept summit and in full view of the enemy emptied burst after burst of fire at the nearest enemy positions. It was not until he had emptied two complete magazines and the section was well on the way to safety that Rifleman Thaman Gurung was killed, shot through the throat.

'It was undoubtedly due to Thaman Gurung's deliberate sacrifice of his life that his platoon was able to withdraw from an extremely difficult position without many more casualties than were actually incurred and it was due in fact to the very valuable information brought back by the platoon that the whole San Bartolo feature was captured three days later.'

Sardar Patel's letter to the Prime Minister
7 November 1950

My dear Jawaharlal,

Ever since my return from Allahabad and after the Cabinet meeting the same day which I had to attend at practically fifteen minutes notice and for which I regret I was not able to read all the papers, I have been anxiously thinking over the problem of Tibet and I thought I should share with you what is passing through my mind.

I have carefully gone through the correspondence between the External Affairs Ministry and our Ambassador in Peking and through him the Chinese Government. I have tried to pursue this correspondence as favourably to our Ambassador and the Chinese Government as possible, but I regret to say that neither of them comes out well as a result of this study.

The Chinese Government has tried to delude us by professions of peaceful intentions. My own feeling is that at a crucial period they managed to instill into our Ambassador a false sense of confidence in their so-called desire to solve the Tibetan problem by peaceful means.

There can be no doubt that, during the period covered by this correspondence, the Chinese must have been concentrating for an assault on Tibet. The final action by the Chinese in my judgement is little short of perfidy.

The tragedy is that the Tibetans put their faith in us, they chose to be guided by us; and we have not been able to get them out of the meshes of Chinese diplomacy or Chinese malevolence. From the latest position, it appears that we shall not be able to rescue the Dalai Lama.

Our Ambassador has been at great pains to find an explanation or justification for Chinese policy and actions. As the External Affairs remarked in one of their telegrams, there was a lack of firmness and unnecessary apology in one or two of our representations that he made to the Chinese Government on our behalf. It is impossible to imagine any sensible person believing in the so-called threat to China from Anglo-American machinations in Tibet. Therefore, if the Chinese put faith in this, they must have distrusted us so completely as to have taken us as tools or stooges of Anglo-American diplomacy or strategy. This feeling, is genuinely entertained by the Chinese despite your direct approaches to them, indicates that, even though we regard ourselves as friends of China, the Chinese do not regard us as their friends. With the Communist mentality of 'Whosoever is not with them being against them', this is a significant pointer of which we have to take due note.

During the last several months, outside the Russian camp, we have practically been alone in championing the cause of Chinese entry into the UNO and in securing from the Americans assurances of the question of Formosa. We have done everything we could to assuage Chinese feelings, to allay their apprehensions and to defend their legitimate claims, in our discussions and correspondence with America, Britain and the UNO. In spite of this, China is not convinced about our disinterestedness, it continues to regard us with suspicion and the whole psychology is one, at least outwardly, of skepticism perhaps, mixed with a little hostility.

I doubt whether we can go any further than we have done already to convince China of our good intentions, friendliness and goodwill. In Peking we have an ambassador who is eminently suitable for putting across the friendly point of view. Even he seems to have failed to convert the Chinese. Their last telegram is an act of gross discourtesy not only in the summary it disposes of our protest against the entry of Chinese forces in Tibet but also in the wild insinuation that our attitude is determined by foreign influences.

It looks like it is not a friend speaking in that language but a potential enemy.

In the background of this, we have to consider what new situation faces us as a result of the disappearance of Tibet, as we know it, and the expansion of China almost up to our gates. Throughout history, we have seldom been worried about our north-east frontiers. The Himalayas have been regarded as an impenetrable barrier against any threat from the North. We had a friendly Tibet which gave us no trouble. The Chinese were divided. They had their own domestic problems and never bothered us about our frontiers.

In 1914 we entered into a convention with Tibet which was not endorsed by the Chinese. We seem to have regarded Tibetan autonomy as extending to independent treaty relationship. Presumably, all that we required was a Chinese counter-signature. The Chinese interpretation of suzerainty seems different. We can therefore, safely assume that very soon they will disown all the stipulations which Tibet has entered into with us in the past. That throws into the melting pot all frontier and commercial settlements with Tibet on which we have been functioning and acting during the last half century.

China is no longer divided. It is united and strong. All along the Himalayas in the north and north-east, we have on our side of the frontier, a population ethnologically and culturally not different from the Mongoloids.

The undefined state of the frontier and the existence on our side of a population with its affinities to the Tibetans or Chinese has all the elements of potential trouble between China and ourselves. Recent and bitter history also tells us that Communism is no shield against imperialism and that the Chinese are as good or bad imperialists as any other. Chinese ambitions in this respect cover not only Himalayan slopes on our side but also include important parts of Assam.

They have their ambitions in Burma also. Burma has the added difficulty that it has no McMahon Line round which to build up even a semblance of an agreement.

Chinese irredentism and Communist imperialism are different from the expansionism or imperialism of the Western powers. The former has a clock of ideology which makes it ten times more dangerous. In the guise of ideological expansion lie concealed racial, national and historical claims.

The danger from the north and the north-east therefore, becomes both Communist and Imperialist. While our western and north western threats are still as prominent as before, a new threat has developed from the north and north-east. Thus for the first time after centuries, India's defence has to concentrate on two fronts simultaneously. Our defence measures have so far been based on the calculations of superiority over Pakistan.

In our calculations we shall now have to reckon with Communist China in the north and north-east – a Communist China which has definite ambitions and aims and which does not, in any way, seem friendly disposed towards us.

Let me also consider the political considerations on this potentially troublesome frontier. Our northern and north-eastern approaches consist of Nepal, Bhutan, Sikkim, Darjeeling and the tribal areas of Assam. From the point of view of communications they are weak spots. Continuous defence lines do not exist. There is almost an unlimited scope for infiltration. Police protection is limited to a very small number of passes. There, too, our outposts do not seem to be fully manned.

The contact of these areas with us is, by no means, close and intimate. The people inhabiting these have no established loyalty or devotion to India. Even Darjeeling and Kalimpong areas are not free from pro-Mongoloid prejudices. During the last three years, we have not been able to make any appreciable approaches to the Nagas and the other hill tribes in Assam. European missionaries and other visitors had been in touch with them, but their influence was, in no way, friendly to India or Indians. In Sikkim, there was political ferment some time ago. It is quite possible that discontent is smouldering there. Bhutan is comparatively quiet, but its affinity would be a handicap. Nepal has a weak oligarchic regime based almost entirely on force; it is in conflict with a turbulent element of the population as well as with the enlightened ideas of the modern age.

In these circumstances, to make people alive to the new danger or to make them defensively strong is a very difficult task indeed and that difficulty can be got over by enlightened firmness, strength and clear line of policy. I am sure the Chinese and their source of inspiration, Soviet Russia, would not miss any opportunity of exploiting these weak spots, partly in support of their ideology and partly in support of their ambitions.

In my judgement therefore, the situation is one which we cannot afford to be complacent or vacillating. We must have a clear idea of what we wish to achieve and also of the methods by which we should achieve it. Any faltering or lack of decisiveness in formulating our objectives or in pursuing our policy to attain those objectives is bound to weaken us and increase the threats which are so evident.

Side by side with these external dangers we shall now have to face serious internal problems as well. I have already asked Iengar to send to the External Affairs Ministry a copy of the Intelligence Bureau's appreciation of these matters. Hitherto, the Communist

Party of India has found some difficulty in contacting Communists abroad, or in getting supplies of arms, literature, etc., from them. They had to contend with difficult Burmese and Pakistan frontiers on the east or the long seaboard.

They will now have a comparatively easy means of access to Chinese Communists and through them to other foreign Communists. Infiltration of spies, fifth columnists, and Communists would be easier. Instead of having to deal with isolated Communist pockets in Telengana and Warangal we may have to deal with Communist threats to our northern and north-eastern frontiers where for supplies of arms and ammunition, they can safely depend on Communist arsenals in China.

The whole situation thus raises a number of problems on which we must come to an early decision so that we can, as said earlier, formulate the objectives of our policy and decide the methods by which those actions will have to be fairly comprehensive involving not only our defence strategy and state of preparation but also problems of internal security to deal with which we have not a moment to lose. We shall also have to deal with administrative and political problems in the weak spots along the frontiers to which I have already referred.

It is, of course impossible for me to be exhaustive in setting out all these problems. I am, however, giving below some of the problems which in my opinion, require early solution and round which we have to build our administrative or military policies and measures to implement them.

(a) A military and intelligence appreciation of the Chinese threat both on the frontier and to internal security.

(b) An examination of our military position and such redisposition of our forces as might be necessary, particularly with the idea of guarding important routes or areas which are likely to be areas of dispute.

(c) An appraisal of the strength of our forces and, if necessary, reconsideration of our retrenchment plans for the army in light of these new threats.

(d) A long term consideration of our defence needs. My own
     feeling is that unless we assure our supplies of arms,
     ammunition and armour, we would be making our defence
     perpetually weak and would not be able to stand up to the
     double threat of difficulties both from the west and north-
     west and north-east.

(e) The question of Chinese entry into the UNO. In view of
     the rebuff which China has given us and the method it has
     followed in dealing with Tibet, I am doubtful whether we
     can advocate its claims any longer. There would probably
     be a threat in the UNO virtually to outlaw China, in view
     of its active participation in the Korean war. We must
     determine our attitude on this question also.

(f) The political and administrative steps which we should take
     to strengthen our northern and north-eastern frontiers. This
     would include the whole of the border i.e., Nepal, Bhutan,
     Sikkim, Darjeeling and the tribal territory in Assam.

(g) Measures of internal security in the border areas as well as
     the states flanking those areas, such as Uttar Pradesh, Bihar,
     Bengal and Assam.

(h) Improvement of our communications, road, rail, air and
     wireless, in these areas, and with the frontier outposts.

(i) Policing and intelligence of frontier posts.

(j) The future of our missions at Lhasa and the trade posts
     at Gyangtse and Yatung and the forces which we have in
     operation in Tibet to guard the trade routes.

(k) The policy in regard to the McMahon Line.

These are some of the questions that occur to my mind. It is
possible that a consideration of these matters may lead us to wider
questions of our relationship with China, Russia, America, Britain
and Burma. This however would be of a general nature, though some
might be basically very important, e.g., we might have to consider
whether we should not enter into a closer relationship with Burma

in order to strengthen the latter in the dealings with China. I do not rule out the possibility that, before applying pressure on us, China might apply pressure on Burma. With Burma, the frontier is entirely undefended and the Chinese territorial claims are more substantial. In its present postion, Burma might offer an easier problem for China and therefore may claim its first attention.

I suggest we meet early to have a general discussion on these problems and decide on such steps as we might think to be immediately necessary and direct quick examination of other problems with a view to taking early measures to deal with them.

Vallabhai Patel
7th November 1950

Comments by Eminent Historians on the Non-use of the Indian Air Force in the Sino–Indian War of 1962

**Comments by Air Vice Marshal Arjun Subramaniam
in his book *India's Wars: A Military History 1947–71*,
HarperCollins, 2016, pp. 256, 257.**

'One of the biggest blunders of the 1962 war was the reluctance of India's strategic establishment to use its superior aerial reconnaissance and offensive air power to blunt the spectacular forward run of the People's Liberation Army (PLA) in both NEFA and Ladakh. While Marshal of the Air Force Arjan Singh has clearly indicated in his book that he was not entirely privy to the reasons why air power was not used in the 1962 war and that the squadrons were ready to go into action, it is quite clear that both Air HQ and the Government of India were fuzzy about what the IAF could do or could not do…

'Air Headquarters did not also contest the exaggerated capability of the PLAAF as conveyed to Prime Minister Nehru by the US ambassador, John Kenneth Galbraith, and chose to go along with the typically restrained interpretation of the time that air power would be unnecessarily escalatory. With joint army-air force structures in place at the corps level, and forward air controllers with the brigades, it is clear that the IAF brass was timid and diffident about forcefully articulating to the army and the political leadership that in an asymmetric situation on the ground, offensive air power could play a stabilizing role, if not a decisive one. If offensive air power had been used in the east, particularly on the Chinese side of the McMahon Line across the Thagla Ridge while the PLA was concentrating its forces, significant attrition could have been caused....

'It would be foolish to surmise that air power would have been a game changer; however, it would certainly have been a face-saver and India's armed forces may have possibly come out of the conflict in both sectors bruised, but not beaten and humiliated.'

Comments by Claude Arpi in his Blog – https://claudearpi. blogspot.com/2019/03/what-if-nehru had used-iaf-in 1962. html
(Relevant extracts of his interview with Wg Cdr Jaggi Nath MVC and Bar)

'China had no air force worth its name on the Tibetan Plateau in 1962. The fate of the Sino–Indian war would have been quite different had India used its Air Force, but the Govt in Delhi chose to ignore the findings of its brave airmen.

'...Pandit Nehru and Krishna Menon were completely switched off from reality.

'Wg Cdr Nath and the Officiating Air Chief AVM Diwan

Atma Ram Nanda were sent to meet the Defence Minister Krishna Menon and they landed in his office. He asked, "Did you see the Chinese soldiers?" I answered, "Yes. I saw them." He said, "That's all right. You may go." That was all – no action was taken. He may have passed on the information to Pandit Nehru but the reaction was the same. There was a total breakdown. They did not know how to handle the situation.

'Later when this information was conveyed to AVM Erlic Pinto and we told him that we could finish them off in no time; he said that the Indian Govt believed that the Chinese had bombers and they could bomb Delhi and other cities. This information was passed from the top by Pandit Nehru and Krishna Menon and the information percolated down. As a result, they decided not to use the Air Force.

'There was no air confrontation with the Chinese, but if we had, it would have been a different ball game. However, there was Zero possibility, as they had no Air Force. The person who should have put his foot down was Aspi Engineer, the Air Chief. Otherwise, why was the IAF not used to support the army which was getting a beating everywhere? If the Govt was still in doubt they could have verified the position and then used the IAF. Can you imagine what would have happened had we used the Air Force at that time?

The info we had was:

(a) The Chinese Air Force was grounded for lack of spares. They were using mainly Mig 17, but as China was having problems with Russia, they did not get supply of spare parts; their planes were blocked. Other planes were in Korea from where they could not be moved.

(b) Even a small plane could not land in Tibet; they had no forward air strip at all. Further, had they used their planes from Korea it would be a one-way trip because they had not fuel to go back.

(c) All this information was available to the Government. What excuse did we have for not using the Air Force?

Extracts of a letter addressed by Wg Cdr Nath MVC* to Air Chief Arup Raha on 10 September 2014 (Courtesy Claude Arpi)

'...It was common knowledge that China was equipped with Migs 15 and 17. Delhi was out of their range. A shortage of spares after falling out with Russia in 1960 had almost grounded the Chinese Air Force.

'...(Meeting with Defence Minister – already narrated)

'Yes, I took pictures of the Northern borders; it was a 3-hour flight. I flew up and down and could see concentrations of the Chinese; I could go around and take pictures. The Chinese could see me and started shooting with their rifles. How could they shoot down an aircraft with their rifles? It was just not possible. The point is they did not have anything. No weapon to shoot down an aircraft. No Air Force!'

https://claudearpi.blogspot.com/2019/02/a-highly-strategic-corridor.html

Last year a publication 'The 1959 Tibetan Uprising Documents': The Chinese Army Documents was released on Kindle. It was a collection of Top-Secret documents of the Military Intelligence of the People's Liberation Army (PLA) dating from the end of the 1950s till the 1962 War.

At that time China had a crucial problem; it did not have an Air Force in a position to take on the Indian Air Force. The compilation of the above papers noted '...disadvantage of the Chinese Air Force is still a problem if case of a conflict with India. Indian jets can start at a low altitude with a full load of bombs and plenty of fuel. Also, India has many airports about a 100 kilometres from the highest peaks of the Himalayas. The short distance and the heavier bomb load that each Indian jet is at least twice if not more than three times more effective than a Chinese aircraft.'

Apart from the fact that many aircraft had been sent to the Korean front and that the Soviet Union had stopped supplying spare parts for the Mig fighter planes, the PLA Air Force had a major hurdle – no fuel for its few planes.

The above findings have two important corollaries; it confirmed that China had no Air Force in flying condition at the time of the 1962 conflict with India and having no spares or fuel.

This raises another issue: Why did the Indian Government, which had all the information about the situation in Tibet, the deployment of the PLA on the plateau and the lack of a Chinese Air Force (Jaggi Nath was never even once attacked or even followed during his regular sorties over Tibet) and why did it not use its jets to pound the PLA concentrations near Thagla Ridge in the Tawang Sector, in Walong Sector of eastern NEFA or in Rezangla in Ladakh?

The answer is woeful leadership. Let us hope the present bosses watch and understand what is happening in this area.

Extract from Shiv Kunal Verma's book *1962 – The War that Wasn't*, Aleph Book Company 2016, pp. 381–382.
'Where were the Boys in Blue?'

'Not only did the IB paint for Nehru a highly exaggerated picture about the PLAAF's strike capability, it was downright dishonest in its overall appreciation. In March 1962, Lieutenant Liu Chengsze of the PLAAF defected to the USA in Formosa (Taiwan). He had earlier approached the Indians seeking political asylum, offering detailed information of the Chinese air capabilities in exchange. The Indians had refused, but the Americans eagerly accepted the offer. However, the gist of Chengsze's information had been shared with the Indian Intelligence Bureau. According to the report, despite having over 2,000 aircraft at their disposal, the Chinese could utilise only a fraction of these from Tibet.'

'The main reason was the complete reliance on the Soviet Union for aviation fuel and spares... with Soviet aid drying up in 1960 after a chill in Sino-Soviet relations, the Chinese were hard-pressed to launch aircraft even in China, let alone Sinkiang and Tibet. Why the Intelligence Bureau chose to deliberately mislead the government and why the Air Chief failed to arrive at an independent assessment will remain another one of the unsolved mysteries of 1962.'

The Plucky One-legged Goan-Gorkha General

– Khushwant Singh
Published in the *Times of India*, 19 January 1992

Believe it or not, we have one in our army. I didn't even suspect that he was handicapped when he walked up briskly to shake hands with me at a party given by Lakshmi and Robin Goswami at Tezpur. I saw him again at the Bangladesh War 20th victory anniversary celebrations. He was moving about among his officers and men, ramrod straight, exchanging jokes and laughing uproariously. He is there because the army found him indispensable.

Goa-born Major General Cardozo, AVSM, is a product of St. Xavier's College, Bombay. He joined the National Defence Academy in Khadakvasla in 1954 and won the President's Gold Medal for being the best all-round cadet. After commissioning, he joined the 5th Gorkha Rifles and won the Sena Medal for bravery in the NEFA operations in 1960.

He fought the Chinese invaders in 1962 and commanded a brigade in Jammu and Kashmir during the Indo–Pak War of 1965. His most glorious exploit was in the 1971 Indo–Pak War when he was dropped behind enemy lines near Sylhet. A BBC broadcast announcing that the Gorkhas had captured Sylhet was heard by both India and Pakistani commanders who were still in control of the city. Cardozo had to drive them out. A day before they laid down arms, Cardozo stepped on a Pakistani mine and one of his legs was shattered. There were no medical facilities available and none of his men would cut his damaged leg. He borrowed a *khukri* from one of his men and with his own hands cut off the damaged limb. He was flown to Pune where he was fitted with an artificial leg.

The army had never heard of a one-legged soldier. Cardozo was offered early retirement, rehabilitation with a gas-petrol agency and free education for his children. He spurned the offers and insisted that he was fit enough to continue soldiering. The army authorities gave in: There was nothing to deter a one-legged man otherwise 100 per cent fit from continuing in service. Cardozo achieved his life's ambition. He is today a Major General and Chief of Staff in Operation Rhino, posted in Tezpur.

Acknowledgements

I would like to acknowledge the help given to me by Major Balwant Singh, my coursemate, who abetted my regurgitation of memories of our days at the Joint Services Wing, the National Defence Academy and the Indian Military Academy, Air Vice Marshal DS Chhabra, PVSM, AVSM who as a Flight Lieutenant at the NDA was my divisional officer-cum-mentor, who taught me that I had only one life to live and that I should live it to the full, Vice Admiral Kaushiva, PVSM, AVSM, VSM who gave me a feedback on my comments as the Academy Cadet Captain of the NDA on the Honour Code, Lieutenant Colonel Hari Singh Sandhu who worked tirelessly to shape us cadets at the NDA to become the best officers in the world, Major General Gopal Gurung, AVSM, SM who went through the chapter 'Nepal and the Gorkhas' and put me right on many aspects of the history of Nepal and the rites and traditions of the Gorkhas, Colonel Prashant Rao of my regiment, who clarified my insight into the tribes of Nepal and recruitment of Gorkhas into the Indian Army, Colonel Abu Tahir, Bir Protik of the Bangladesh Army, Major S. Kipgen, SM, and Major JV Raju who shaped my vision regarding the command of troops by battle casualties, Nilanjana Ghosh

Bardan, the wife of an officer of the 4th Battalion the 5th Gorkha Rifles (FF) who painstakingly went through the chapters and gave her forthright comments and constructive suggestions, Brigadier Madhav Prasad, VSM, who put me wise about what it was like to be part of the 1st Course JSW and who was unfailing in his encouragement throughout my writing of this book, Nalini Samuel who always responded to my call to correct syntax and grammar, my brother Colin and my class mate Julius Chagas Pereira who walked me down memory lane to revive our days spent at St. Xavier's School, Shekufey Irani who helped renew old memories of happy days spent at Mathura and my association with her parents – Lieutenant General Jehangir Sataravala, MBE, MC and Mrs Perin Sataravala, Brigadier Arun Bhimrao Harolikar, MVC, the brave and indefatigable Commanding Officer of the 4th Battalion the 5th Gorkha Rifles (FF), whose outstanding leadership during the 1971 War resulted in containing two Pakistani brigades and the Sylhet Garrison and the ultimate surrender of over 8,000 Pakistani soldiers and whose writings and discussions helped in putting together the story of what happened at Sylhet during the 1971 War, General Arun Vaidya, PVSM, MVC*, AVSM, who believed that battle casualties could command units and who encouraged me to apply for command of an infantry battalion, Field Marshal Sam Manekshaw, MC, the most loved and respected Chief of the Indian Army, who by his vision and moral courage helped to carve an outstanding victory over Pakistan and to push the Indian Army to have a 're-think' on the future of battle casualties, Generals 'Tappy' Raina, MVC and Krishna Rao, PVSM, subsequent Army Chiefs who opened up promotion for the war disabled with no restriction to rank or appointment, Lieutenant General AM Vohra, PVSM, who believed in me and was my pillar of support in my struggle for command of an infantry battalion,

Lieutenant General NSI Narahari, PVSM, who encouraged and supported me to prove myself as an infantry battalion commander when my battalion was part of the brigade he commanded, Lieutenant General JFR Jacob, PVSM, whose frequent dialogues and writings gave me a better perspective of what really happened during the 1971 War, to Clari and Shilpa Cardozo in whose homes in Bolton and Singapore I wrote the first draft of this book and who read through the chapters and made constructive suggestions. To Pramod Kapoor and Priya Kapoor who were the first who asked me to write this book because they felt I had led an interesting life and my story could be a source of motivation for others. Adil Chhina, about the same time, was the first person to say that my story needed to be told and offered to write the book himself.

My very special thanks to Meghna Girish who painstakingly did the first and subsequent edits of the book before it went to the publishers and for her sterling advice, ideas and recommendations in the content and design of this book which has made it what it is today. She owns this book as much as I do.

To Manish Bawa who gave me his time and technological expertise to do what was necessary to bring to life the illustrations and photographs which appear in this book. Thank you Manish.

To Neelam Narula and Isha Maniar the editors of this story who painstakingly went through the text time and again to make my story error-free and interesting.

John Master's book *A Bugle and a Tiger* has been my inspiration for this book. His life, and of those of us who have been trained at the National Defence Academy and who have served with the Gorkhas is astonishingly similar. His book is a must read for all officers of the Gorkha Brigade.

Lastly, I am grateful to Priscilla my wife, for constantly being around while good-naturedly allowing me to spend time away from her in the evening of our lives and helping to give this book the right perspective.

This is a factual story that goes back nearly eight decades and I have written this narrative to the best my memory can recall. I have changed names of persons to protect privacy, except when individuals are part of known history and those who have confirmed that it is alright to quote their names.

However, I accept full responsibility for what is stated in this story.

Index